Latina Performance

D0108090

Unnatural Acts: Theorizing the Performative

Sue-Ellen Case
Philip Brett
Susan Leigh Foster

The partitioning of performance into obligatory appearances and strict disallowances is a complex social code assumed to be "natural" until recent notions of performativity unmasked its operations. Performance partitions, strictly enforced within traditional conceptions of the arts, foreground the gestures of the dancer, but ignore those of the orchestra player, assign significance to the elocution of the actor, but not to the utterances of the audience. The critical notion of performativity both reveals these partitions as unnatural and opens the way for the consideration of all cultural intercourse as performance. It also exposes the compulsory nature of some orders of performance. The oppressive requirements of systems that organize gender and sexual practices mark who may wear the dress and who may perform the kiss. Further, the fashion of the dress and colorizing of the skin that dons it are disciplined by systems of class and "race." These cultural performances are critical sites for study.

The series Unnatural Acts encourages further interrogations of all varieties of performance both in the traditional sense of the term and from the broader perspective provided by performativity.

Latina
Performance:
Traversing
the Stage

Alicia Arrizón

INDIANA UNIVERSITY PRESS

BLOOMINGTON & INDIANAPOLIS

PN
2270
.M48
A77
1999
40631649

This book is a publication of

Indiana University Press
601 North Morton Street
Bloomington, Indiana 47404-3797 USA

www.indiana.edu/~iupress

Telephone orders 800-842-6796
Fax orders 812-855-7931
Orders by e-mail iuporder@indiana.edu

© 1999 by Alicia Arrizón

A portion of chapter 2 appeared as "Soldaderas and the Staging of the Mexican Revolution," in *The Drama Review: The Journal of Performance Studies* 42, no. 1 (Spring 1998), and it appears here in a new form with permission of MIT.

All rights reserved

No part of this book may be reproduced or utilized in any form or by any means, electronic or mechanical, including photocopying and recording, or by any information storage and retrieval system, without permission in writing from the publisher. The Association of American University Presses' Resolution on Permissions constitutes the only exception to this prohibition.

The paper used in this publication meets the minimum requirements of American National Standard for Information Sciences–Permanence of Paper for Printed Library Materials, ANSI Z39.48-1984.

Manufactured in the United States of America

Library of Congress Cataloging-in-Publication Data

Arrizón, Alicia.
Latina performance : traversing the stage / Alicia Arrizón.
    p.   cm. —(Unnatural acts)
Includes bibliographical references and index.
ISBN 0-253-33508-6 (cloth : alk. paper). —ISBN 0-253-21285-5 (pbk. : alk. paper)
    1. Mexican American theater. 2. Hispanic American drama (Spanish). 3. Hispanic American women in literature. 4. Hispanic American women. 5. Hispanic American lesbians.   I. Title.   II. Series.
    PN2270.M48A77   1999
    792'.089'68073—dc21   99-11577

1   2   3   4   5   04   03   02   01   00   99

Augustana College Library
Rock Island, Illinois 61201

For Gina Marie Ong

"I painted my own reality"

—Frida Kahlo

CONTENTS

Illustrations

Acknowledgments

Special gratitude is offered to the Chicano Studies Research Center and the Institute of the American Cultures at the University of California, Los Angeles, where I was a visiting scholar (1994–1995). At UC Riverside, I want to thank the Vice Chancellor's office, The Center for Ideas and Society, and the Institute for Mexico & the United States (UC Mexus). The financial support of these organizations has contributed to the enhancement of my research.

Acknowledgments are extended to many people: those performance artists, dramatists, and intellectuals whose works have shaped and inspired my own work, and my friends and colleagues who guided me in the final preparation of the book. The inspiration and support of scholars such as Sue-Ellen Case and Diana Taylor have been instrumental to me. I dearly respect their contributions in the field and fully admire their intellect. Working with them (in the international feminist group of IFTR, the performing identities group, etc.) has been an enlightened experience. Sue-Ellen, one of the editors of the series, along with Susan Foster and Philip Brett, helped me achieve my analytic prowess. With her special personal touch, Susan Foster inspired me to find my own voice. I wish to express my sincere gratitude to Joan Catapano, who is the sponsoring editor at Indiana University Press.

I also wish to thank my friends and colleagues who in one way or another are involved in my intellectual journey: Lillian Manzor, David Román, Josie Saldaña, Jennifer Brody, Marta Savigliano, Margie Waller, Sharon Salinger, Susan Rose, and Inés Salazar. My connection with them is substantiated by different levels of sisterhood (and brother-hood). In this group I also want to include Vicki Ruiz, who made comments on the first draft of chapter 4; and Yvonne Yarbro-Bejarano, who provided copies of her own unpublished work which helped engage my ideas with hers. I really appreciate their friendship, generosity, and intellectual support. Special thanks to Kathy Mooney, who read my manuscript and offered suggestions for clarity.

My deepest gratitude to my father and mother, Francisco Arrizón and Ofelia Peña, for having instilled in me the belief that I could accomplish any goal I set for myself. I love you both very much. I also want to thank my sisters and brothers, nieces and nephews, for their love and patience. I hope to have more time in the future to visit more often. My appreciation to extended members of my family, Wil Villa and Olga Vásquez, for their unconditional love and support, which are always well received. Finally, Gina Marie Ong, who transformed my life with her love so that I can write. I dedicate this book to her.

El otro, la mudez que pide voz
al que tiene la voz
y reclama el oído del que escucha.

[The other, muteness that begs a voice
from the one who speaks
and demands the ear of the one who listens]

Introduction

These verses from one of the most prominent Mexican poets and dramatists of this century, Rosario Castellanos (1925–1974), embody the struggle of the suppressed subject who wishes for a voice, who longs to be heard. The quoted verses are from the poem "Poesía no eres tú" (Poetry Is Not You), a title she also used for her compiled volume of poetry, published in 1971. I consider it very appropriate to begin my book with these verses because it is in this poem that Castellanos counters the ultra-romantic vision of the nineteenth-century Spanish poet Gustavo Adolfo Bécquer. In Bécquer's poem "¿Qué es poesía?" (What is poetry?), the poetic subject responds, "Poesía eres tú" (Poetry is you). Writing during Spain's Romantic period, Bécquer depicted the female body in the conventional idiom of his day—as delicate and docile, materialized in beauty and harmony. She was the sex of poetry and the object-muse of that period's romantic imagination. Bécquer's verses have gradually come to epitomize Romantic poetry. This poem of his is still "performed" each year in poetry festivals and memorized by literature students in classes throughout the Hispanic world. I can clearly remember having to learn "¿Qué es poesía?" by heart as an assignment in the first Hispanic literature class I took as an undergraduate.

Castellanos' creative response, which reverses Bécquer's cliché, underscores the presence of a voice who speaks and a receptor who must listen. I find Castellanos' subversive imagination especially intriguing because she proposes radical ways to reverse the order that portrayed the female body as a static creature of attraction, an object of desire. By subverting form and content, Castellanos proposes alternative ways to imagine and witness. She demands a critical receptor. By using her poem to transgress the production of meaning, she not only transforms the objectified, docile body into an active subject, she demands to be listened to rather than simply "admired." What was once a mute object becomes the speaking subject.

Evoking Castellanos as a referent is an especially appropriate way for me to open *Latina Performance* because her interest in the interaction of "self" and "other" centered on the struggle to find a voice within silences. For Latinas in the United States, this effort to be heard is an ongoing battle shared by artists, intellectuals, and academics striving to become visible in a world dominated by ostracism, alienation, and shame. Like the voice in search of a receptor in Castellanos' subversive transfiguration, the topography of the Latina body alters the sites of marginality to create a radical entree into existence. A first step in this process of making ourselves "real" is to acknowledge the power of language in identity making—thus the insistence on the use of the term "Latina," as opposed to the masculine gender inflection, "Latino." The split between the a/o, giving preference to the feminine construction and Spanish grammatics, ideologically challenges the site of the homogeneous and the location of the gendered subject. Now her body is placed in a position of power. She is a witness, spectator, and protagonist of the silence and suppression her body speaks against: the cultural tyranny embedded in a history and society which has attempted to make her submissive, obedient, mute, and powerless. The Latina subject I bring into focus in this book is the antithesis of that "model." My subject is the one who replaces whispers with shouts and obedience with determination. In challenging her assigned position, she begins to transform and transcend it. She is the radical intellectual, the taboo breaker, the feminist dramatist. She is the transgressive, the lusty and comical performer, the queerest among us. She represents "difference" and seeks to uncover and confront the very space where her body converges or intersects in a performance that comprises her subjectivity and ethic cultural sense. Following the lead of the subversive imagination that Rosario Castellanos demonstrated earlier in this century, Latinas today bring a rebellious sensibility to the task of dismantling the structures that have defined, silenced, and marginalized them.

In choosing to use the term "Latina" rather than "Hispana" I have made a deliberate political decision. I give preference to this term in order to uphold discursive notions of identity which surpass the static condition implicated in the term "Hispanic." Neither Latina nor *Hispana* represent racial categories. They are deliberate linguistic constructs, with specific histories and legacies. The notion of Latina is the pretext of my own cultural and academic formation. My approach to the term is a liberating one that allows me to embrace multiple ethnic categories, such as Mexican American and Cuban American; to recognize various ideological determinants, such as Chicana and Nuyorican; and to acknowledge and support the determining connotation implicit in the label "women of color." Thus, in embracing the term Latina, I am adopting a position that problematizes the reality of women who live in a divided utopic world. Latinas are American, and yet, at the same time, they are not "Americans." Latinas comprise a multiracial and multiethnic community whose multiple and diverse voices are long overdue to be heard. *Latina Performance* is a step toward raising the volume and shattering the silence.

Much as Latinas themselves must struggle to be heard, the field of Latina/o Studies occupies a position on the margins. It has received little recognition—or even attention—either in mainstream media or in U.S. universities. With very few exceptions, neither the field's critiques nor its creative narratives are discussed or quoted by Anglo Americans. On those rare occasions when Anglo Americans do turn their attention to Latina/o studies, it is most often to challenge the concepts of "difference" and "diversity" in the name of preserving multiculturalism, all the while ignoring the cultural plurality that defines the configuration of Latina/o identity. I do not hope to reach such an audience with this book. Aside from the reader who is my most important concern—*mi comunidad latina*—I address my work to those who are interested in going beyond the political correctness of "multiculturalism." The reader who would engage in the quest *Latina Performance* represents must be capable of understanding the real implications of diversity, beyond mere celebrations of "otherness." My work centers on marginality, on border space(s), and it is this uneasy, complicated, and contradictory state that the reader must be willing to inhabit. She or he must engage with me, my narrative, and their own subject position in order to capture the body and embodiment of the Latina subject who is and will remain in process, overdetermined and yet emergent. The interdiscipline of cultural studies where I locate the Latina body negotiates various kinds of boundaries that human societies construct. My approach in *Latina Performance* resists the view of culture and life as static conditions. Instead, it insists that they are both products of dynamic processes.

In presenting this book to such readers and to others concerned with the formation and development of feminist discourses, my goal is to expand the possibilities of two necessary fields: Latina theater and Performance Studies. My book focuses on identity politics but at the same time explores performative and theatrical activities. I attempt to locate the Latina subject whose work as dramatist, actress, theorist, and/ or critic helps to further define the field of theater and performance in the United States. All these areas of study intertwine and represent an interdisciplinary method, a practice associated with Ethnic Studies and the pluralistic eclecticism it inspires. For while interdisciplinary studies in the academy are certainly encouraged by the institutional pluralism of contemporary life, their methodologies allow us to map many forms of cultural production that need to be studied in relation to the humanities and society. With the help of contemporary cultural studies, interdisciplinary analysis offers a link between conceptual theory and material culture. The work presented in this book moves in and out between each of these epistemologies. The parameters of interdisciplinary analysis, I believe, define the role of the intellectual, pressing for certain kinds of change.

The transitions I make in the process of analyzing the many facets that I believe make up Latina identity are designed to mirror the functionality of theater, culture, and performance. Thus, my discussion ex-amines the dynamics of a cultural politics that flows through the interstices of gender, ethnicity, race, class, and sexuality. I do not claim to unite the many distinct positionalities of Latinas. Instead, I aim to thread together the separate strands of a critical consciousness rooted in the transhistorical connections of nonstatic identities.

The trajectory traced in Chapter 1, which sketches the connections between the formation of Latino groups and significant historical events (i.e., migration, annexation, and exile), is an essential foundation for grasping the specific configurations in later chapters. It is, for example, important to recognize the discursive configurations of a Mexican American identity in order to accurately locate the theatrical and performative subject *before* the development of the Chicano movement. In this context, my discussion in Chapter 1 emphasizes the complexity, diversity, and historical specificity of identity formation in order to bring into sharper focus the contributions of Latinas—women from many different ethnic backgrounds and with different political and sexual orientations—whose work predates as well as postdates the Chicano movement, *el movimiento* or *la causa*. I focus on the ways in which "Latina" gets constructed—geographically, politically, histori-

cally, and discursively—in order to present a framework that will rein-
force the structure of later chapters. Although the historical overview
presented in Chapter 1 helps me unmask the multiple sources of
identity formation, I am most concerned with the implications of the
colonial legacy, as it is these far-reaching effects that are most crucial
for comprehending the political economy of theater, its practice and
theory, in relation to the subject's post-Spanish and neocolonial state.

In Chapter 2, I focus on a Latina theatrical legacy fostered by two
early figures of the Mexican American stage: Beatríz Escalona (La
Chata Noloesca), an actress, producer, and director; and Josefina Niggli, also an actress, dramatist, and director. Both women were leading
participants in a generation of artists who developed an infrastructure
sufficient to sustain a theatrical tradition in the U.S. As theater workers
who were affected directly and indirectly by the Mexican Revolution,
Escalona and Niggli demonstrate the eclecticism of the Latina theatrical tradition. Escalona's theatrical characterization—La Chata Noloesca—became a legendary symbol in the history of Spanish-speaking
popular theater in the U.S. Niggli's contributions helped stimulate an
interest in (and preservation of) folkloric theater in the 1930s. Her play
Soldadera, which I analyze, stages the participation of women in the
Mexican Revolution, characterizing the protagonist of "La Adelita," a
very popular *corrido* (song), as a hero of the revolution. In this context,
I also analyze the song as a way to critique the gender and cultural
relations embedded in the historical subjectivity of this protagonist as
she appears in various (other) texts. Throughout Chapter 2, as I employ
the tools of literary criticism, textual analysis, and historical interpretation to gain a deeper understanding of the problematic identity of the
soldier-woman Adelita, I am guided by insights from the work of contemporary feminist scholars. Just as Anna Macías, Clara Lomas, María
Herrera-Sobek, and Shirlene Soto have attempted to reconstruct the
dynamic participation of women in various contexts during the Mexican Revolution, so I attempt to construct and deconstruct romantic
notions of the revolutionary subject in the contexts of culture and
drama as I examine how the *soldadera* has been variously represented
and misrepresented. Adelita, whether in popular songs or in plays,
represents a contested paradigm that demands further critical reflection.

Positioning Niggli's work in connection with La Chata Noloesca—as
the embodiment of an emerging Mexican American aesthetics and
identity—provides the necessary background for looking at a more
evolved stage of that new synthesis, as it is incorporated in Chicana
issues. Chapter 3 discusses the cultural specificity of Chicana identity

and its context in Chicano theater. At the same time, the chapter theorizes the notion of performance as an autonomous system of production, separate from both the dramatic text and its representation. In exploring the work of Chicana performance artists Laura Esparza (*I DisMember the Alamo: A Long Poem for Performance*) and Nao Bustamante *(Indigurrito)*, the third chapter highlights the role of performance as a means for appropriating mechanisms of cultural and political mediation that go beyond the stage. Humor, parody, and subversion are denominators of the Chicana performance artists in this section. As it was in La Chata's day, humor is again an indispensable tool among Latinas in contemporary performance art. The work of Laura Esparza, Nao Bustamante, Monica Palacios, and Carmelita Tropicana is defined by these artists' satiric and transgressive sensibilities. As an essential ingredient in Latino culture, humor is also a characteristic of the plays I discuss in Chapter 4, but there it is not my focus.

In Chapter 4, I deal with issues I consider elemental for the cultural survival of Latinas. I return to the Latina subject to explore identity in the context of migration. I examine three plays: *Latina* (by Milcha Sánchez-Scott), *Coser y cantar* (by Dolores Prida), and *Simply María or the American Dream* (by Josefina López). My analysis shows how reality and theatricality become consolidated by economic sanction and cultural survival. The representational and theatrical space provides a framework for examining geographical and allegorical "borders" as cultural paradigms through which new kinds of identities are forged.

Chapter 5 presents the concept of the gendered self as one which is constructed inseparably from sexuality, race, and ethnicity. In analyzing the work of Monica Palacios (*Latin Lezbo Comic: A Performance about Happiness, Challenges and Tacos*) and Carmelita Tropicana (*Leche de Amnesia/Milk of Amnesia* and *Carmelita Tropicana: Your Kunst Is Your Waffen*), I wish to establish a discourse that questions "queer theory" and also challenges the implications of other signifiers that mark the power structures of self-representation and the politics of lesbian identity. It is precisely this aspect of performance art—the opportunity it makes available to women of color to use their racialized and sexualized bodies as a metaphor to intervene in the system of representation—that makes this medium so attractive to Latinas (and others).

The trajectory traced by the ordering of the topics I address in this book is a reflection of the way I view the constant and complex negotiations that shape identity formation, even as they alter and (re-)imagine it. From the general perspectives laid out in Chapter 1, where I establish

the continuous reenactment of Latina subjectivity and identity formation, to the radical alternatives presented in Chapter 5, where the
lesbian body parades in a lusty performance of self-representation
pinpointing race, ethnicity, and sexuality, the contents of this book mark
and unmark the possibility of materializing the sites of "difference" within "difference." Selecting figures such as La Chata and Josefina Niggli
from an early phase of Latina theater allows me to contemplate in
Chapter 2 the transhistorical subject who also "traverses" identity: the
Mexican American crosses the borders of time to become transformed
later into *La chicana mestiza*. This progression of identity formation in
my book divides but consolidates Chapters 2 and 3, in which the
subject's bodily display directly confronts patriarchal domination and
cultural oppression. These same regimes of power are central in Chapter 4's analysis of the plays by Milcha Sánchez-Scott, Josefina López,
and Dolores Prida. Making the play *Latina* the chapter's central focus
offers me an opportunity to reinscribe the potential gestures that sanction the survival of cultural identity within class stratification. Finally,
throughout *Latina Performance*, poetry (dramatic and theatrical) is inter-
sected in the analysis, much as it "traverses" the gestures that shape
performance as a cultural practice.

The specific theatrical and performative texts examined in *Latina
Performance* were selected because they offer a means of weaving together strategies that privilege horizontal relationships. My reading of
the selected pieces considers theater, performance, and feminism as
representative of the vital motive forces of this period and of my generation as a Chicana, lesbian, and academic. I wish to emphasize that
although my own feminist and cultural approach to theater, identity
formation, and performance embraces very subjective angles, I do not
intend these as absolute, but rather as dynamic and forever in process.
I believe that it is essential to keep in mind that identity, like culture, is
never static. It is a phenomenon always in transition.

It is this sense of *movement* at the core of identity that underlies my
special interest in the impact of concepts of time and space within
diverse cultural traditions, including Latino, Third World, and Anglo
European theory and criticism. My methodology embraces a cultural
studies approach to dramatic and performative texts. Making explicit
the relations between performance art and theater was one of the
motivations for writing this book. By blending theater and performance,
I want to mark a theatrical tradition that signals an equivalence between
the two categories: Their parallelism provides a critical model for inscribing the way the interposition of the two forms enables the opposi-

tion, autonomy, codependence, and even coincidence, of each category. My study's interdisciplinary character corresponds to the nature of theater itself, where the cross-referentiality of performance art mirrors the cross-referentiality of identity. It is within this framework that the discussion in *Latina Performance* engages the complexity of identity formation and explores the impact of power relations on women's writing, gender, sexuality, and performance.

On an allegorical level, Latinas as women of color may be understood as a heterogeneous trope in a continuous process of invention and re-creation, positioned in opposition to the rigid and restrictive practices of patriarchy, colonialism, and sexual oppression. The goal in showcasing the work of the artists analyzed here is to redefine Latina identity (and subjectivity) as a site of cultural and political contestation, imaginary or real. Theater and performance art play an important role in that redefinition. The blending of the two in my text corresponds (in theory) to the demarcation of the site of hybrid cultures, including that within forms and systems of production. Indeed, the various shifts evident around the terms "theater" and "performance" reside in the configurations of "body" and "embodiment," which are in constant negotiation. As discursive notions of performativity, both theater and performance converge in the term "mirror." Both intersect in an act in which meaning, always ephemeral, is unmasked, transfigured. This book, then, is situated in multiple contested spaces where meaning is not absolute. The identity of performance is inseparable from the materialization of discursive conventions into which it is ostensibly integrated. It is the site where your voice and mine coalesce in a performance of affirmation and skepticism. In a performance of intercultural mediation in which the utterance is split between two or more cultures, the subject is inevitably divided between at least two worlds and two languages. Caught between the First and Third Worlds, the subject in *Latina Performance* interacts in a performance of cultural transference. It is this cultural transaction that validates the reciprocities of discourse, to the degree that the "dominant" grammars of representation are decentered by inserting the "dominated" into it. This intrinsic heterogeneity permeates every aspect embedded in the critical negotiation of this book, both as a concept and as practice. Theoretically, I am invested in the analysis of cultural production. Its potential counter-hegemonic function is a crucial element in understanding the grammars of the divided self. The subjects of *mestizaje*, transculturation, representation, and self-representation informed my approach to theater, performance, and dramatic art.

I have selected a group of artists (and intellectuals) who could help me trace a tradition, one that begins with an emergent Mexican American aesthetics and continues through a queer activism. My book contemplates identity in the past—"traversing" geographical, historical, and political borders—but contemporizes the subject into discursive categories that make her aware of the collective legacy of which she is a part. Thus, the act of reading this book should not be a passive experience. It is a conversation with me, and between ourselves. The women I include in my book speak to us when they perform, write, or sing. They tell us who they are—their secrets, their stories and pains. They laugh and cry while imaging and contesting the sense of meaning and desire, memory and hope.

Latina Performance

In Quest of Latinidad: Identity, Disguise, and Politics

ONE

The contradictions embedded in colonialism shape the creative contributions of Latina artists, writers, and performers. Their work is now and always has been the result of a theatrical *mestizaje* which represents the ongoing conflict inherent in the merger of two worlds: Europe and America. The invisibility of women in the production of theater must be understood as connected in part to the overall powerlessness of women in Latin America. In many sectors of society, this powerlessness has been reinforced by patriarchal and Christian values. In particular, the *marianismo* and *machismo* within the margins of gender roles and their definitions are sustained by the idealization of the female subject posited in the cult of the Virgin Mother Mary and further codified by the dictates of an intensely patriarchal society.

Because it is through Latinas' identity as post- and neocolonial subjects that the political economy of theater, its practice, and its theory must be defined, I begin with a historical overview of identity formation. The framework provided in this chapter emphasizes the political and theoretical definitions of group identity, as well as its diverse racial and cultural roots. It also ties together the histories of various groups, such as Mexicans, Puerto Ricans, Cubans, and Central Americans in the U.S. Further, in sketching a general outline of the trajectory of identity generation, this chapter makes explicit the shared transitory nature connecting the significant historical events of annexation, migration, and exile. Finally, in recognizing "Latino" as a homogeneous, male construction, the discussion simultaneously emphasizes the multiple determinants of the gendered construction "Latina."

The narrative in this chapter is intended to emphasize a common ground that brings the subjects in question together, in solidarity. I believe, however, that acknowledging distinctions embedded in the configuration of *Latinidad* (Latin-ness) is the most powerful way to communicate the importance of this concept. The formation of a strong, positive group identity—one that recognizes and embraces heterogeneity—is key to escaping the shackles of a colonized subjectivity. My analysis complements Chandra Talpade Mohanty's position that the notion of colonization "almost invariably implies a relation of structural domination, and a suppression—often violent—of the heterogeneity of the subject(s) in question."[1]

Histories and Politics of Traversing: Against Homogeneity

> The sense of collective identity ("Latin America") stems less from a history of shared community than from the shared history of *opposition* to the colonial powers. Latin Americans may not all know about or like each other, but by and large they feel intense animosity toward the United States, which has become the latest in a long history of colonizers.[2]

In this passage from *Negotiating Performance*, Diana Taylor draws attention to the shared history of Latinos in relation to their post-Spanish colonial subjectivity. *Negotiating Performance* discusses the political contestation which not only shapes the heterogeneous character of the term "Latin American" and its hybrid variants but also influences diverse modes of representation. In her "Opening Remarks," Taylor expands the categories that mark the hybridity of identity formation and theatrical and performative practices. Of special importance is the contribution *Negotiating Performances* makes by recognizing the centrality of border cultures as a field of study and suggesting new models for future research in the area.[3] My book is one such effort. *Latina Performance* expands the conceptualization of a field that, in embodying politics and performativity, provides a site for critical discourses across disciplines. It continues the search for open-ended definitions of *Latinidad* and the sense of self. I am convinced that the development of Latino and Latina studies within theater and performance (and other disciplines) must start with a quest for the pluralism that *necessarily* perpetuates specific cultural practices that challenge both colonial and imperialist U.S. discourses and recognize the geopolitical implications of space. In this context, the idea of *unidad latinoamericana* must be defined as a "unity" consolidated in the struggles of liberation. The essential unity is one not of languages and origin, but of problematics. The very complexities of *Latinidad* may be the crucial distinguishing mark of Latino culture and identity in the Americas. For David Román and Alberto Sandoval, the development of this notion has been motivated by the "crisis of categorization and this tension between competing political ideologies; it arrives on the scene as a nostalgic reinvocation of the markers of a cultural heritage and homeland—wherever that may be—for the *gente* by the *gente*."[4] The "reinvocation," as marked by Román and Sandoval, emphasizes the vernacular representation of Latino cultures and identities. For them, *Latinidad* disseminates a counteracting mediation against racism and imperialist practices.

Although the term "Latino" refers to people of Latin American descent living primarily within the United States, the word should not be interpreted as denoting a homogeneous racial or ethnic group. Latino people are as diverse as any other cross-section of the population in the U.S. In its embrace of heterogeneity, *Latinidad* mirrors the multiple identities that form the Latin American territory. Thus, the term "Latin American" may be seen as representing an abstract unity composed of multiple ethnicities: Mexicans, Argentineans, Puerto Ricans, Cubans, to name only a few. In the United States, this eclectic unity is denied, replaced by the illusion of homogeneity implicit in the use of a single category, Hispanic, which hides the multiple experiences of what is in fact a heterogeneous community. Popular wisdom maintains that "Hispanic" was a "bureaucratic invention" of the federal government, designed to homogenize the Latino community, at least on paper. Following the recommendation of a task force on racial and ethnic categories, the Department of Health, Education, and Welfare (HEW) adopted Hispanic as an official category in 1973. When the Census Bureau and other government agencies, along with many large institutions and businesses, also began using the term, its mainstream acceptance was assured.[5] Thus, the word "Hispanic" came to be associated with the Establishment and with a politics of identification that accepts the notion of the "melting pot" as a category of unity and equilibrium. A nonthreatening label that eludes negative stereotyping, Hispanic transforms the diversity of national origins into a single category. This aspect of the term—its suppression of the multiple specificities of Latin Americans in the United States—combined with its origin as a bureaucratic convention, led many groups to reject it in favor of Latino. The latter term has the clear advantage of allowing otherwise diverse individuals to signify their shared identity as post-colonial subjects, as well as their present status as members of a neo-colonial, underdeveloped, and exploited Third World community in the United States.

Despite the obvious difficulties in trying to represent in a single word the multiple experiences of Latinos, it remains a worthy goal. Assumptions about the nature of Latino identity differ, in keeping with gender and language. Of course, in Spanish, the o/a split is crucial for signifying gender. In this book, I use the gender-inflected term "Latina" to consciously mark the distinction between the masculine and feminine construction of group identity. The term Latina contests the silence and marginalization of the "feminine," not only in language but in dominant discourses. I view the term Latina as marking the in-between-ness embedded in the geopolitical spaces where identity formation occurs. My aim here is to use Latina as a broad category that embraces a political and cultural movement in the United States, where the politics of identity are crucial. As a critical site of gender deconstruction with strong political implications, Latina subjectivity deals not only with the subcultural claiming of public agency, but also with the experience of marginality as well as with the desire to become powerful and conspicuous. As a performative signifier, the construction of the Latina body is also an inquiry into the possibilities of revolutionary subjectivity. The construction of a revolutionary entity that can transform Western "democratic" social structures requires the support of cultural institutions such as theater and performance art. Thus, the construction of the Latina subject and the performative mediation are linked by necessity in the process of cultural production. In *Latina Performance*, the performative as grammars of identity (de)formation relays a message in favor of a politics of articulation and proclaims power and the social body. Within a binary heterogeneous/homogeneous system of representation, the performative mediation in grammars of identity intervenes in dominant discourses because it proclaims the presence of a marked *differentiality*. Self and Other coalesce in a performance of multiple determination. Thus, the performative as an act of speech or grammars of identification in *Latina Performance* is understood to describe a set of conditions that precede the subject in question as well as the accountability of that conditional state. In such a case, the "citationality" of discursive configurations serves to mediate the possibility of anti-hegemonic agency, which directs and delimits the subject in question in different ways. To use Judith Butler's notion of the performative, the term "Latina" responds to the "linguistification" of a multi-delineated body that contests the ontological status of sexuality, gender, and race. For Butler, the performative registers the "linguistification" or the "verbal conduct" in the context of what she calls "sovereign perform-atives."[6] Her definition of the performative questions the Foucaultian conviction on power and its contestation, which is somehow her own logic in proposing a revised sense of the performative. Butler's views seem to move into a more challenging sensory space in which different genres of "signifying" are paradoxically positioned. She is concerned not only with forms of "harmful speech" (and acts), but with the relation of speech and action: hate speech, pornography, and the homophobic declaration of the military against homosexuality. Butler's discussion of the performative considers the grammars that exercise a compelling power and significantly marks the site in which power *performs*.

To grasp the full meaning of Latina requires an understanding of the ongoing historical and sociopolitical processes of immigration, annex-ation, and exile that have formed the Latino community as a whole. The evolution of the Mexican population in the borderlands, especially in Texas and California, provides a clear example of this cycle.

Latinos: Annexation, Migration, and Exile

In the 1840s, westward expansion in the United States was ignited by the combined stimuli of the idea of Manifest Destiny and the discovery of gold in California. Of the two, the ideology of Manifest Destiny, which sanctified imperialism as the embodiment of the will of God, was perhaps the most devastating for Mexicans. The Mexican-American War (1846–1848) was a direct consequence of the nation's belief in its holy right "to overspread and to possess the whole of the continent which Providence has given us for the development of the great experi-ment of liberty and federated self-government. . . ."[7] In blatant disregard of Mexican sovereignty, U.S. troops precipitated a lopsided war that resulted in the annexation of a prosperous territory containing rich farmlands and natural resources such as gold and oil. Moreover, the U.S. gained control of parts of the Pacific Ocean, generating further economic development. Meanwhile, as Rodolfo Acuña has noted, "Mexico was left with its shrunken resources to face the advances of the United States."[8]

The Treaty of Guadalupe Hidalgo, which formally ended the war, guaranteed Mexicans who remained on the northern side of the border U.S. citizenship, with all of its attendant rights (including the right to own property and the political liberty to preserve one's language and cultural values). However, the treaty, like others that the federal government signed with the indigenous peoples of North America, was never upheld. The government breached its agreement by violating the clauses that guaranteed respect for the cultural autonomy and material property of Mexicans living in the U.S. In the aftermath of the war, when the U.S. was rapidly developing as one of the most powerful empires in the world, Mexicans who chose to remain in the U.S. were subjected to the power and domination of Anglo expansionists. Lured by adventure and capitalist ideals, these Yankee explorers justified their imperialism as the will of "God." They believed themselves to be the "chosen people." Indeed, it was the alleged superior "racial" traits of Anglo-Saxons which became the impetus for American expansion and empire-building. Later, this same self-representation would provide the basis for white supremacy. Most Mexicans living in the U.S. during the nineteenth century were considered a class apart, separate from the Anglo-Saxons, who increasingly insisted upon themselves as a homogenous biophysical entity. The myth of racial purity and superiority became consonant with prevailing beliefs that each race had a unique quality, ordained by God. Thus, the relations between the "dispossessed" people and their "conquerors" came to be understood as "forever" fixed. In this way, the conquest of the Mexican Southwest transformed the Mexicans into a doubly, triply conquered people — subjugated militarily, they were also vanquished commercially, administratively, and culturally.

Overt acts of discrimination against the *mestizo* people increased as the Mexican population in the Southwest grew. With the emergence of the Ku Klux Klan in 1915, the ideology of white supremacy found a near-perfect vehicle. Lothrop Stoddard's *The Rising Tide of Color: Against White World-Supremacy* (1920)[9] identified brown people such as Mexicans as a threat to white supremacy. This type of literature, which helped shape the politics of racial hatred practiced by the Klan, continues to find an audience today. In California, the passage of Proposition 187 in the 1994 gubernatorial election cycle and Proposition 209 in the 1996 presidential election cycle are clear manifestations of a discriminatory politics aimed at an ethnic minority that is fast becoming a demographic majority.

Mexicans who lived in the United States at the start of this century felt compelled to assimilate, to accept the host country's political and cultural systems, despite their repressive and discriminatory aspects.

One outgrowth of the earliest efforts to adapt and accommodate to mainstream American society was the development of a politically conservative, middle-class Mexican American identity, epitomized by LULAC, the League of United Latin American Citizens. Founded in 1929, LULAC championed the twin causes of education and equality throughout the 1930s. LULAC members fought for state laws that would end discrimination against Mexicans and claimed to speak for the Latino population. Nevertheless, the organization's ideology was that of a rising middle class who saw assimilation as a necessary strategy for advancement. LULAC members felt threatened by the radicalism embraced by other groups and their organization did not, according to Rodolfo Acuña, serve the interests of the poor: "[T]hey felt they could achieve their goal—which was to become capitalists—in a dignified manner like 'decent' people. Their method was to work within the system and not in the streets."[10] Indeed, LULAC's constitution clearly defined the group as nonpolitical. The time would come, however, when political activism among minorities would not be restricted to "radical" fringe groups.

During and immediately following World War II, increased opportunities for ethnic and racial minorities helped promote a sense of political awareness in these communities. By the early 1960s, among blacks, the call for equal rights was in full swing and Mexican Americans were not far behind. *El movimiento,* which gave voice to the community's opposition to entrenched political and social discrimination, may be characterized in terms of its two main stages: the early period, from the mid-1960s to 1973, and the "post-Chicano movement" period, from the mid-1970s to the present. During the first stage, characterized by radicalism, nationalism and social protest unified the struggle for civil rights. Hidden within this unity, however, was an age-old, patriarchal and heterosexist hierarchy that placed women in *el movimiento* far below their male counterparts. This was the fault line along which the movement divided, marking the advent of its second stage. Women and queers, committed to developing a politics of visibility and difference within a dynamic movement, helped usher in the postnational period by displacing the static predicament of *chicanismo*. Women activists, writers, dramatists, and other cultural workers are now much more visible in the continuing struggle of Mexicans and other Latinos to counter white, Anglo cultural domination. Some critics deny the existence of this second stage, maintaining that the Chicano movement died out in the 1970s. I join Cherríe Moraga in asserting otherwise; the movement did not die, it "was only deformed by the machismo and homophobia of that era and coopted by [the] 'hispanicization' of the eighties."[11]

In the Chicano movement (and in other Latino contexts), efforts to build a sense of community and/or national identity typically have been undertaken in an environment rife with unresolved ethnic, cultural, and racial questions. For example, the concept of *la familia chicana*, saturated with sexism, homophobia, and internal oppression, once served as the movement's mandate, its rallying call for the collective participation of all members of the community. This *familia* ideology directly— and negatively—affected the movement's heterosexual women participants: "[W]omen were, at most, allowed to serve as modern-day 'Adelitas,'" Moraga recounts, performing the "'three fs,' as a Chicana colleague calls them: 'feeding, fighting and fucking.'"[12] The movement's tendency to perpetuate traditional structures simultaneously sustained the power of the patriarchal father figure, who tried to remain in charge in both the public and private spheres. Same-sex desire, because it is unencumbered by the cultural bonds implicit in the foundations of community, nation, and *la familia*, was/is seen as threatening.

In the late 1970s and 1980s, heterosexual women began to organize against the repressive structures that systematically reproduced their subjected position in *el movimiento*. Gays and lesbians, however, continue to suffer the effects of homophobia, which is an especially effective form of sexism. As a social institution, heterosexism validates and reinforces the spirit of homophobia through its linked assumptions that everyone is and must be heterosexual, since heterosexual behavior represents the norm and constitutes the "natural" experience of humanity. In Suzanne Pharr's words, "heterosexim and homophobia work together to enforce compulsory heterosexuality and that bastion of patriarchal power, the nuclear family."[13]

It was not by accident that the Chicano movement alienated some very significant female, lesbian, and gay leaders. Nor is it simply bad luck that the type of unified *familia* the movement envisioned has never come about. A political commitment to race and ethnic awareness must include a commitment to queers, as well. Moraga made this clear in an early work:

> I guarantee you, there will be no change among heterosexual men, there will be no change in heterosexual relations, as long as the Chicano community keeps us lesbians and gay men political prisoners among our own

people. Any movement built on the fear and loathing of anyone is a failed movement. The Chicano movement is no different.[14]

For intellectuals such as Moraga, Gloria Anzaldúa, and myself, the impact of homophobia and sexism within the Chicano community and in other Latino contexts, and the oppressive definition of gender roles in these environments, are subjects that require a serious critique. Our intellectual roles as activists, cultural workers, or academics represent a challenge linked to a concern for a body which constitutes itself in critical relation to a set of hegemonic social and cultural orders. In fact, our practices as queer intellectuals not only attempt to subvert these oppressive orders, but have become an indication of the contradictions they constitute. As dialectical-oppositional significers, these contradictions constitute binary relations between knowledge and ignorance, between power and abdication, and between compulsive heterosexuality and queer politics. Thus, the work of queer academics, artists, and activists strives to reach out for alliances across identities and spaces to deal with new cultural forms and new political subjects.

Moraga argues that *el movimiento* "has never been a thing of the past, it has retreated into subterranean uncontaminated soils awaiting resurrection in a 'queerer,' more feminist generation."[15] Moraga's radicalism proposes redefining the concept of *la familia chicana* in a manner that would provide a sense of location for Chicana lesbians. She offers "queer Aztlán," a community of mythic capabilities that could embrace all of its people, including heterosexuals. In Moraga's view, queer Aztlán is a particularly potent cultural metaphor for redefining the Chicano movement in the 1990s:

> Since lesbians and gay men have often been forced out of our blood families, and since our love and sexual desire are not housed within the traditional family, we are in a critical position to address those areas within our cultural family that need to change. Further, in order to understand and defend our lovers and our same-sex loving, lesbians and gay men must come to terms with how homophobia, gender roles, and sexuality are learned and expressed in Chicano culture.[16]

Moraga's "imagined community" (to use Benedict Anderson's concept) will be able to liberate itself from the sexism and homophobia that have continuously damaged *el movimiento*. Thus, queer Aztlán becomes the site of the utopic. It is a divided entity of hybridized cultures which negotiates a prioritized space equivalent to the affirmation of identity politics. In this mythical "promised land" (whether it be Moraga's

Aztlán or the "queer nation" that ACT UP! proposed when it formed in 1987), the negotiation of space and identity politics juxtaposes the operations of "queer" with ethnic categories.

This negotiation is precisely what Sue-Ellen Case proposes when she questions the functionality of queer as a strategy of the white, middle-class urban activist. By identifying the importance of identity politics, Case suggests ways to make the applicability of the term 'queer' more substantial. Having juxtaposed "ethnic models with new, queer ones, we can now turn to the rise of Queer Nation, and the succeeding operations of the term 'queer.'"[17] In Case's view, the functionality of queer breaks up lesbian and gay orthodoxies, making possible new alliances across gender and other categories. In Moraga's account, the queering of her homeland and her community are predicated on different arguments, but they have the same political implications. Moraga envisions a *movimiento* that will represent women, students, queers, working-class people, farm workers, and other Latinos. She calls for the kind of collective action that will affirm a politics in which "la chicana indígena stands at the center and heterosexism and homophobia are no longer the cultural order of the day."[18] While Case defines multi-culturalism as an effect of ethnicity within the definition of queer politics, Moraga adapts Queer Nation to Aztlán as a crucial argument against homophobia and sexism: "Chicana lesbians and gay men do not merely seek inclusion in the Chicano nation; we seek a nation strong enough to embrace a full range of racial diversities, human sexualities, and expressions of gender."[19]

The Chicano nation Moraga envisions calls for forming coalitions beyond the confines of separatist agendas. She proposes a queer politics in which men and women and members of various ethnic groups would work together and learn from each other. I question the practicality of this proposal. In any heterogeneous group, there will always be individuals and/or subgroups who rise to the top and, once there, redefine the "original" agenda. In the feminist movement, for example, white middle-class women still overshadow women of color; in the university, heterosexual white men still hold the reins of power and conservatively "govern" white women as well as women of color. The structures that sustain the social hierarchies within radical, "liberal," or conservative settings are of long standing and have proven difficult to eradicate. This entrenchment is especially clear in imperialist nations like the U.S., where the social order is justified in terms of a capitalist ethos that is intertwined with a possessive, individualistic subjectivity. A queer politics such as Moraga urges is attractive insofar as it presents a possible challenge to our diverse sexual, political, and cultural histories. However, I would support Case's "multicultural" vision if it could stake out a politics that would always require the presence of an empirically determinable pluralism, one that would decenter the "dominant" culture—democratically speaking—and would attain equality and reciprocity. A commitment to pluralism does not ensure unity, but it does provide a forum for negotiations over identity, representation, and cultural production. From the Treaty of Guadalupe Hidalgo and the Mexican American experience to the Chicano movement and queer Aztlán, multiple tensions characterize every effort to build a united community from diverse peoples.

Latino identity: Puerto Rican annexation and immigration. An additional important source of Latino heterogeneity may be traced to yet another nineteenth-century act of imperialism. In 1898, as part of the settlement of the Spanish American War, the United States confiscated Puerto Rican national territory. With the passage of the Jones Act in 1917, Puerto Ricans became citizens of the United States. Since then, and especially in the 1920s and the 1930s, Puerto Rican immigration to the mainland has been steady. After World War II, the number of immigrants grew substantially. Until recently, Puerto Ricans on the mainland have settled mainly in New York City and surrounding areas, and in Chicago. Since 1980, however, this regional concentration has expanded to include Los Angeles, Philadelphia, and Miami. Like other ethnic and racial minorities, Puerto Ricans on the mainland were galvanized by the civil rights movement of the 1960s; during this period the community began to actively participate in affirming their rights as citizens—including the right to gain elective office.

One striking aspect of the Puerto Rican migration is its "circular" character. This community has developed a cultural identity in direct colonial bondage to the United States. As Juan Flores has explained, this bondage "evokes the relation, above all, between Puerto Rican people here and there, between the expressive life of the migrant population and the long-standing traditions of struggle and articulation of the Island culture."[20] Flores speaks of the long-lived traditions of struggle that characterize the indigenous Island culture and the conflict inherent in the neo-colonized subject position imposed by life on the mainland.

These separate traditions also have coalesced to create a third identity, the Nuyorican. As the "promised land" of Puerto Ricans, New York City becomes the urban landscape imprinted in the making of a new identity. Flores suggests that by "[l]ooking at New York, the Nuyorican sees Puerto Rico or at least the glimmering imprint of another world to which vital connections have been struck."[21] This traversing notion of cultural identity resonates in the work of Nuyorican poet Sandra María Esteves. In one of her poems, "Here," the recovery of hybrid roots provides a glimpse of cultural intersections and contentions:

> I am two parts/ a person
> boricua/ spic
> past and present
> alive and oppressed
> given a cultural beauty
> . . . and robbed of a cultural identity.[22]

Esteves uses very strong images to express the sense of displacement. Even beyond this word imagery, however, her dramatic configurations evoke the contradictions that connect the divided self—"alive" but "oppressed," at once deceived and sustained by her culture. Critics often compare Esteves, who was born in the Bronx, to the poet Julia de Burgos, who was a significant presence in the previous generation of *émigrés.*[23] Esteves' poetry, written exclusively in English, deals with her personal experience as an urban Latina living in New York City. As a Nuyorican, she is constantly confronted by the conflicts of living between two cultures and languages. In "Here," the dramatic revelations repeatedly express this sense of alienation. Esteves must continually incorporate a new language and culture into the "sweetness" of the Boricua:

> I speak the alien tongue
> in sweet borinqueño thoughts
> know love mixed with pain
> have tasted spit on ghetto stairways
> . . . here, it must be changed
> we must change it

Boricua ("borinqueño" in the poem) is a powerful identity marker which places the subject against hegemonic reasoning.[24] Esteves' poem expresses a sense of separation. She invokes the process of transculturation itself as a way to counteract the estrangement of cultural identity from its origins. The mechanism of the subject's transculturation is synonymous with the embodiment of a divided sensibility and subjectivity. It alters collective and individual identity, transforming the positionality of the one who speaks. Esteves' poetic subject struggles in a fragmented world, but the powerful poetic voice provides the work with a sense of continuity.[25] This progression is evident in another of her poems, written in 1990. "Puerto Rican Discovery #5, Here Like There," again clearly expresses the sense of continuity that is also readily apparent in much Nuyorican music, poetry, and theater:

> Like there in Puerto Rico,
> mountains and sea wage vain attempts
> to purify the plastic layer
> Breathless and tight over its victims,
> a flag stuffed luscious,
> laying to rot in ambivalent warehouses
> of aborted children
> from an indifferent
> . . . mother.[26]

As poetic reflections, the spaces "here and there" represent the distinction between the mainland and the Island. The symbolic and performative discourse through poetry accompanies the yearning of motherland to such a degree that the poetic subject asserts the cultural and historical syncreticism of the beloved Island. The first, "here," reflects the state of ambivalence, of mixed feelings, always in contradiction. The second, "there," looks to the Island for direction and meaning. Flores notes that the poet's decision to search "there" for guidance "cannot be tested for its historical or even geographical authenticity, since it is initially conjured for metaphorical, emblematic reasons."[27] The performative resonance attests the rejection of authenticity, supporting the process of the subject's transcultural experience. Thus, the subject's poetic voice and imagination become the result of resistance and reaffirmation. The utterance's concern responds not only to the political ramifications embedded in the production of the collective self, but to the encounter of worlds and cultures.

Symbolically, the in-between-ness of migrant communities, of colonized and neo-colonized cultures, becomes a continuous form that is often expressed through the formation of a new identity. For Puerto Ricans, the term Nuyorican captures the neither "here" nor "there" quality of their daily lives on the mainland. For both Chicanos and Puerto Ricans, the in-between sites of geopolitical borders, U.S./Puerto Rico and U.S./Mexico, constitute transitions of space that induce the subject into a state of *nepantla,* as she/he moves in and out, from one place to another. As a middle territory, *nepantla* is the uncertain terrain one crosses in the transition from the present identity to a new one. This condition, Gloria Anzaldúa points out, is negotiated "when changing from one class, race, or gender position to another."[28]

The Nuyorican identity of New York City's Puerto Rican community affirms the existence of a new cultural marker. It negotiates the process of transculturation, producing new meaning implicated in the cultural transference of bodies ready to be re-embodied and re-visioned. Norma Alarcón compares the two terms, Nuyorican and Chicana, pointing out that each was invented to generate a critical space for articulating similarities and differences between the two components of the United States/Puerto Rican Island dyad and between the two components of the United States/Mexico dyad. Alarcón defines the slash between the countries as "a conscious cultural and political intervention in which the territories on either side of the slash play a role of transformation for the subject posed on the slash itself."[29] The slash represents the middle part that divides, but also, paradoxically, unifies a subjectivity that is always poised to change, alter, and adjust. Because this border refuses to accept a single, definitive sense of self, interrogation of national, political, cultural, racial, and sexual identities must be ongoing.

Latino identity: Cuban exile and immigration. Other important strands in the formation of Latino identity in the United States include the Cuban population. The largest and most visible influx of Cubans to the United States came following the overthrow of Fulgencio Batista by Fidel Castro's forces in 1959. Like Puerto Rico, Cuba was acquired by the United States as a consequence of the Spanish-American war. Unlike Puerto Rico, it was ruled by the U.S. government for only three years—Cuba acquired its independence in 1902.

The first Cuban migration to the United States occurred in 1868, in response to an increased demand for labor fueled by the growth of a new tobacco industry in Key West and Tampa, Florida. But most Cuban immigration has occurred in the years since Castro took power in 1959. The first postrevolutionary group to flee Cuba consisted mainly of the white middle classes, who were the most adversely affected by the institution of a communist state and the nationalization of the island's economy. The unsuccessful Bay of Pigs invasion in 1961 prompted an increase in Cuban naturalization, as many who had fled Castro's Cuba resigned themselves to living in the U.S. permanently. More Cuban exiles arrived throughout the 1960s, airlifted as part of the U.S. government's ongoing efforts to discredit Castro's regime. This politically conservative first generation of Cuban exiles quickly succeeded in establishing themselves in the U.S. business world, especially in construction, real estate, tobacco, restaurants, television, and newspapers. This secure economic position has helped this earlier generation of Cubans to acquire excellent education for themselves and their children. As a result, unlike Chicanos and Puerto Ricans, they have been able to consolidate an impressive amount of sociopolitical power in communities like Miami.

The most recent large Cuban immigration to the United States, the *Marielitos*, took place in 1980. This migration was made up of darker-skinned people of lower socioeconomic status. These newcomers received a chilly welcome when they arrived in the United States, partly because of a downturn in the U.S. economy and partly because the media portrayed this wave of exiles as composed mainly of criminals, homosexuals, and the mentally ill. Miami's Cuban community was disgusted by the new arrivals, perceiving them as a threat to the established community's "golden" image. The significant socioeconomic differences between the older community and the newcomers remain. The group who came in 1980 tend to be, relative to the older generation, economically and socially disadvantaged. This socieconomic position, in turn, shapes their daily life experiences and gives them more in common with Puerto Ricans and Chicanos. However, unlike Chicanos and Puerto Ricans, for close to twenty years, Cubans could cross the border in only one direction. When, two decades after the revolution, it finally became possible for Cubans to travel back home, this "generation" of Cubans exiled in the U.S. began to come to terms with their displaced identity. The struggle to reclaim one's full self by recovering this lost memory is what Carmelita Tropicana performs in *Milk of Amnesia/Leche de Amnesia* (see Chapter 5 for a discussion of this work).

Latino identity: South American exile and immigration. Of course, not all immigrants who come to the U.S. find the kind of well-established (if disapproving) community that the *Marielitos* faced. Peoples exiled by repressive dictatorships in the Southern Cone have become an increasingly noticeable presence in the U.S. since the early 1970s: these groups include people from Argentina, Chile, Uruguay, and Brazil. By the 1970s, the Southern Cone's most important governmental positions were occupied by technocrats, individuals who had come to power after successful careers in large bureaucracies, private or public corporations, or the armed forces. These functionaries implemented national modernization programs, under the control and domination of the armed forces. The political system that emerged by the 1970s reflected both the breakdown of the popular sector and the rise of monied interests representing groups backed by large amounts of foreign or domestic capital.

The magnitude of the United States' involvement in the process of militarization in Latin America is difficult to assess accurately. The victory of the Left in Chile, the ongoing skirmishes with guerrillas, the rise of social movements, and the increasingly strident demands of political activists finally alerted the United States to the threat to its geopolitical interests posed by the spread of socialism in this part of the continent. Commenting on the election of socialist Salvador Allende in Chile in the early 1970s, Henry Kissinger summed up the United States' position with regard to Latin American politics this way: "I do not see why we need to stand by and watch a country go Communist due to the irresponsibility of its own people."[30] To combat such "irresponsibility," the U.S. supported military regimes by bankrolling their campaigns against alleged "subversive" elements. Moreover, by legitimizing the military systems and advising them in their initial political processes, the U.S. undoubtedly assured the triumph of the military takeovers. Augusto Pinochet, for example, relied heavily on material, training and strategy provided by the U.S. government. Ironically, many of the people who fled these U.S.-supported Latin American authoritarian regimes saw "el Norte" as their salvation.

Latino identity: Central American exile and immigration. More recently, political upheaval and the existence of armed resistance movements in El Salvador, Guatemala, and Nicaragua have spurred another large-scale exodus. Among those emigrating to the U.S., the greatest number are from El Salvador; the second greatest, from Guatemala. Because of these newcomers' undocumented status, it is impossible to calculate their precise numbers. Many Salvadorans, Nicaraguans, and Guatemalans who have filtered into the U.S. over the past 15 years consider themselves to be political refugees. It can safely be assumed that most of them still have not been granted that legal status, however. The U.S. Refugee Act of 1980 provided that any individual present in the U.S. had the right to apply for asylum. However, this status is only granted to those individuals who can demonstrate a well-founded fear of persecution in their native country. Most of the refugees from Central America have witnessed the deaths of parents, relatives, or friends. The bare fact that they are willing to leave their homeland, culture, language, friends, and family, knowing that they are unlikely to be able to return, should be ample proof of the seriousness of the danger that surrounds them in their own countries. It is not. In fact, new immigration laws and guidelines require that members of certain refugee communities from Central America be summarily returned to their homelands, with no regard for their safety once returned. Many political refugees discover when they reach the U.S. that they have simply exchanged one set of problems for another.[31] Undergoing a harrowing journey through Mexico and a terrifying border crossing, these "traversers" finally arrive in Los Angeles or another border city, only to discover a far harsher reality than they expected. Economic hardship is complicated by the additional burden of pressures from the dominant society to deny/cast off one's "old" identity and assume a new, "more acceptable" one. For Latinas, especially, these demands, with their underlying elements of patriarchy and sexism, can be overbearing. (The complex experiences of the cross-border subject are discussed in Chapter 4.) The next section examines some of the ways in which Latinas constitute a Third World community within the U.S. and discusses the challenges Latina writers and artists have mounted to the neocolonial subject position assigned to them.

U.S. *Latinas: Women of Color and* Tercermundistas

> My name is Coco Fusco, and actually, I was born in the U.S. and genetically composed of Yoruba, Taino, Catalan, Sephardic, and Neapolitan blood. In 1990, that makes me Hispanic. If this were the '50s, I might be considered black.[32]

> To posit some objective "Hispanicity" common to everyone remotely connected to Spain or born in a Spanish-speaking country is a state-imposed hegemonic project that culturalizes economic and political oppression.[33]

An unmasking of the multiple sources of identity is crucial to an understanding of the Latina subject in the United States. In the passages quoted above, Coco Fusco and Martha E. Gimenez expose the diversity within and between U.S. Latinos. Each is aware of the complex social, historical, political, and personal dimensions that constitute group identification. Fusco raises important questions about the heterogeneity embedded in the term "Hispanic"; and Gimenez explicitly rejects the idea of "hispanicity," noting its association with cultural domination in the U.S. Both Gimenez and Fusco remind us that Latinos (or Hispanics) are distinguishable not only by race and class, but also by generational processes of migration. Despite the importance of the processes of migration, the history of Latinos in the U.S. has often been viewed with little or no regard for the diverse types of *émigrés*, the reasons for their emigration, or the timing of their arrival in the United States.

Gimenez considers the term "Hispanic" a bureaucratic invention that eradicates the diverse histories among U.S. Latinos and between these Latinos and the newly arrived immigrants from Central and

South America. While she observes the contradictions embedded in both terms, Latino and Hispanic, Gimenez prefers to use the former, "for it grapples with the historical links between people who, while living both north and south of the border between the U.S. and Latin America, do have a common history."[34] Fusco rightly problematizes the homogeneity implied by ethnic designations and affirms the African legacy that is a significant, though typically unexamined, element in Latin American and Caribbean cultures.[35] Latinos' tendency to marginalize their African and indigenous roots while celebrating their Hispanic heritage is both an outgrowth of a colonial subjectivity and a mechanism for perpetuating the domain of "the subjected." The colonized subject continuously abolishes her/his own identity by invalidating the multiple determinants that may intersect within the broader categories of race or nation.[36]

Latina theater and performance may be understood as bringing together the subject of a post-Spanish colonial history in relation to the multiple entities subsumed within the term "Latin American" and within the categories of ethnicity, race, and sexuality. Given this perspective, understanding the role of theater and performance requires first considering the location of Latinas as a Third World community in the U.S. The genderization signified by the a/o split, by separating the space of male hegemonic representation, privileges the female subject's self-governing position within a collective identity. The term Latina signals the complexity and heterogeneity of identity, a construction that reinforces the subject's agency and multiple determinations. Historically, in the intricate realm of First World power, the subject has prevailed. In this context, Latinas, as women of color, identify with a Third World politics which resists both historical and symbolic systems of domination. It is crucial to note that the marker "women of color," frequently used in the U.S., has no similar meaning in Latin America. As Diana Taylor explains, "the term 'people of color' is at best meaningless in Latin America; at worst, it reenacts U.S. dominance for it is only from the vantage point of the United States that all Latin Americans, regardless of race or class, are 'people of color.'"[37] The artist or intellectual in Latin America often speaks from a position of power; he or she may speak "*for* the marginalized, but not *from* the margins."[38] Beginning in the nineteenth century, indigenous people and blacks, viewed through a paternalistic/materialistic lens, were portrayed as part of the "barbaric" component of a "civilization" in the process of modernization. In this century, the use of racial and cultural categories "disguises" the more complex relationships between the geopolitical reality of

Latin American neocolonialism and a "distinguished" culture that continues to favor European standards.

In the introduction to her book, *Third World Women and the Politics of Feminism,* Chandra Talpade Mohanty has noted that the terms "women of color" and "Third World women" are often used interchangeably. She argues that these groups constitute "a political constituency, not a biological or even sociological one."[39] From a theoretical perspective, a Third World politics strives to form coalitions among women who identify with a common context—one in which the feminist subject is located as the explicit embodiment of overlapping networks of power. In Mohanty's words, "it is [T]hird [W]orld women's oppositional *political* relation to sexist, racist, and imperialist structures that constitutes our potential commonality."[40] Thus, a Third World women's politics attempts to compensate for what the dominant culture has failed to embody. This is why a politics of allegiance among Third World women is of paramount importance if we are to maintain our self-autonomy and avoid being tokenized within mainstream society. For women of Latin American descent, this exclusiveness is a legitimate part of the process of identity formation and reformation. Women who choose to identify as Latinas, to resist the term Hispanic, make a consciously political determination.

In (re-)claiming their identity as Latinas, artists and writers such as Fusco and Gimenez and Vicioso (discussed below) have demonstrated a willingness to acknowledge and embrace their African heritage as well. This attitude sets them apart from most academics and intellectuals in the United States, Latin America, and the Caribbean. The Dominican poet Chiqui Vicioso explains how the experience of living in New York City was pivotal in helping her to discover her identity as a black Caribbean:

> In the United States, there is no space for fine distinctions of race, and one goes from being "trigueño" or "indio" to being "mulatto" or "Black" or "Hispanic." This was an excellent experience for me. From that point on, I discovered myself as a Caribbean *mulata* and adopted the Black identity as a gesture of solidarity. At that time, I deeply admired and identified with Angela Davis, and ever since then, I have kept on identifying myself as a Black woman.[41]

Vicioso's identity formation as a black *caribeña* is crystallized by her own migrant and marginal position in New York City, where she discovers herself as a woman of color. From being just another *dominicana* of the Caribbean, she comes to terms with her own African-ness as a way of consolidating her place among other women of color in the United States. Vicioso's identity is fundamentally political, and she speaks of Angela Davis as an influential role model. A powerful figure in the 1960s and 1970s, Davis was a key source of feminist thinking and activism. She created a more accurate history of black women, bringing to attention and preserving a tradition of black women's activism, and at the same time, questioning traditional accounts of reproduction.[42]

The discursive configurations included in the notion of "woman of color" are ambiguous and contradictory. Because of, rather than in spite of, this unruly eclecticism, the term represents a crucial politics of identification among Latinas and other minority women who seek to de-identify with the dominant white feminist movement. Whether their skin is dark, black, or white, Latinas in the U.S. speak of the "racialization" of culture as a counter-hegemonic project. After the publication of *This Bridge Called My Back: Writings by Radical Women of Color* (1981), edited by Cherríe Moraga and Gloria Anzaldúa, the concept of women of color emerged as a counter-subjectivity capable of demonstrating the differences between Third World women and Anglo Americans (an important distinction long avoided within Eurocentric feminist debates). As Moraga and Anzaldúa noted in their introduction, *Bridge* was originally conceived as a project to consolidate the Third World feminist movement in the United States. The editors suggested that Third World women thinking of joining or forming a broad-based political movement consider the following:

> 1) how visibility/invisibility as women of color forms our radicalism; 2) the ways in which Third World women derive a feminist political theory specifically from our racial/cultural backgrounds and experience; 3) the destructive and demoralizing effects of racism in the women's movement; 4) the cultural, class, and sexuality differences that divide women of color; 5) Third World women's writing as a tool for self-preservation and revolution; 6) the ways and means of a Third World feminist future.[43]

Launching a Third World feminist movement in this country has proved to be easier in theory than in practice, a fact *Bridge* attests to, as Moraga has noted in the foreword to the book's second edition. At the theoretical level, the notion of women of color or Third World feminism trains attention on the multiple faces and voices of minority women in the United States. The writers in *Bridge*—Latinas, African Americans, Asian Americans, and Native Americans—discuss their systematic exclusion from the dominant white culture and from white academic, feminist discourses. They invoke a collective identification for women of color, hoping to span the multiple differences of a silent community. As Norma Alarcón has pointed out, "[l]ike gender epistemologists and other emancipatory movements, the theoretical subject of *Bridge* gives credit to the subject of consciousness as the site of knowledge but problematizes it by representing it as a weave."[44] Alarcón proposes a multiple-voiced subject who resides in resistance to contending notions of the politics of self-representation. As a process of deidentification, this act of contestation attempts to deconstruct dominant formulations of the theoretical subject of feminism.

In *Bridge*, the writers deconstruct the space of the dominant subject (whiteness) by constructing a productive site for rewriting the arrangements of gender, class, race, ethnicity, and sexuality. The importance of constructing one's identity within a collectivity and supported by enduring alliances is reinforced by Chiqui Vicioso's *testimonio*. She explains, "I had to discover that I was part of a certain geographical area, and then, that I was Latin American."[45] Vicioso's marked identity is shaped by the recurrent migrations of Afro-Caribbeans to the inner cities of the United States; Latin-ness is discovered within terms of racial relocation. This ongoing process creates and re-creates the conditions for the production of a multi-layered hybridity within Latina/o cultures and languages. Even though not all Latinas are black or brown, and some speak only English, some only Spanish and some Spanglish, the complexity embedded in national-cultural markers of identity formation must be related to that which defines Latinas/os in general, and Puerto Ricans, Dominicans, Colombians, Mexicans, Chicanos, etc., in particular.

As a Chicana who views her *mestizaje* as the site of utopic hybridization—a metaphor of political interpretation and identification—I have learned to deal with this complexity. My position, then, recognizes the pluralism implicated in the ongoing process of defining Latina-ness as a project committed to building coalitions not only *among* ourselves, but also *between* ourselves and other women of color. Latinas, who identify *as* and *with* women of color, must attempt to extend their allegiances beyond the privileged—and related—discourses of colonialism, homophobia, and patriarchy. Chicanas, like many other Latinas in the United States, perceive themselves as part of a mother culture that has been "raped": violated by the order of colonialism and cultural tyranny since the sixteenth century when the Spaniards invaded Mexico and other nations in Central and South America and the Caribbean.

The repression of female sexuality finds its roots in the colonial experience. A legacy of betrayal among Chicanas and other Latinas reinforces their perception of cultural violence and exploitation. The historical and mythical representation of La Malinche as a paradigm of this legacy of betrayal has been noted repeatedly by artists, critics, and historians. The first victim of the Spanish colonization, La Malinche was known for her ability to speak and understand many different languages. She became Hernán Cortés' mistress and translator. She became, as well, the intermediary between two cultures. In her poem "La Malinche," Carmen Tafolla writes:

> Yo soy la Malinche.
> My people called me Malintzin Tenepal
> The Spaniards called me Doña Marina
> I came to be known as Malinche
>   and Malinche came to mean traitor.
> They called me—*chingada*
>   Chingada.
> (Ha—¡Chingada! Screwed!)[46]

Tafolla's representation of La Malinche as the "fucked one" is a deliberate reflection of the still-current popular perception of La Malinche in terms of her symbolic subjectivity as *la chingada*. In Mexico and in other Latino contexts, the label *malinchista* signifies a traitor and associates the one so labeled with a legacy of betrayal.

Later in her poem, Tafolla explains Malinche's noble ancestry and her role in helping the Spaniards to defeat the emperor Moctezuma. At the end of the poem, the poetic subject comes forth to clarify and transgress Malinche's subjectivity as the "fucked one":

> But Chingada I was not.
>   Not tricked, not screwed, not traitor.
> For I was not traitor to myself—
>   I saw a dream
>   And I *reached* it.
>   *Another world.* . . . .
>   la raza.
>   la raaaaa-zaaaa . . . (p. 199)

In Tafolla's final articulations, La Malinche becomes the mother of *mestizaje*, of a new race in a "new world." The poet's dramatic account attempts to create a more sympathetic view of Malinche's actions. Tafolla challenges the long-standing accusation that La Malinche betrayed her race, and she rejects the tradition that perceives La Malinche as *la chingada*. At the same time, the historical/mythical poetic references Tafolla uses remind us of the effects of La Malinche's paradigm in defining the racial and sexual identity of Chicanas, specifically, and of other Latinas, more generally.

The sexuality of Latinas has typically been defined with reference to male desire and colonial domination. The *sensuality* of Latinas is flaunted and exploited in the popular media, but most of the time, their *sexuality* is subjected to internal and external cultural domination. From the actively heterosexual to the politically visible lesbian, Latinas' sexuality, like the sexuality of all other women, is closely tied to the patriarchal system. Moraga explains this relationship clearly, noting that female sexuality is systematically regulated, whether it is through the Church or the State.[47]

It is in this context that Latinas deconstruct their colonized position. They address and then reject the homogeneity embedded in a dominant culture that, bypassing the significance of ethnicity, race, and sexuality, tries to censor their multiple subjectivities. Ironically, the very experience of being denied the full domain of self-conscious representations allows Latinas to invent, formulate, and recreate a sense of continuity and community rooted in the diversity and pluralism of their experience. It is by becoming a subject in this shared process of cultural mutation that the dramatists and performance artists I discuss in this book free themselves from the tropes of hegemonic representation. As premier venues for self-expression, theater and performance art are logical choices for Latinas as they seek to enact their selves, and in so doing, to contribute to a collective act of identity making. But, as the next section chronicles, even in the "new theater" tradition that developed in the wake of the Cuban revolution, old values and entrenched sexual hierarchies have often prevailed. Thus, at the same time as they are staging their own liberation, Latinas are also engaging in a struggle to free theater and performance art from the bonds of a male-dominated and male-defined political economy.

The Transformation of the Stage across Borders

It is understood that the radical transformation of the theatre can't be the result of some artistic whim. It has simply to correspond to the whole radical transformation of the mentality of our time.[48]

Toda pieza de teatro es un ajuste de cuentas, un enfrentamiento inmediato con la sociedad. La escritura teatral es una escritura agresiva por su misma naturaleza, está hecha para ser llevada a la escena, y la escena tiene, no sólo la falta de pudor de todo arte, sino un subrayado agregado por la corporeidad de los actores, por la confrontación física entre lo que sucede en el escenario y el espectador que escucha y sobre todo "ve."[49]

[Every theatrical piece is a whole, an immediate confrontation with society. By nature, theater itself is an aggressive form of writing: it is written to be taken to the stage, and the stage needs more than what any other artistic form demands: It needs the actors' corporeality and the physical encounter between what will happen on stage and the spectator, who listens, but most important, "witnesses."][50]

Both Bertolt Brecht and Griselda Gambaro envision, in their respective historic moments, an important connection between theater and change in society. Brecht's clear definition of life as a model for theater was a product of his prolonged opposition to the established theater, which he considered superficial, mindless entertainment. Brecht's idea that theater could be—indeed, should be—more than entertainment for an educated economic elite took hold in Latin America during the early 1960s. As Latin American theater began to examine reality as a historical and social process, a dialectic method of production, Brecht's ideas were crucial. According to critic and playwright Augusto Boal, Brecht "taught us that our obligation as artists was to shed light on reality, not only to reflect and to interpret it, but to try to change it."[51] Brecht also influenced the structure of modern theater in Latin America. Since the 1960s, most playwrights have replaced the Aristotelian model of dramatic components with Brecht's independent scenic units. The latter permit contrast in three main areas: the "hero" or the human being as the subject of theater; the structure of the play; and the incorporation of the spectator within the dramatic action.

In addition to the Brechtian influences, several other factors contributed to the development of an attitude of revolt in Latin American theater. *The Theater and Its Double* by Antonin Artaud (1938) and *Political Theater* by Erwin Piscator (1929), were influential, as were Beckett's and Ionesco's absurdist orientations. But perhaps the most significant external event was the triumph of the Cuban revolution in 1959. It is important to bear in mind that the Latin American movement referred to by some critics as "New Theater" evolved in a specific social, political, and economic context, one significantly impacted by the Cuban revolution. To translate and paraphrase the ideas of Guatemalan critic Manuel Galich, this theatrical movement, "nuevo teatro," is an outgrowth of a revolutionary ideology that demystifies history, denounces imperialism, situates oligarchy within society, and explicitly outlines the problems of the proletariat (i.e., the oppressed majority) as emanating from the despotic decrees of the ruling minority.[52] It is this larger intellectual framework that gives the theatrical movement its distinctive dynamic in Latin America.

But for some, such as Diana Taylor, the word "new" in the name of this movement is more symbolic than actual. She questions the real vitality of "nuevo teatro." In *Theatre of Crisis: Drama and Politics in Latin America*, Taylor explicitly counters the views of several commentators, including the position that Beatriz Rizk takes in *El nuevo teatro latinoamericano: Una lectura histórica*; the practical definitions that Eliana Boudet offers in *Teatro nuevo*; and Marina Pianca's discursive configurations in *Diógenes*.[53] These three critics have defined the "new theater" as overlapping with "popular theater." Taylor dismisses this attempt to generalize "new theater." She rejects the equation of "popular" with "new" when the two terms are "posited in such a way as to reflect and authorize each other," because this will, she believes, "tend to place the subject above discussion and criticism, rather than—as their claim insists—open the field to inquiry."[54] For Taylor, the theatrical movement that developed after the Cuban revolution is not necessarily characteristic of the periodization of theater. Rather, the revolutionary spirit set the stage for a new beginning, "new men and women." Taylor believes that what emerged was a "theater of revolution" that was able to gain worldwide attention. The Cuban revolution, by shaping a collective perception mediated through cultural images, created a sense of national and international identities.

Efforts to develop national identities, with the revolutionary aim of raising the sociopolitical consciousness of the masses, were instrumental in creating a collective dynamic that attested not only to collective creations, but also to the politics of group action. This collectivist vision, which informed theater movements in Argentina (Libre Teatro Libre), Chile (El Aleph), the U.S. (El Teatro Campesino), and Uruguay (El Galpón), among others, viewed theater as serving society by attempting to change it through struggle and cultural resistance.[55] The theater that flourished under these circumstances revolutionized existing ideas about mass culture, and especially about the uses of theater for purposes other than elite entertainment. The goal was to raise public awareness and stimulate response to political, social, and economic injustices, while at the same time striving to incorporate previously marginalized rural sectors into the national consciousness and culture of their home countries.

In the United States, this kind of activist theater developed under the direction of Luis Valdez, who founded El Teatro Campesino in 1965. The influence on Valdez of Brecht and of the revolutionary theater movement sweeping Latin America is clear. From the beginning, Valdez's company's theatrical politics were connected to the struggle for civil rights and the discrimination suffered by farm workers (see Chapter 3). El Teatro Campesino performed "actos" (acts or sketches) in which contemporary social and/or political issues were addressed in a very comical way. Valdez is commonly termed the "father" of Chicano theater; his approach profoundly affected Latino theater traditions in the U.S. and elsewhere.[56]

Although Valdez's revolutionary concepts were crucial to the development of Chicano theater, his vision tended to marginalize women. Yolanda Broyles-González's critique of gender relations in El Teatro Campesino corrects many misconceptions concerning the role of women in the development of the company. Broyles-González's feminist approach and her interest in "marginal voices and perspectives" have led her to search for and to recover "the silenced history [of women] and reconceptualize the established historical record. . . ."[57] Not only does she try to deconstruct the male-centered cultural history of El Teatro Campesino; more importantly, she explores the ramifications of the company's sexist orientation and male dominance: "The women's self-image remained at odds with the images of those unable to see women in their wholeness; the issue of women's roles was consistently deflected."[58] By displacing the limitations of the Chicano theater movement, Broyles-González centers Chicanas' long-overlooked contributions and their involvement with El Teatro Campesino. Her feminist perspective destabilizes the male-centered, monolithic image of the group's orientation.

Following Broyles-González's critique, and going beyond the nationalist ideologies of the Chicano movement, I focus (in Chapter 3) on the work of Chicanas who, by undermining patriarchy, create a performative space for themselves. As the arguments in this book stress, the configuration of a geopolitical space beyond hegemony and patriarchal domination is crucial. From my perspective, the performative, representative, and theatrical subject comes to rest in the formation of identity, its development and subversion. *Latina Performance* not only "traverses" identity, it demarcates that which is *in between* and *within* the distinctions and abstractions of the aesthetics of theater and performance.

Final Articulations

The nexus of performance and theater, Elin Diamond suggests, "is precisely the site in which concealed or dissimulated conventions might be investigated."[59] Noting that performativity is a constant negotiation between an act in process and a function already instituted, Diamond emphasizes the political contestation of performance in relation to the social body that comprises the sense of history and cultural production. Both the theatrical and performative subjects must constitute a sense of placement but also a feeling of displacement. I want to place performativity between the conventions and reiterations of theater and performance art: It is the site where aesthetics and the political *must* embody that which is (un)representable, progressive, and mimetically produced. Thus performativity "traverses" both the theatrical and performative in such a way that political contestation becomes "utteractive," a transgressive imposition where a witness and performer are posed collectively in the production of meaning. That is the space where women and others at the margins *transcend* the realm of the subjected. In societies where women are perpetually defined in terms of their endemic subordinate position as subject, their only publicly sanctioned roles are those of mother and/or wife. Historically, Latinas have been subjected to twin repressions—the hegemonic force of colonialism and the suffocating power of patriarchy. They have not had a strong tradition in theater. The absence of women among playwrights, performance artists, directors, and producers is especially striking in comparison to their relative visibility in other expressive forms, such as fiction and poetry. In this context, performativity becomes the site of reflection, where flesh-and-blood experiences are concretized in symbolic representations that begin to undo women's historic oppression.

As Argentinean Griselda Gambaro explains, the lack of Latina women's participation in theater may be traced directly to socially imposed limits:

> Y sé que si en America Latina las mujeres no hacen todo el teatro que quisieran, no innovan como directoras de escena en la medida deseable, es porque recién ahora están adquiriendo aquella experiencia del oficio que les estuvo vedada. Si no alternan la escritura, el cine, el teatro, la televisión, como sus hermana europeas, es porque el medio les impone barreras de índole ecónomica y política.[60]
>
> [And I know that in Latin America women don't produce as much theater as they would wish, they don't innovate as directors as much as they may like;

this is because they just recently started to work in an area that has been prohibited. If they do not alternate their writing, film, theater, television as much as their European sisters, it is because of the barriers imposed by politics and economics.]

Gambaro notes women's lack of participation not only as playwrights, but as producers and directors. In cataloguing the difficulties that women face in theater production, Gambaro considers the political economy associated with theater to be decisive.

Implicit in the importance of the "economics" of theater is another constraint. To succeed, women must become public, visible, and active subjects in the field. Latin American women have pursued careers as writers of poetry and fiction since the eighteenth century. But novels and poems are mostly written — and read — in private. Theater, by contrast, requires a collective participation in public. This is a significant distinction; theater production spans the public and private spheres. Women were/are far less likely to succeed in a space where their presence — their bodies and their intellects — must be publicly displayed. It is this aspect of theater that is most responsible for curtailing the participation of women on stage, particularly in patriarchal cultures.

The female gender repression encoded in traditional formulations of culture is also reproduced in male-dominated theater. As a result of women's marginalized position in the dramatic arts, female characterization typically has been left to the artistic manipulation and control of male writers and producers. Historically, this has resulted in a long tradition of envisioning and casting women as no more than symbolic objects. Latinas in contemporary theater emphatically reject the marginal spaces and narrow roles meted out to them. Instead, they insist on a new vision — one that pushes back the limits of patriarchy and creates an open site for proud bodies, strong voices. In so doing, Latinas today continue a long tradition of women struggling to be heard. From the colonial period through the nineteenth century and into the early twentieth century, Latin American women have shown the determination and defiance required of desiring subjects who hope to express themselves and participate in public life. It is this legacy, along with a Mexican American theater tradition that evolved among the communities of exiles who fled the chaos of the Mexican Revolution in the early twentieth century, that Latinas draw on as they define a place for themselves in the U.S. contemporary stage. In the next chapter, I explore the impact of migration and exile on Latina theater traditions in the U.S.

The Mexican American
Stage: La Chata Noloesca
and Josefina Niggli

TWO

The trajectory of the Latina theatrical tradition that my book configures is firmly rooted in a culture of migration. A distinctive Spanish-language theater tradition in the U.S. was initially motivated by the needs and demands of a displaced people—the Mexican citizens who fled their homeland for the asylum of *el norte* after the Mexican Revolution (1910–1917). In this chapter, I take the career of La Chata Noloesca as a beginning point to chart the growth of the theater tradition on which contemporary women dramatists and performance artists draw as they forge a new Latina identity. The foundation of that tradition is intertwined with the development of a Mexican American aesthetics that emerged from the cultural upheaval following the Mexican Revolution. That new aesthetics shaped the dramatic contributions of Josefina Niggli, this chapter's other major focus. Her work helped to sustain a theatrical tradition that expanded the body and upgraded the quality of theater fare in the U.S. By connecting the cultural legacies of Josefina Niggli and La Chata Noloesca, I demonstrate the specificities of a rich eclecticism, tracing both related and distinct elements in the development of theatrical production before the Chicano movement. La Chata and Niggli held quite different places in the emerging culture of the Mexican American period, yet both recognized the common core of their community as based on a consciousness of historical collectivity and pluralistic sensitivities.

Given the political and economic conditions that constrained Mexican American communities in the early twentieth century, the accomplishments of women like La Chata Noloesca and Josefina Niggli seem all the more remarkable. La Chata truly broke new ground, even beyond her influence as a director and producer. Her creation of the theatrical character La Chata, who actualizes a lusty comic tradition on stage, is an extraordinary accomplishment. La Chata's participation in the public domain as an actress, director, and founder of a traveling troupe defied the power dynamics that would normally have restricted her actions and her influence. With her artistic sensibility and powerful sense of freedom, she succeeded innovatively in a male-dominated field where women usually have been absent or marginalized. The cultural, economic, and political boundaries that La Chata had to break through in the first half of this century remain almost as firmly in place today. I place her in the center stage of a Mexican American aesthetics in order to provide a more specific angle of analysis.

First, I sketch the history of "La Adelita," a popular musical composition in which a *soldadera* (soldier woman) of the Mexican Revolution is in the key subject position. Then, I turn to two works: the book *Francisco Villa y La Adelita* by Baltasar Dromundo; and the play *Soldadera*, written by Josefina Niggli. Both present La Adelita as a soldier, but in Dromundo's book, the central tension involves the gender and power relations of domination embedded in the larger social and cultural context. Niggli's play is more nuanced. Niggli's dramatic works and contributions were a product of her upper-middle-class position and her intellectual and academic formation as part of the dominant ("mainstream") society in the U.S. Niggli's class position and status reflect her location within a developing middle-class community of Mexican skilled workers and professionals who had escaped the upheaval of the revolution by moving to the north. Unlike La Chata's artistic formation, which had its roots in the world of the working class and in popular culture, Niggli's artistic talent was supported by her formal studies in the field of theater. I examine Niggli's contributions because I view her work as a creative effort to link her experiences as an exile in the United States to her remembrances of the life and culture of her beloved homeland, Mexico. Her plays and stories bear witness to the efforts of a generation that tried to respond innovatively to the new materiality of life in the United States by forging a bi-sensibility that transformed two separate cultures into a new synthesis.

The Consolidation of New Theatrical Traditions after the Mexican Revolution

There is no doubt that the dynamics of Latin American theater from south to north of the U.S.-Mexico border underwent a revolutionary transformation in the 1960s. The triumph of the Cuban revolution in 1959 reinforced the march toward a new Latin American stage that would demand a reevaluation of the cultural systems embedded in a bourgeois and conventional theater and spell the extinction of the established order. Indeed, the "dialectical theater" initiated by Brecht was aimed at incorporating a vernacular vision into theater productions. The social and political implications of the radical change that followed in the wake of the Cuban revolution have a historical counterpart in the effects of the Mexican Revolution on theater tradition in the U.S. The upheaval caused by that revolution also inspired a new generation of theater workers to overcome adverse conditions by building a sense of community and identity through the theater.

The Mexican Revolution transformed many aspects of life for Mexicans already residing in the U.S. and for newcomers escaping the upheaval at home. A culture of exile began to develop as a product of the migration that occured during and soon after the revolution. According to Tomás Ybarra-Frausto, the exiles "brought with them certain attitudes that became pivotal in the subsequent development of popular theatre in the Southwest."[1] Moreover, this refugee culture "expanded the customary theatrical experiences of the settled residents." In particular, the Mexican Revolution inspired the development of popular theater in the form of the *carpa*, or tent theater, and the *teatro de revista*, a short one-act burlesque renowned for comic characters such as the *pelado* (underdog) and the *vedette* (singer-dancer-actress). According to Ybarra-Frausto, after the Mexican Revolution, the *teatro de revista* promoted a popular base for an emerging national culture:

> Being politically partisan, the *revista* functioned as a tribunal for the debate of national issues. Its essence was an acerbic, critical stance personified in the irreverent *pelado* and the insouciant *vedette* both of whom added a sparkling levity to serious social concerns. It was this light touch expressed in witty plots, hummable music and memorable, if somewhat risqué jokes that made it possible for the *revista* to survive the various post-revolutionary regimes in Mexico and cross the border into the Southwest.[2]

The *teatro de revista*, with its vernacular language and bold anti-establishment attitude, attracted audiences from all strata of Mexican society and played a crucial role after the Mexican Revolution in consolidating a type of revolutionary and innovative theater. The *revistas* replaced the naturalism embedded in the Mexican tradition since the nineteenth century with a confrontational aesthetics which posited the subject of performance against the metaphysics of Eurocentrism. By celebrating the rebel who rejects conformity and ridicules the predominant norms of middle-class "decorum," the *revistas* motivated and helped establish the beginnings of a new sense of self-identity.

At the same time, the *carpas,* which were rooted in the popular tradition of the circus, were also drawing large audiences. These performances were based on vivid representations of specific character types in semi-improvised, impetuous clowning situations. Ybarra-Frausto has pointed out that the spirit of the *carpa* tradition intentionally promoted satire, parody, and travesty: "*Carpa* performances were fluid, open, semi-structured presentational events with direct audience interactions."[3] In these folkloric spectacles, *corridistas* and *declamadores* often enhanced the repertoire with their songs and dramatic poetry readings. Over time, these itinerant performers became respected figures. It was this group of troubadours who helped sustain the fight for liberty by singing the ballads of the revolution—La Cucaracha, La Valentina, El Pato, and La Adelita:

> Si Adelita se fuera con otro
> la seguiría por tierra y por mar.
> Si por mar en un buque de guerra
> si por tierra en un tren militar.[4]
> Adelita, por Dios te lo ruego,
> calma el fuego de esta mi pasión,
> porque te amo y te quiero rendido
> y por ti sufre mi fiel corazón.

> [If Adelita should go with another
> I would follow her through land and sea.
> If by sea in a battleship
> if by land on a military train.
> Adelita, for God's sake I beg you,
> calm the fire of my passion
> because I love you and I cannot resist it
> and my faithful heart suffers for you.][5]

"La Adelita" was one of the most popular songs of the Mexican Revolution. According to some sources,[6] this ballad was originally inspired by a Durangan woman named Adelita who had joined the

Maderista movement at an early age.[7] Troubadours made the song—
and Adelita herself—a popular emblem of the revolution. As Baltasar
Diomundo put it, "las guitarras de todas partes se iban haciendo eruditas
en ese canto hasta que por fin la Revolución hizo de ella su verdadero
emblema nacional"[8] [guitarists from all over were becoming experts on
that song, and then it became the true emblem of the Revolution].
Significantly, Adelita's last name, as well as the last names of many other
soldier-women, remained virtually unknown. However, the popular
songs composed in these women's honor contributed enormously to
preserving their fame and to documenting their role in the revolution.
Shirlene Soto has pointed out that "Two heroines of the revolution,
Adelita and Valentina, were considered 'the essence of Mexican femininity,' and the *corridos* written to honor them had widespread popularity."[9] Over time, Adelita's name began being used to refer to any female
soldier who participated in the Mexican Revolution, so that "Adelita"
gradually became synonymous with *soldadera* (soldier-woman). Today,
among women in both Mexico and the United States, Adelita is a
symbol of action and inspiration, and her name is used to mean any
woman who struggles and fights for her rights.

During the decade of the revolution, Mexicans flooded north across
the border into the relative safety and security of the United States.
From the 1920s on, Spanish-language theater flourished within this
population movement across the five southwestern states. Nicolás Kanellos has documented the development of Spanish-language theaters
and performance tradition in the U.S. from their origins in mid-nineteenth century California through 1940. He traces the impact of the
Mexican Revolution as follows:

> Theatrical activities expanded rapidly when thousands of refugees took
> flight from the Mexican Revolution and settled in the United States from
> the border all the way up to the Midwest. During the decades of the
> revolution, many of Mexico's greatest artists and their theatrical companies
> came to tour and/or take up temporary residence in the United States; some,
> however, would never return to the homeland.[10]

The new migrants from the Mexican Revolution, along with U.S.
Mexicans, consolidated their intellectual and cultural search for community through this new theatrical movement, which expressed their
struggles to survive and maintain their traditions and values in an
increasingly hostile world. A rising tide of Anglo American nativist
reaction against Mexicans coincided with the coming of the First World
War in 1914, and with a higher demand for Mexican workers. While

the impact of the Mexican Revolution intensified discrimination against immigrants and U.S. Mexicans, theater professionals throughout the world flocked to Los Angeles, which was then the heart of the motion picture enterprise for the United States and Latin America. Kanellos suggests that this influx of movie professionals enhanced live theater invaluably: "Hispanic impresarios and directors from throughout the United States and northern Mexico would come to Los Angeles to recruit talent for new touring companies."[11]

By the late 1920s and early 1930s, the Spanish-language theater in the United States was at its peak. Traveling companies brought the *carpa* tradition to rural areas and small cities, while in large urban areas like San Antonio and Los Angeles, there were regular nightly performances of everything from *teatro de revista* and melodrama to vaudeville. In Los Angeles, for example, eight theaters were solely dedicated to the presentation of such diverse theatrical genres as the *zarzuela*, *revistas*, comedy, and *tandas de variedad* (vaudeville spectacles). Ybarra-Frausto calls this period the golden era for Spanish-language theater in the United States. He describes a typical scene:

> Waiting patiently in long lines, the spectators were dazzled by the thousands of electric lights brilliantly lighting the *marquesinas* announcing international stars like the great doyenne of the Mexican theater, Virginia Fábregas, the renowned Cuban *cupletista*, Pilar Arcos, the premier *declamadora*, Bertha Singerman, from Buenos Aires, and such new crowd pleasers as Dolores del Rio, Ramón Navarro and Tito Guízar. From Paris, Barcelona, Madrid, Buenos Aires, La Habana and Mexico City, the cavalcade of stars always included Mexican American performers who began developing their own legions of fans.[12]

Meanwhile, in Hollywood, filmmaking was becoming a booming but highly discriminatory industry. Latinos, especially Mexicans, were practically banned from the financial and technical side of Hollywood film productions. Ironically, there was more room for people of color in front of the cameras than behind them. The 1920s saw the growth of the phenomenal popularity of the "Latin Lover" and the vamp/femme fatale, a trend that allowed a few Latino performers, most notably Dolores del Rio and Ramón Navarro, to rise to star status.

The daughter of a Mexican bank president and member of the ruling class, del Rio had migrated to the United States with her family to escape the upheavals of the revolution.[13] She was twenty-one when she was discovered by a Hollywood director. Del Rio debuted in *Joanna* (1925) and starred in *The Loves of Carmen* (1927). She had established herself in aristocratic roles as well as in popular ones by the time sound was introduced to movie-making. Even she, however, was not immune from discrimination. In 1931, she turned down a role that she believed denigrated her identity as a woman and as a Mexican. *La Opinión*, the Los Angeles Spanish-language newspaper, reported that del Rio would not accept the role she was offered in *The Broken Wing* because she refused to be depicted as a "cantinera" (bartender) who rejects a "Mexican bandit" for a white American pilot. The Mexican American actress Lupe Velez apparently had no such scruples; she accepted the role. Both del Rio and Ramón Navarro also had to combat publicity releases that falsely identified them as Spanish. Each insisted on being identified as Mexican.[14]

Del Rio's impact was not confined to Hollywood films; she greatly influenced the way some female roles would develop on the live stage, as well. In the *teatro de revista* and *carpas*, the *vedette* often would imitate the glamour of Hollywood actresses. Del Rio's influence is clearly demonstrated in the film *La carpa* (1993), directed by Carlos Avila.[15] The two actresses who work at the *carpa* depicted in the movie try to imitate del Rio. In a scene in which the older woman (Dora) is teaching the younger one (Isabel) how to be seductive and irresistible, the two describe their aim: to be "like the movie star, Dolores del Rio." During the *carpa* performances in the movie, Dora dances a number entitled *fantasía*. In this act, the female performer moves to the rhythms of very seductive music. The male characters, who later discuss the *fantasía* act, explain it as a performance in which the woman is supposed to show her *curvas peligrosas* (dangerous movements). Isabel is not yet ready to perform the *fantasía*; however, she is being trained to do it in the near future. She is clearly very excited by the prospect of one day performing that act and being able to imitate the glamour of Dolores del Rio.

Del Rio's film portrayal of the vamp/femme fatale perpetuated an image that negatively stereotyped Latinas and narrowed the roles that Hollywood would make available to them. As Antonio Ríos-Bustamante has noted, Hollywood stereotyping positively characterized Latin Americans as people of great beauty and attractiveness; however, this outcome does not offset the fact that "stereotyping both reconfirmed and catered to existing subliminal and conscious prejudice against Latinos and other ethnic, racial groups by Anglo Americans and Europeans as well as by elitist Latin Americans and Spaniards."[16] Ríos-Bustamante points out that this kind of racial prejudice restricted many brown-skinned actors and actresses to a very limited range of film roles: "[S]tereotyping and exclusion were especially acute for Latinos and Latinas of mestizo and mulatto appearance who were relegated to the greaser, bandido, and 'native' bit or extra roles."[17] Even Dolores del Rio acknowledged (in 1978) that Latinos in Hollywood during the 1920s and 1930s fell into one of two categories: the light-skinned, who were able to land roles as whites; and the darker-skinned, who were inevitably cast as servants or criminals.[18] Light-skinned and Spanish-looking, the phenomenally attractive del Rio had no trouble getting "white" roles. By contrast, Lupe Velez, who many considered a "Mexican spitfire," had to be content with fewer roles and a limited celebrity.

The nativist hysteria sweeping the country in the 1920s also affected the way Hollywood films depicted Mexicans and other Latinos. In the 1930s, the Universidad Autónoma de México undertook a formal study of Hollywood's attitude toward Latin Americans. The study concluded that the film industry had no difficulty understanding the Latin American people as a lucrative mass market for the exportation of films. However, in portraying the culture and history of Mexican Americans and other Latinos on screen, Hollywood showed a willing disregard for both accuracy and respect.[19]

The situation was different in live theater. Unlike the film industry, theater was decentralized and not dependent on the monied interests of Anglo financiers. As the popularity of Spanish-language theater grew, opportunities for performers and playwrights alike multiplied. Most of the traditional constraints on women's participation in theater remained unchanged, but certain women, like La Chata Noloesca, were able to break free in remarkable ways.

From Vedettes to Comediennes: "Atracciones La Chata Noloesca"

> Through humor, "La Chata Noloesca" reminded us of one of our highest spiritual privileges, the ability to confront adversity with cheer. Through the universal spirit of laughter, she understood Aristotle's ancient formula: "Of all living creatures, only humans are endowed with laughter."[20]

La Chata Noloesca (1903–1979; born Beatriz Escalona in San Antonio, Texas) was the preeminent comedienne of the Spanish-language theater that emerged after the Mexican Revolution. Over the course of her long career, La Chata was a glamorous actress, a gifted comedienne, and the manager of her own highly successful theater company.

She was the only Mexican American comedienne from Texas to travel throughout the U.S., Mexico, and Cuba with her own company. She was also the first San Antonian to make her theatrical debut in Mexico and the first to introduce Mexican vaudeville at the Teatro Hispano in New York City. La Chata's characterizations drew heavily on clowning and miming techniques; the core of her repertoire was centered on the embodiment of ideas through physical action. Movement and gestures were central—her performances rarely developed a plot line. According to Tomás Ybarra-Frausto, La Chata's sketches were "confrontational situations between authority figures and underlings."[21] The portrayal of such comical situations was common in the 1930s.

The transitions in La Chata's performing identity—from an early emphasis on sensuality to her later comic routines—not only revolutionized Mexican American theater, but also guaranteed her a continuing place in show business. As a veteran performer in West San Antonio, as late as 1976 she was featured in the pages of *The San Antonio Light*, signing a contract for what she called "La Chata Review." In launching this "return," La Chata hoped to revive the tradition of Spanish-language vaudeville: "We will be presenting serious drama skits once in awhile in which Castillian Spanish will be used instead of the funny Tex-Mex used in the other slapstick shows," she announced.[22] Ybarra-Frausto, in summing up La Chata's many contributions, described her as "la figura del donaire" (a figure of much class) on the Mexican American stage.[23]

La Chata's interest in theater began at the age of thirteen when she worked in the box office at the Zaragoza Theater in San Antonio. As she grew up, she was influenced by the touring theatrical groups which came to San Antonio during and after the revolution. At age seventeen, working as an usherette and selling tickets at San Antonio's Teatro Nacional, she began to form her own ambition to sing and dance. In 1920, the acclaimed Areu Brothers came to perform at the Nacional, and they took her with them on tour. Her first performance took place in El Paso at the Teatro Colón. Following her debut, she married José, one of the Areu Brothers, and they toured the U.S.-Mexican borderlands.[24]

At this early stage of her career, La Chata (who at the time still used her given name of Beatriz) imitated the grace and glamour of film stars such as Dolores del Rio and aspired to the charm of Dorita Ceprano, a vaudeville *vedette* whose stage performances and voluptuousness (see Figures 1 and 2) were causing a sensation at the time.[25] To performers such as La Chata, Dolores del Rio and Dorita Ceprano were archetypes

FIG. 1. *Dolores Del Rio in the late 1920s. Del Rio became a role model; she was a phenomenal figure in the late 1920s and 1930s with her "glamour and grit." She started her artistic career in the Spanish live theater. This photo is from* Hispanic Hollywood: The Latins in Motion Picture *(1990).*

FIG. 2. *Dorita Ceprano embodies the attractiveness of the* vedette, *whose emerging femininity introduced a cosmopolitan mood in the theater. This photo is a souvenir postcard given out at her performances. Benson Latin American Collection, University of Texas at Austin.*

of beauty and glamour. A collection of photographs of La Chata (pre-served in scrapbooks that her daughter, Belia Camargo, donated to the San Antonio Conservation Society) shows how Noloesca shaped her beauty to conform to the alluring look of 1920s Hollywood. See, for example, the snapshots reproduced here (Figures 3, 4, and 5), where she poses seductively, exalting her sensuous *mestizo* body. The pictures capture a consciously provocative femininity. Taken in the 1920s, they reflect La Chata's preliminary phase, before she discovered her incred-ible comic sensibility. The photos show La Chata asserting her subjec-tivity in a performance of sex appeal and fashion in which the body is paramount. According to Kanellos, the 1920s were the years when La Chata was considered beautiful.[26]

More important than La Chata's grace and charm in advancing her early career, however, was her participation in José Areu's distinguished troupe. María Teresa Marrero argues that La Chata "came into [her] own through a large dose of personal talent and charm, but not without the advantage of being married to a prominent theater director."[27] It is true that La Chata very quickly became acclaimed across the Southwest and that she overshadowed her husband. I believe, however, that La Chata's marriage to Areu was a strategic necessity for her as a female in that generation: her marriage legitimated her presence on stage. It was her own strength and talent that made it possible for her to succeed in what has always been the most "masculine" of cultural forms.

In 1930, when the Areu group went to Los Angeles, La Chata separated from her husband and started her own company, "Atracciones Noloesca." This name, which she fashioned herself, is a creative rear-rangement of the letters of her maiden name, Escalona: Noloesca. She remarried in California and traveled to Mexico frequently until 1936, when she returned to San Antonio. By this time La Chata was recog-nized as the only Mexican American comedienne promoting the vaude-ville style across the border states. Kanellos relates La Chata's daughter's explanation of what motivated her mother to become a comedienne: "she answered that La Chata had always been so inclined, especially when singing humorous couplets, but that [she] also had grown fat and could no longer make it as a beautiful chorine."[28]

Thus, in the 1930s, Beatriz Escalona shed her stylish look of the 1920s and transformed herself into a comic persona who would imitate the tradition of the *pelada*, a street-wise, fast-talking character. Accord-ing to Kanellos, La Chata "developed a picaresque style that allowed her character to survive and ironically get the upper hand at all times."[29] She created her own comic look, often wearing ruffled print dresses and

FIGS. 3-5. *La Chata Noloesca in the 1920s. Photos courtesy of the San Antonio Conservation Society.*

FIG. 6. *La Chata Noloesca in the 1970s. Photo
courtesy of the San Antonio Conservation Society.*

oxford shoes with flashy rolled-down socks. She also wore two saucy-
looking colored ribbons in her hair, false eyelashes, and abundant
makeup. Ybarra-Frausto sums up her look this way: "The overall im-
pression was [of] a pert, clever, yet vulnerable maiden."[30] It was this
inventive character that took the place of the dazzling femininity of the
earlier years. The role of La Chata came to define Escalona's theatrical
core—a combination of artful slapstick and constantly changing facial
expressions and body movements. She sustained this character for more
than 40 years, through her last performance in 1977 (see Figure 6).

In 1941, La Chata performed in Havana, Cuba, at the Teatro Alcázar.
By this time, her company had expanded to sixteen members, including
dancers, musicians, singers, and comedians. After her trip to Cuba, she
was engaged to perform in New York City for two weeks at the Teatro
Hispano. She ended up being held over for sixteen weeks.[31] She remained in New York for more than a decade, though she returned to
San Antonio regularly to visit her mother. In the late 1950s, La Chata
moved back to San Antonio permanently. There she worked in radio

and television, doing programs on KCOR and KWEX-TV. In 1975, when she turned seventy-two, a tribute to her was organized in San Antonio to celebrate her fifty years in show business. Many talented groups from San Antonio performed in her honor and more than one thousand fans were present. Also in 1975, La Chata was given a diploma of honor by the National Association of Actors in Mexico City. In 1976, despite not having undertaken vaudeville shows in many years, she returned to the stage at the Joy Theater, which began presenting vaude-ville shows on weekends. Her last performance was a benefit show in August 1977.[32]

As an influential performance artist whose career spanned many generations, La Chata Noloesca broke many barriers. She divorced the husband who had "discovered" her talents and then went on not only to establish her own company, but also to become the most visible female representative of Mexican American theater. In spite of all the problems associated with economics and gender politics, La Chata Noloesca shaped the history of the Mexican American stage. It is precisely be-cause of the courage, talent, and perseverance of performers such as La Chata that it is possible today to trace, as I do in this book, a theatrical tradition among women of Latin American descent in the United States. A second important influence in that tradition is the work of the dramatist Josefina Niggli, a near-contemporary of La Chata.

Josefina Niggli, La Adelita, and Other Soldaderas

As a privileged upper-class writer during the 1930s, Josefina Niggli took part in the intellectual search for community that characterized the emerging Mexican American upper and middle classes during the Mexican American period. Her writing developed as a product of her Americanization, mediated by such institutions as the family, the Cath-olic Church, and the educational system. Moreover, her ideological consciousness was shaped by the ideas of the exiled Mexican *ricos* who settled in San Antonio, Texas between 1908 and 1914.[33] This is in marked contrast to La Chata, whose theatrical legacy was directly linked to the more marginal sectors of society. Niggli's writing reflects her desire to make the Anglo American public appreciate the Mexican experience in the U.S.[34] For example, in the play *Soldadera*, Niggli centers Adelita, a soldier of the revolution, as a way to dramatize the folklore and the historical setting that recognize the courage and valor of women who fought in the revolution.[35] More generally, portrayals of "the Mexican" and an exploration of her own Mexican-ness, carefully translated and adapted for a foreign audience, are the core themes of Niggli's work.

Given Niggli's class position and artistic interests, it should not be surprising that *Soldadera* is suffused with a marked idealism and romanticism. This one-act play (with a full-length form) was the first theatrical representation, north or south of the border, of the participation of female soldiers in the Mexican Revolution. Niggli's editor, Frederick H. Koch, described this play as embodying "the heroic struggle of Mexican Valkyries in the Revolution of 1910."[36] The play depicts this participation in strong, vivid terms, referring to "the women who left their homes and dragged along after their men, cooking for them, tending their wounds, guarding their ammunition, fighting when necessary."[37] Niggli uses the drama to explore women's heroic role in the revolution and to illustrate the personal and ideological motivations that made them active protagonists. Adelita is presented as a hero who sacrifices her life for the revolutionary cause. The dramatist describes the characterization of Adelita this way: "She is the poetry of the Revolution, and the beauty, and she who has seen almost nothing of death finds life very gay" (p. 57).

This depiction of Adelita as "the poetry of the revolution" is understood through the theatrical lyrism embedded in the musical composition. Niggli represents Adelita, other female soldiers, and the revolution in romantic terms. She views them all through the lens of her own reality, one significantly shaped by the circumstances of her upper-middle-class life and her participation in a particular generation in U.S. society. Her formative years were divided between Monterrey, Mexico, where she was born (in 1910), and San Antonio, Texas (where she was sent in 1913, to escape the disruption of the Revolution). Niggli started her writing career in 1928, when her father financed the printing of her first book, *Mexican Silhouettes*, a collection of poems; she also published poems and short stories in magazines such as *Mexican Life* and the *Ladies' Home Journal*. As Niggli tells it, her career owed much to the no-nonsense approach of one of her teachers. Sister Mary Clement, of Incarnate Word College, locked Niggli in a room and would not let her come out until she had written a piece for the *Ladies' Home Journal* short story contest. Niggli won second prize in that competition and later also won the National Catholic College Poetry Award.

During the late 1920s and 1930s, Niggli became very popular in San Antonio, where she was writing and producing for KTSA radio (55.5 AM). After receiving her B.A. in 1931, she began to study playwriting at the San Antonio Little Theatre. In 1935, Niggli decided to join the Carolina Playmakers, a graduate program at the University of North Carolina at Chapel Hill. She completed her M.A. degree with *Singing Valley*, a play produced by the Carolina Playmakers in 1936. These were very creative years for Niggli. In addition to *Soldadera*, she wrote three historical plays about Mexico—*The Fair God*, *The Cry of Dolores*, and *Azteca*. During the late 1930s, she returned to Mexico to work as stage manager for Rodolfo Usigli, a well-known Mexican dramatist who was at that time directing the theater department at the Universidad Autónoma de México. In 1956, Niggli was hired to teach English and drama at Western Carolina University, where she headed the theater department until her retirement in 1975.[38]

When *Soldadera* was originally performed, all the characters except Maria (who was played by Niggli) were played by Anglo Americans, including the role of Adelita. For Niggli, the Mexican spectator/protagonist—on both sides of the border—remained absent. Her didactic system of representation was specifically crafted to target Anglos. The system of production in *Soldadera* (and in general) was a means of demanding her rights as a Mexican American, of making herself heard by the Anglo majority, of making herself known and "visible" as an ethnic "other." Niggli's dramatic work embodies Mexican-ness as an inscription which marks ethnic subjecthood as a model for performing identity. This is evident in Figure 7, where Niggli is pictured in festive attire, wearing a traditional *serape* over her left shoulder and allowing her wide straw *sombrero* to ride across her shoulders. Her expression is narcissistic; she seems to be engaging in a deliberate performance of Mexican folklore.

Most of Niggli's plays, including *Soldadera*, were originally produced by Professor Frederick H. Koch and performed by the Carolina Playmakers for Anglo American audiences. Rodolfo Usigli has noted this regrettably narrow focus: "Her source is essentially Mexican, but the treatment strikes in certain ways as a deliberate one, intended for a foreign public."[39] Focusing on a "foreign public," he makes clear, simultaneously implies the *absence* of a Mexican audience. This was disturbing. An admirer of Niggli's work, Usigli ranked her highly among such contemporaries of Mexican theater as Celestino Gorostiza, Xavier Villaurrutia, and Amalia de Castillo Ledón. Still, he did not hesitate to criticize Niggli's failure to write for the Mexican audience of the 1930s, as his closing remarks in the foreword to *Mexican Folk Plays* demonstrate:

FIG. 7. *Josefina Niggli in the 1930s. She poses performing the folklore embedded in most of her plays. Reprinted from Niggli's* Mexican Folk Plays *(1938).*

It has been my contention for some time that we will be in no position to promote the advent of a poetic theatre in Mexico so long as we do not have a true realistic drama created by playwrights well possessed of their craft and of the necessities and limitations of the theatre. I will, therefore, take this opportunity to excite Miss Niggli to write something along this line in Spanish to give the contemporary audiences of Mexico an occasion to appreciate her talents and to rejoice at the appearance of a new Mexican playwright. (p. xx)

Niggli countered this criticism by maintaining that "The United States needed the folk drama more than Mexico. I wanted people to know the wonderful world south of the border and that there was something besides Europe."[40]

For Niggli, the essence of the "wonderful world" of Mexico lay in its vividness, its dramatic potential. She was not concerned to bring to her audiences an understanding of the complex realities of life in Mexico, nor was she interested in examining the dilemmas facing Mexican Americans. She evoked instead a kind of magical world summoned from objective knowledge and memory, a gauzy mixture of the real and the imagined. Niggli's artistic imagination was dominated by her yearning for her beloved Mexico, and by the conflict entailed in trying to integrate her cultural and social heritage with Anglo society. Her (unsuccessful) solution to the difficulties of blending her two heritages was to place the Mexican world wholly in the past and situate the inevitable process of assimilation in the present. A poem she wrote, included in the introduction to *Mexican Folk Plays*, clearly illustrates her strongly nationalistic sensibility:

> Mexico, my beloved,
> is not the clashing of cymbals
> not the curving of vermilion sails
> over the heart
> of the wind;
> it is not
> a vivid slash
> across the mouth
> of the world.
> But when the moon touches the silken waves
> of the Lerma,
> and the carnations
> breathe their scents
> into the souls of a thousand birds
> forcing them to sing
> of something
> they but dimly understand—

this, my beloved,
is Mexico. (p. vi)

Faced with the crisis of the Great Depression, Niggli uses her poetic imagination to try to capture the Mexican soul as the essence of her own identity. Mexico is a "landscape" with a colorful and rich past; Mexico is La Adelita and the many soldier women who fought for the ideals of the revolution. Thus, she brings to center stage the women who joined the revolution, making the protagonist of "La Adelita"—the song—a hero. Although Niggli preserves Adelita's bravery, she undercuts it by attributing to her heroine an overwhelming naivete and romantic idealism. Nevertheless, Niggli's feminist consciousness in *Soldadera* properly problematizes the tension that involves the age-old equation of male power and female subordination embedded in the historical subjectivity of her protagonists. She makes "La Adelita" the pretext of her play. I do the same in this book.

Staging Gender Relations and Other Settings: Francisco Villa against La Adelita

Si Adelita quisiera ser mi esposa,
si Adelita fuera mi mujer,
le compraría un vestido de seda
para llevarla a bailar al cuartel. (p. 38)[41]

[If Adelita wanted to be my wife
if Adelita would be my woman,
I would buy her a silk dress
to take her dancing at the barracks.]

Clearly, Adelita's identity, and in particular her subjectivity as a soldier of the revolution, has been shaped and reshaped many times and in many contexts. I consider it very important to trace the connections between various treatments of Adelita and the gender and power relations embedded in the larger social, political, and cultural environment because almost from the beginning, the meaning of the song and the role of its subject have been given different, often conflicting, interpretations. As the battle hymn of Pancho Villa's troops, "La Adelita" expressed the sensitivity and vulnerability of men, emphasizing the stoicism of the male rebel soldier as he confronts the prospect of death:

Si supieras que ha muerto tu amante,
rezarás por mi una oración,

por el hombre que supo adorarte
con el alma, vida y corazón. (p. 39)

[If you find out your lover has died,
say for me a prayer,
for the man that adored you
with soul, life and heart.]

Here the speaking subject of "La Adelita" feels sorrowful at the prospect of dying in combat and never seeing his beloved again, but he accepts his likely death after expressing his love. In this guise, "La Adelita" is a song of hope, based on virility, and the name Adelita becomes a metaphor for love in times of war. Similarly, in other versions of the song analyzed by the feminist scholar María Herrera-Sobek, Adelita's bravery and revolutionary spirit are lost in the sexism and machismo of male soldiers who are focused on passions, love, and desire as they face combat:

Recordando aquel sargento sus quereres
los soldados que volvían de la guerra
ofreciéndole su amor a las mujeres
entonaban este himno de la guerra.[42]

[The sergeant was remembering his loved ones
when the soldiers were returning from the battle
offering their love to the women
They would sing this song of war.]

As one of the protagonists in Niggli's drama, La Adelita pays tribute to the bravery of women who joined the revolution, an involvement often ignored in the written history of Mexico. As a soldier in the troops of Francisco Villa, La Adelita became known as one of his most courageous soldiers. It is this characteristic that Baltasar Dromundo makes the subject of his short book, *Francisco Villa y La Adelita*. He uses folklore as a source of information about two legendary figures: General Francisco Villa, the leader of powerful revolutionary troops in the northern state of Chihuahua and a champion of agrarian reform; and Adelita, a soldier-woman whose beauty and courageous acts during the revolution attracted much attention. Dromundo includes a version of "La Adelita" that he maintains is the original composition of an anonymous troubadour of the Mexican Revolution. He presents the story of Adelita, narrating a significant event in her life and dramatizing the situation by combining his prose with dialogue between his protagonists, Adelita and Francisco Villa. As a text within a text, the musical composition increases the dramatic tension of the story Dromundo presents:

> Ya no llores, querida Adelita,
> ya no llores, querida mujer,
> no te muestres ingrata conmigo,
> ya no me hagas tanto padecer. (p. 39)

> [Don't cry anymore, my beloved Adelita,
> don't cry anymore, my beloved woman,
> don't be hardhearted with me,
> don't make me suffer anymore.]

In Dromundo's book, Adelita is described as a *norteña* (a woman from the north) who is a beautiful and courageous soldier, but also a heartbreaker. She is depicted as a major figure among the followers of Francisco Villa. According to Dromundo's anecdote, the day the General first noticed Adelita, she had been selected to give the speech at a banquet held in his honor. Adelita was romantically involved at that time with Francisco Portillo (also known as *el güero*), who was regarded as one of Pancho Villa's most courageous *dorados*.[43] Villa, unaware of Adelita's and Portillo's romance, found the young woman's beauty and sagacious personality irresistible. That the General followed up his feelings with immediate action was not surprising since Villa was widely known as a passionate and daring man — and a womanizer.

In Dromundo's rendition, while Villa and Adelita are having a conversation, the General suddenly grabs her violently and kisses her: "Cerca de la puerta se detuvo Villa y bruscamente tomó a Adelita entre sus brazos y la besó" [near the door Villa stopped and he violently grabbed Adelita in his arms and kissed her].[44] Although this scenario is absurdly romantic, in its melodrama it resembles images from commercial films produced in Mexico since the 1930s, in which the beautiful *señorita* is always seduced, conquered, and loved or "dishonored" by a handsome *charro*. More significantly, in Dromundo's anecdote, gender relations are indirectly problematized so that domination comes to determine the protagonists' interrelated subjectivity. Moreover, this narrative encapsulates the manly power of a nation that subordinates the female subject, a symbolic paradigm of colonization. After the Spanish conquest of Mexico, women's subordination, already instituted in both countries, was reinforced by the impact of caste and race. Anna Macías asserts that "Undoubtedly *machismo* ('extreme male dominance') and its counterpart, *hembrismo* ('extreme female submission'), have been pervasive in Mexico, in part because of the Aztec subordination of women and even more because of the Spanish colonial experience."[45]

Dromundo presents a very dramatic text in order to explain the situation which links Adelita with General Villa. The central event in Dromundo's narrative—in which Villa imposes his power and strength on Adelita—is easily interconnected with the larger narrative of machismo and sexism in which the male protagonist imposes his power and maleness on a female. My reading of Villa's imposition centers representations of superiority and inferiority in relation to gender differences and sexual power. Villa's compulsive behavior is an affirmation of his superiority; Adelita's submission is inevitable. The physical and metaphysical force evident in Villa's action is self-explanatory: "It is force without the discipline of any notion of order: arbitrary power, the will without reins and without a set course."[46] In Dromundo's narrative, Adelita—in her beauty and intelligence—is the seducer. She is Eve. Francisco Villa's action is predestined by his masculinity. His attitude is never questioned; it is understood that his act is produced by instinct.

Villa's actions embody the representation of manly power as the generative force of his condition as a *macho*, and, of course, historically speaking, as the General. Whether Adelita liked or disliked Villa's imposition, or whether her flirtation (as it was described by Dromundo) induced the General to commit such an act, are irrelevant to my argument. I am much more concerned with the effects produced by the representations of sexual power and gender relations. Mexican poet and philosopher Octavio Paz believes that the inferiority of the female stems from her sexuality (specifically, her vagina), which he defines as an open "wound" incapable of healing. The macho's essential attribute is manifested by his capacity for penetrating that "wound." According to Paz, "the macho represents the masculine pole of life," and he feels superior because he cannot be made to "open."[47] The "real meaning" of *macho*, Paz says, "is no different from that of the verb chingar and its derivatives. The *macho* is the *gran chingón*."[48]

In the Freudian scheme of thought, the female's lack of a penis contributes to her inferiority. For Freud, this connection between sexuality and human experience was a product of established, subliminal processes that could be exposed and perhaps modified through psychoanalysis. In Paz's work, the obsession with the verb *chingar* is a manifestation of his own internalized racism. Emma Pérez has suggested that Paz's inferiority complex "holds less power than that of his symbolic white father, *el conquistador*."[49] Authoritarian and patriarchal, both Freud and Paz became trapped in the circles of complex paradoxes involving women, sexuality, and male domination. In Dromundo's narrative, this paternal law seems to support the association of power with masculinity and with Villa's role as the General. The bipolar relationship between Francisco Villa and Adelita is a dramatization of the culture of the superior-inferior dyad—the complex set of rules and rights embedded in the position of "master" (the General, the man) and the "subordinate" (the soldier, the woman).

Although Dromundo's textual treatment of "La Adelita" centers the song's narrative nature, it is important to remember that the story first gained currency as a popular ballad, a *corrido*. Thus, the story was and is integrally bound to its performance. In Mexico, the *corrido* developed as a unique tradition of the lower classes. In giving presentation to the illiterate masses and recounting (often satirically) stories of current interest, the *corrido* resembled the English ballad of the seventeenth century. But while the English ballad was printed and then transmitted orally, the *corrido* was first performed and then printed, often anonymously. Sometimes the printed ballads were sold for one or two cents each. Since *corridos* were transmitted orally before being transcribed from memory, versions of any single song varied across troops and between any one performer (or group of performers) and another. During the revolution, *corridos* were sung not only for the glorification of soldiers, but also to disseminate news of national import. "La Adelita" served as a model for the glorification of the female soldier who became the potential lover, girlfriend, or wife of combat soldiers. The performative functionality of "La Adelita" lies in its enactment of real—albeit contested—history. As a text within a text, the ballad is useful analytically because it helps expose the performance of gender relations rooted in the upheaval of social transformation.

The story of Adelita in Dromundo's text does not end with the narrative of male imposition and cultural revenge. Portillo, witnessing the way in which Villa grabs his sweetheart Adelita, automatically draws his gun, intending to kill the General. But then he hesitates, caught in the web of the master-subordinate relationship. He cannot kill his superior. He backs away, shooting himself, instead. Adelita runs toward the dead body of her beloved Portillo and embraces him, crying out. Francisco Villa, looking confused and upset, asks for an explanation:

> —¿Qué sabes de esto?
> —Era mi novio—, repuso Adelita sollozando
>
> [What do you know about this?
> "He was my boyfriend," Adelita replied, sobbing]. (p. 37)

Villa's reaction is to blame Adelita. In his eyes, she created the
situation by deliberately seducing him. In retaliation, he asks her to
leave his troops, and Adelita agrees. She joins General Domingo Arrieta's
forces, but later disappears and then returns to Villa's army disguised as
a male soldier. Hiding her beautiful face under the shadow of a wide
straw hat, she passes as one of his brave *dorados*. Adelita dies in combat
in 1915, during one of the bloodiest fights of the Villistas (the first battle
of Celaya). After the battle, when Francisco Villa is walking around
among the dead bodies of his *dorados*, he finds Adelita's corpse. Very
moved and surprised, Villa declares, "¡Era un dorado!" acknowledging
her bravery. Dramatically, he takes Adelita's dead body in his arms and
gives orders for it to be buried beside Francisco Portillo's grave. With
Adelita, the woman, dead, all that remains is "La Adelita," the song:

> Y Adelita se llama la joven
> que yo quiero y no puedo olvidar;
> en el mundo yo tengo una rosa
> y con el tiempo la voy cortar. (p. 38)

> [And Adelita is the name of a young woman
> who I love and I can't forget;
> in the world I have a rose
> and in time I will cut it.]

Romantic and Folkloric Sites: Plotting Revolutionary Subjects

In *Soldadera*, as Niggli translates the folklore of Mexico and gives form
to history and tradition within the medium of the theater, she emphasizes her country's dramatic, passionate qualities. The play's stark setting is more meant to impart a particular atmosphere than to capture a
specific, historical site:

> The rocks are rugged spikes of stone against the dark blue sky. Here is no
> flowery green softness, no delicacy of outline, but a grim fortress built by
> nature against the valley below. What vegetation exists is sparse and scat-
> tered. Perhaps a yucca palm stands aloof from the organ cactus that rears its
> pointed leaves here and there, while small round cacti, studded with thorns,
> wear scarlet flowers for crowns. (p. 55)

This romantic vision of the stage represents a camp in the middle of the
desert, located in the Sierra Madre Mountains, near the capital city of
Saltillo in the northern state of Coahuila. Niggli's staging of the desert
symbolically represents the terrain characteristic in the northern states

of Mexico where Villa's troops gained control. While she uses rich metaphors to describe the staging in natural terms, the portrayal of the desert captures real geographics. Set in the spring of 1914, the play's action involves an event in the life of a group of *soldaderas* who support the Villistas. Their task is to guard the rebels' ammunition, which is stored at this camp. When the play opens, "It is the hour just before dawn, that hour when even nature seems to be asleep, and the only moving thing in all that silence is the figure of a woman standing on the high rock that shields a part of the path from view" (p. 59).

Among the characters are Maria, the sentinel (played by Niggli);[50] Concha, the leader (Gerd Bernhart); The Blond One (Christine Maynard), guarding the ammunition; and Adelita (Barbara Hilton), the youngest of the group. Two other soldiers are Cricket (Phoebe Barr) and Tomasa (Jessie Langdale). There is also The Old One (Mary Lou Taylor), a woman whose son was killed by the *federales*, their enemy. The enemy forces, known as *pelones* during the revolution, are the "rich ones" in the play. The action develops when The Rich One (Robert du Four), a spy who has been captured by the women and is being held in the camp, pretends support for the revolutionary cause and takes Adelita as his chosen target. He tries to seduce her in order to obtain information that later will be sent to the enemy.

Addressing the content of this play, Usigli asserts, "It is my feeling that, if presented to a Mexican public, the treatment of *Soldadera* would have to be somewhat different to be altogether satisfactory" (p. xix). I agree. Niggli's dramatic idealization of the Mexican subject makes her work more suitable for the very audience she wanted to reach—the Anglo American public of the 1930s, most of whom knew nothing about the Mexican Revolution. That she was consciously trying to transmit to an Anglo audience a sense of the culture and folklore of the country she loved is evident in the notes she wrote to accompany *Soldadera*. For example, when she introduces very specific cultural markers such as "mescal," she explains: "Mescal is a colorless liquor made from the sap of maguey" (p. 58). Later, she includes another footnote to explain the significance of "Maguey: type of cactus found extensively in Mexico. Grows exceedingly fast—three feet in a night. The sap of the maguey is used as an inebriating drink, called mescal" (p. 103). And, to explain the meaning of the word tequila, she remarks, "This is refined mescal" (p. 101).

Niggli introduces the subject of Francisco Villa in a song.

MARIA: One thing always gives me laughter,
　　　　Pancho Villa the morning after.
　　　　Ay, there go the Carran[c]istas . . .
　　　　Who comes here?
THE OTHER WOMEN (*joining in the chorus*): Why, the Villistas.
　　　　Ay, Pancho Villa, ay Pancho Villa,
　　　　Ay, he can no longer walk.
　　　　Because he lacks now, because he has not
　　　　Any drug to help him talk! Ay-yay! (p. 64)

The protagonists joyfully sing and dance "La Cucaracha" (cockroach), a famous musical composition popular with the Villistas and Carrancistas in the north. The ballad tells the story of a cockroach who can travel no further without marijuana. This refrain became symbolic among the revolutionaries, for whom travel and fighting had become a way of life. Niggli reworked some verses by substituting "Francisco Villa" for "la cucaracha."[51] Again, Niggli includes a footnote to provide her audience with basic information about Villa: "Pancho Villa was the leader in the north of the Agrarian Revolution of 1910. His followers were called Villistas. He was opposed to the government of Venustiano Carranza whose followers were known as Carran[c]istas" (p. 64).[52]

Notes like these, which place the Mexican world wholly within cultural markers, demonstrate the didactic nature of Niggli's approach to theater. At the same time, her system of representation was intended to transcend all geographical and psychological borders, and in so doing reveal the richness of her culture. In that sense, her writing also displays her efforts to transcend her own state of exile. Tensions and unresolved conflicts remained, however, as plays like *Soldadera* make clear. Although Niggli uses the Mexican Revolution and the role of female soldiers mainly as an intertext in her play and infuses the action with didactic romanticism, she never strips her key female characters of either strength or spirit. When she incorporates some verses of "La Adelita," it is Concha, the strong, brave leader of the group, who sings the song:

> If Adelita should go with another,
> If Adelita should leave me all alone,
> I would follow in a boat made of thunder,
> I would follow in a train made of bone. (p. 73)[53]

Concha is depicted as a "woman of the earth." She is a fearless, combative, and vehement *soldadera*:

As dirty as the rest of them, there is strength that flowers in her body and sets her above and beyond them. Born of the earth, it is the earth's pulse that she has for her heart. She is the one who keeps these fighting, snarling women together . . . who can punish with a sure, cold hand, but at the same time can heal their wounds. As merciless as the wind and rain, she is as warm and healing as the sun. (p. 74)

Concha is a force comparable to the strong elements associated with Mother Nature. A loving woman, she is also capable of going to extremes, if circumstances require.

Concha embodies the dramatist's feminist vision to problematize gender roles and the conflict of domination. For example, Concha is challenged by their prisoner, whom she has threatened to torture, with the words: "But you [are] women. . . . not hardened soldiers" (p. 94). Men and women are posited in separate and distinct categories. Even in times of war, one can be only a woman, never a "hardened soldier," suggests The Rich One. Here gender interrelations are placed within the context of male domination and hegemonic ideology. These relations, Jane Flax suggests, "have been concealed in a variety of ways, including defining women as a 'question' or the 'sex' or the 'other' and men as the universal (or at least without gender)."[54] Concha rejects the prisoner's presumption regarding the weakness of the female sex:

> Concha (*more to herself than to him*): Are we women? Sometimes I
> wonder. The Old One who cooks our food . . . she saw her son
> crucified by men of your kind . . . another one saw her son
> hunted down by dogs for the sport of it. That doesn't make
> women, my friend. That makes something worse than the
> devils in hell.
> The Rich One: But I had nothing to do with their sorrows. Why do
> they want to torture me?
> Concha: You called Adelita a symbol of the Revolution. Well, you're a
> symbol to us. You're a symbol of all the hate and horror that
> the Rich Ones have made for us. There are no men here to
> tell us what to do. We stand alone. You are merely the victim.
> That is not our fault. (p. 94)

These exchanges between Concha and the prisoner are perhaps the most powerful articulations in Niggli's dramatic text. In representing class struggle as the main conflict of the Mexican Revolution, while also capturing as a subtext the internal struggle over gender differences, these passages define the playwright's feminist and ideological consciousness well. Niggli's characters' dialogue embodies some of the important ideals of the revolution, including the demand for extensive reforms that would distribute land to the indigenous people, *mestizos*, and other dispossessed communities.[55] *Soldadera's* theatricality connects directly with a powerful discourse of class struggle in which the rich are understood to be the enemy of the poor. Niggli's ideological formation, then, represents the revolution as an act against the Mexican bourgeoisie.

In fact, the Mexican Revolution arose in response to social evolution motivated by the Díaz regime and the generation of the so-called "Científicos." At the turn of the century, with the development of industry, railroads, and the freedom to acquire wealth, materialism and dehumanization were championed as models of modern life. Of course, it was a type of modernism and freedom in which not all classes could participate. Concha strongly believes in the revolution as a class struggle, as is clear in her remarks to The Rich One: "You're a symbol of all the hate and horror that the Rich Ones made for us. There are no men here to tell us what to do" (p. 94). As a true *soldadera*, she defends the ideals of the revolution with passion and bravery:

> THE RICH ONE (*sneering*): I suppose you women think you can stop the *Federales*, now you know so well they are coming.
> CONCHA: I'll stop them, never fear. They'll be making a nice warm nest for you on the tail of Grandfather Devil. (p. 96)

While Concha represents the force that holds the women in the group together, young Adelita is depicted as childlike. She is the essence of vulnerability. Sweet and innocent, she readily believes the lies The Rich One tells her and tries to persuade her fellow *soldaderas* that he is trustworthy.

> ADELITA: This man is different. He believes in the Revolution. Why, he even knows the words of ADELITA . . .
> TOMASA (*sneering*): What does he know about the great song of the Revolution?
> ADELITA: He's crazy about the Revolution and he wants to know all about us, what we think about, how we live, everything.
> MARIA: And I suppose you tell him everything, eh? Not that the news will do him any good, when he is dead.
> ADELITA: He says that if he hadn't sworn an oath to the *Federales*, he'd like to join Hilario.
> THE BLOND ONE: So he tells you that, eh? That eater of cow's meat.
> MARIA (*jibingly*): And she believes him.
> ADELITA: Why shouldn't I believe him? What do you know about him? Any of you? You've never spoken to him . . . not seriously you haven't.

CRICKET: Didn't I capture him?
ADELITA: You? It was Concha. (p. 71)

It is Adelita who represents virtue. She wants to save The Rich One's life, and she becomes distraught over the cruelty of the women whom she loves and respects. Listening to the group deciding what to do with their prisoner, Adelita is appalled by their plans.

> CONCHA: Adelita! Come here, child.
> ADELITA: I don't want to touch you. I don't want to touch any of you. You are not the women I used to know . . . you're not the women who used to carry me around on your backs when my mother died. You've changed, all of you, horribly changed! Why, you're just like you're dead to me. All of the goodness and sweetness that used to be in you . . . it's dead! (*Crouches on the ground, crying bitterly.*)
> TOMASA: This is the Revolution, not a nursery.
> ADELITA: What do you know about the Revolution? It's beautiful, it's glorious, it's heroic. It's giving all you've got to freedom. It's dying with the sun in your face, not being eaten to death by little red ants in a bottle. If this is your Revolution, I don't want to see it . . . I don't want to see it!
> CONCHA (*standing*): Yes, this is the Revolution. We had to forget how to weep, and how to be kind and merciful. We are cruel, because the Revolution is cruel. It must crush out the evil before we can make things good again.
> TOMASA: Crush it lower than earth.
> CONCHA: Adelita, Adelita, for you there is tomorrow, but for us there is only yesterday. The Revolution is a fire that flames up and destroys, and we are the fire.
> THE BLOND ONE: Burning, burning, let us burn them all.
> CONCHA: We are the flame, calling to flame, and we are the earth calling to earth, and we are the tempest blowing across the sky! (p. 109)

Niggli uses rich metaphors to address the nature of the revolution, both poetically and ideologically. The power of these dramatic representations is reinforced in the weaknesses and strengths of her protagonists.

Beyond these symbolic representations, the portrayal of Adelita as unlike the rest of the members of the group gains additional import in the final outcome, when she becomes their unexpected hero. Concha discovers that the enemy troops are on their way to the camp to destroy the rebels' ammunition. The group's plan requires a sacrificial victim — one of the women must throw a bomb at the troops as they arrive. This means certain death for the woman who agrees to do the deed. The intended hero is Cricket, but at the last moment she becomes immobilized by fear. Adelita steps in and takes Cricket's place, giving up her own life without hesitation.

> CRICKET (*screams*): No! Not me! (*Runs down, flings herself on her knees and throws both arms about* CONCHA'S *knees.*) I wouldn't have a chance in a landslide. I don't want to die. Not me! I was only fooling. I didn't mean what I said. Please, Concha, not me, please. I don't want to die.
> CONCHA: Choose quickly, my friend. Would you rather have Tomasa's red ants eating out your eyes?
> (CRICKET *screams and flings both arms up over her face.*)
> ADELITA (*running toward them*): Wait! I will throw it. (*She snatches the bomb from Concha.*)
> CONCHA (*horrified*): No!
>   ADELITA (*strikes* CONCHA *with her free arm and knocks her to the ground*): This is the Revolution! The sun will be in my face!
> (*She flings back her head after the triumphant cry and* THE RICH ONE, *seeing the path free, gives a desperate pull, dashes past the women, and up the path.*)
> THE RICH ONE (*screaming to the Federales*): Back, you fools, back!
> ADELITA (*running up the path after him*): Long live the Revolution! (p. 113)

Adelita is killed, but the ammunition is safe. Her bravery is exalted in this final act. The innocent and sweet Adelita sacrifices her life for the revolution. This event represents Niggli's idealization of Adelita's character; the dramatist's sense of poetic justice makes Adelita the symbol of the revolutionary cause. Beyond Niggli's romantic metaphors, however, lies her rich ideological and feminist consciousness. She is intent on revealing the courage of women who fought in the revolution, and therefore, she makes Adelita a hero. Carmen Salazar Parr and Genevieve M. Ramírez, in "The Female Hero in Chicano Literature," discuss *Soldadera* and consider both Adelita and Concha heroes.[56] They make a comparison between Adelita and the mythical Ifigenia. Although noting similarities in the two characters' sweetness and innocence, they point out a major difference, as well. Adelita's self-sacrifice is motivated by her own conscious will in support of the revolution; Ifigenia's sacrifice was influenced by her father, Agamemnon. They describe Niggli's *soldaderas* thus: "Niggli's women are not the stoical *mujeres sufridas* (women who are submissive to a social station imposed by male-dominated society and their maternal obligations); instead, their form of self-sacrifice is their deliberately assumed role as active agents" (p. 50).

Niggli's *soldaderas* are both theatrical subjects and products of the

FIG. 8. *The Rich One, Concha, and Adelita* (sitting). *A scene from the
original production by the Carolina Playmakers at Chapel Hill, North
Carolina (February 27–29, 1936). Reprinted from Josefina Niggli,*
Mexican Folk Plays *(1938).*

dramatist's dialectical imagination. Her marked discursive conventionalism, evident in the play's many romantic metaphors and its fanciful
staging, is intertwined with a feminist consciousness. Contradictions
abound: Anglo women play Mexican *soldaderas*; they wear clean and
colorful skirts and shawls; they are surronded by basketry and cacti
meant to evoke folk art and a warm, exotic countryside. (See Figure 8.)
At the same time, the theatrical subject is hard-edgedly formulated on
the ideological premise of the revolution. The playwright's message is
clear. Despite her childlike qualities, Adelita is revealed in the end as an
aggressive, valiant hero. Beyond the folklore and subjective historical
interpretation presented in *Soldadera*, Niggli's depiction of Adelita and
the other female soldiers centers the courage and bravery of these
women. The song "La Adelita" and the character Adelita become
powerful intertexts which help to reconstruct the subject of history in

relation to the courageous participation of women. Adelita's self-sacrifice was inevitable, as was the dramatist's metaphoric discourse. But this conventionalism helps to increase the dramatic tension and the cultural condensation, as Niggli's identity, too, is affirmed as feminist and as Mexican American.

The play closes with the women in the camp softly singing verses of "La Adelita":

> CONCHA: Well, she got to them in time. The ammunition is safe.
> Aren't you glad? Aren't you happy? Hilario can fight on for the Revolution. You should show how happy you are. You should sing. Yes, sing, you devil's vomit, sing!
>
> If Adelita should go with another,
> If Adelita should leave me alone . . .
>
> (*As the women slowly join in the song,* CONCHA *stops singing, and her outflung arms drop slowly to her side.*)
>
> THE WOMEN (*singing softly*):
>
> I would follow in a boat made of thunder,
> I would follow in a train made of bone.
>
> (*The curtains close.*) (p. 114)

Metatheatrical and representative of folkloric interventions, "La Adelita" functions in *Soldadera* as an explicit link between history and popular culture. This use of the song is found in Dromundo's work, as well. In his narrative, the song breaks the monotony of the anecdotal. In Niggli's play, "La Adelita" is a theatrical metaphor embedded in the emerging construction of Mexican American identity. This construction is heightened by Niggli's sense of Mexican-ness, which provided a consciousness of joy touched by the American-ness underlying the economy of the play's stage production.

The fact that most of the characters in *Soldadera* are played by Anglo Americans is not an accident. As members of the Carolina Playmakers at Chapel Hill, the actors and actresses who brought Niggli's work to life were students in the department of dramatic arts, headed by Frederick Koch (editor of Niggli's folk plays). Indeed, the Carolina Playmakers gained a national reputation on the American stage as the founders of folk theater. As a student at Chapel Hill, Niggli was influenced by Koch, who defined folk theater as a performance concerned with "legends, superstitions, customs, environmental differences, and the vernacular of the common people."[57] Thus, Niggli's construction of Mexican American identity is intertwined with the folklorization of culture. The theatrical methodology she learned at Chapel Hill shaped the way Niggli expressed herself, resulting in a bifurcated image of the Mexican American. One aspect represents the legacy of her culture and traditions, while the other reflects the reality of her present condition as a playwright for Anglo American society.

Despite the dire economic conditions of the 1930s, which were detrimental for Mexican Americans, Niggli was able to succeed as a dramatist, novelist, director, actress, and teacher. Being in North Carolina during the 1930s was crucial for her development as a dramatist. The Playmakers at Chapel Hill provided her with the necessary space to create and develop her career as an artist of eclectic aptitude. Had she remained in San Antonio, she might never have succeeded; the Depression devastated theater workers in the Southwest through forced and voluntary repatriation. As a Southwestern artist who achieved great popularity, Niggli became the first dramatist of Mexican descent to have her previously produced material published. *Lo mexicano* (Mexican-ness) provided authentic material for a series of plays which deal in a colorful and theatrical way with the memories of her own exile. In *Soldadera*, Niggli represents the struggle of women and their active participation in the revolution. In romantic terms, she "stages" herself as one of these women. Indeed, Niggli's revolutionaries are the subjects of specific historical circumstances, but their staging becomes a reflection of her own experience at Chapel Hill.

The Role of Women in the Revolution: Adelita and Other Rebels

Whether the Adelita celebrated in songs and plays was a real, historical subject or a mythical figure composed of bits and pieces of women who took part in the Mexican Revolution has not been definitively established. María Herrera-Sobek, for one, questions whether there was an actual Adelita. She presents the well-known argument that Adelita was a nurse and not a fighting *soldadera*. Herrera-Sobek's sources claim that during a personal interview, a woman named Adela Velarde recounted her involvement in the revolution. Adela insisted that Sergeant Antonio del Rio Armenta, a member of General Carroncista's troops, had written the song in her honor. Mortally wounded in combat, del Rio had died in her arms, after declaring his secret love for her.[58]

If Adela Velarde was not a fighting soldier, many others were. Among the photographs in his *Biografía ilustrada del General Francisco Villa 1878–1966,* Gustavo Casasola includes a picture of two unidentified *soldaderas* (see Figure 9). One carries a sword; the other holds a gun. Both women stare defiantly at the camera and appear ready for combat. These women capture the spirit of the Revolution; with their aggressiveness and indigenous beauty, they look like models of the fighting *soldaderas.*[59]

Most of the *soldaderas* who joined the front lines of the revolution were *mestizas* or indigenous women. Sometimes they went into combat carrying their children on their backs. Some *soldaderas* were teachers who left the classroom to join or support the troops. They risked their lives and left their families to take part in the revolution. Regardless of their backgrounds, female participants in the Mexican Revolution did whatever was needed—they fought, foraged for food, cooked, nursed the wounded, and performed many other essential services.[60] I had the honor of speaking with one of these women. In Mexico in 1986, I met Justina Carrasco, a *mestiza.* Doña Justina was then 94 years old and very proud to have participated in the Mexican Revolution. Called "mi coronela" [colonel] by some people in her community, she was well known and respected by all. Doña Justina confirmed that at one point during the revolution, women fought on the front lines. Of course, many of them also took care of wounded soldiers. For example, Apolinaria Flores, a *curandera* (healer), was a source of faith and hope for the Zapatista rebels.

Among Las Adelitas there were rich as well as poor, educated as well as uneducated women.[61] Some upper-class women fought not with guns but with words. These aristocrats, rebelling against the ideals of their own social class, were important advocates of an ideology of resistance and contributors to the development of revolutionary feminist consciousness. Despite the intensity and integrity of their struggle for social reform in a society where the conflicting role of women demanded redefinition, these pioneering rebels have not received the credit that is their due. In noting the diverse role women played during Mexico's crisis, Anna Macías observes

> Yet, except for occasional references to *soldaderas,* most historians of the revolution have ignored the active role of Mexican women as precursors, journalists, propagandists, political activists, and soldiers. Only artists and novelists have given serious attention to the way the revolution victimized millions of women and, outside of religious publications, there has been a

FIG. 9. *Two defiant* soldaderas, *ready for combat. Reprinted from Gustavo Casasola's* Biografía Ilustrada del General Francisco Villa *(Mexico: Editorial Gustavo Casasola, 1969), p. 67.*

vast silence concerning the active role women played in opposing the anticlerical aspects of the Mexican Revolution.[62]

Macías further contends that it was from the status of these women that the Mexican feminist movement of the 1920s and 1930s drew its power. Feminists of this generation gained limited rights during the revolutionary period. For example, divorce was permitted for the first time, and the 1917 Constitution endorsed some rights for working women. During this time, women began to write extensively and were published in books, magazines, and newspapers.

One important feminist voice among the aristocrats was that of Leonor Villegas de Magnón. A vehement critic of dictator Porfirio Díaz, Villegas was a conspirator and a willing participant in the Mexican Revolution.[63] She rejected both the ideals of the aristocratic class and the traditional role assigned to women in Mexican society. Villegas emigrated in 1910 from Mexico to Laredo, Texas, where she began to write for a Laredo newspaper and became a member of the Junta Revolucionaria (Revolutionary Council). In her introduction to Villegas' memoir, *The Rebel*, Clara Lomas describes the author this way:

> Villegas de Magnón protagonizes an "aristocratic" rebel whose task is to immortalize the border activism of *los fronterizos*, to move them from a marginal backstage to center stage. Her story provides yet another instance of the struggle for authority and interpretative power waged by the various revolutionary factions of the borderlands through one of the most powerful mediums of their oppositional discourse, the alternative press.[64]

Villegas de Magnón supported the ideals of the Mexican Revolution. In using her writing as a tool of liberation and intellectual growth, she joined many other women of her generation (e.g., Sara Estela Ramírez, the Villareal sisters, Jovita Idar, and other members of *La Voz de La Mujer* and *Pluma Roja*) and contributed enormously to greater political and socio-cultural awareness at the turn of the century. Clara Lomas has pointed out that in their writings these women expressed different ideological positions with regard to nationalism, religion, and anarchism. In spite of these differences, however, they all consistently rejected the many restrictions imposed by gender inequality and sexual oppression, and thus all helped to shape a feminist consciousness on both sides of the border. In much the same way as the participation of women in the revolution has been overlooked as a historical subject, these women's writings and ideology have gone unrecognized. "These women's stories and publishing efforts, nonetheless, capture the realities of a people, the significance of whose daily existence transcends the limitations imposed by political and national borders."[65]

It is not unusual for the writings and activities of women, and especially those of feminists, to be wholly absent from the annals of history. Often, however, women's deeds and words are not so much deleted as they are transformed beyond recognition. This process of redefinition is strikingly clear in the case of "La Adelita." Historically, the subject position of Adelita represents the female revolutionary. In many versions of the song, however, little mention is made of her participation as a soldier. Instead, Adelita is viewed as an object of male desire. As María Herrera-Sobek has observed, the transformation of Adelita into a love object "became problematic for the troubadour since he or she could not employ the classic form of the heroic corrido; a more flexible structure, a more lyrical framework, had to be employed to fit the romantic contents of the ballad."[66]

In order to discuss the status of Adelita, Herrera-Sobek compares in detail the form and content of two versions of "La Adelita" taken from the Guerrero Collection.[67] One version leaves Adelita's status unclear; the other more obviously presents her as a soldier.[68] As a historical figure, Adelita was a soldier-woman, attracting attention with her military uniform—cartridge belts slung across her chest, a rifle hung on her shoulder—and her bravery. Adelita's revolutionary subjectivity represents the feminist spirit of the revolution, but in many well-known renditions of the song "La Adelita," that spirit has been distorted by the romanticization of her subject position as a lover of men. This exaltation of the romantic (and doomed) subject is also the core of a theatrical production by the Mexican Players. In 1937, at the Padua Hills Theatre,[69] Charles Dickinson directed *La Adelita*, a play loosely based on an episode in Pancho Villa's life. The program notes summarize the plot this way:

> The Mexican Players of the Padua Hills Theatre present a dramatic legend of the revolution based upon a folk tale woven around Pancho Villa's favorite song, "Adelita," and portraying the vivid life of his followers, their loyalty, spirit, the invaluable services given them by their women without which their campaign would have been futile, and especially the supreme sacrifice of Adelita.[70]

In this play, the dramatic action takes place in 1924 when Victoriano tells his daughter, Maria, Adelita's legend. After hearing the legend, Maria falls asleep and her dream becomes the story line of the play. The stage lights fade and the scene shifts to a time ten years earlier. Francisco

Villa is there in Maria's father's *cantina* (bar). While the General is being shaved, his followers dance and sing Villa's favorite music. In this version of the story, Adelita has been promised to the soldier Mariano, who is away on a spying expedition. In her fiancé's absence, Adelita discovers that she loves Pancho Villa who, in turn, realizes the intensity of his feelings toward her.

In the second scene, Adelita finds the General talking with a young woman whom he is asking to sing the new song, "La Adelita," as a surprise for his sweetheart. The scene is interrupted by soldiers who announce Mariano's return. Once Mariano has reported that the *Federales* are far away, the group begins to plan a celebration. Meanwhile, Adelita, who paid no attention to the actual conversation between the General and the young woman, is overcome by jealousy and suspicion. She tells Mariano that Villa sent him on the spying expedition only as a way of getting rid of him so that he, Villa, could woo Adelita. Mariano and Adelita then begin to plot Villa's assassination while they dance "La Cucaracha." The *fiesta* is in progress when Villa announces the surprise he has arranged for Adelita. Although she realizes the mistake she has made, Adelita cannot tell Mariano, since it would make him even more jealous. When their dance ends, instead of bowing low, she throws herself in front of Mariano's gun, receiving the bullet meant for the General (see Figure 10).[71]

The play not only disembodies the story of Adelita, it transforms this courageous soldier-woman into a powerless victim of her own passions, and it does so at the hands of an Anglo director. Dickinson's play "kills" the legacy of women such as Adelita, Valentina, and many other *soldaderas* who influenced the feminist consciousness of artists such as Josefina Niggli. The formation of the revolutionary subject in Niggli's play through characters like Concha, and the promotion of the revolutionary cause through Adelita's self-sacrifice, are distorted and weakened by the emphasis on Adelita's jealousy in the play directed by Dickinson. This type of romanticism subordinates the female subject: Adelita's self-sacrifice results from her own jealousy; she is not a hero. She is simply a victim of lust.

Still, not all representations of Adelita have tried to de-emphasize her role as a *soldadera*. In fact, as a paradigm of the female rebel, the *soldadera* was a source of inspiration for many people during and after the revolution. The work of the artist Guadalupe Posada (1852–1913) is important in this regard. During the revolution, Posada used *calaveras* (skulls or skeletons) as characters in his drawings in order to address the

FIG. 10. La Adelita, *produced and directed by Charles Dickinson. This production was cast with the members of the Mexican Players at Padua Hills Theatre. In the last scene, Adelita dies after receiving the bullet meant to kill General Francisco Villa.*

subject of the revolution as a social manifesto.[72] As a part of his *calavera* collection, he created the *Calavera revolucionaria*, representing a woman soldier riding a horse among the rebellious troops (see Figure 11).[73] More than 25 years later, in homage to this same revolutionary protagonist, Josefina Niggli created *Soldadera*.[74]

Determining what constitutes representation and misrepresentation can be problematic. What one understands to be the relation between the real and its distortion, between what something is and what it can be imagined as, involves subjective judgment. From the musical composition of "La Adelita" to Dromundo's narrative of deception and Niggli's folkloric theatricality, the gendered position of the protagonist is repeatedly represented in romantic concepts. In the song, the subject clearly becomes the object of sexual desire, but in both Dromundo's narrative and Niggli's play, the protagonist is a fighting soldier who dies in com-

FIG. 11. Calavera revolucionaria *by José Guadalupe Posada (1852-1913). This skull was produced around 1910 or later. It is a representation of the soldaderas who rode, marched, and fought with the rebellious bands against the federals. Reprinted from* Posada's Popular Mexican Prints *(1972).*

bat. As a true tribute to the inscription of Adelita's legendary subjectivity, both authors present her as a hero of the revolution. However, in Dickinson's production this heroism is transformed: the protagonist becomes a casualty of her own desires. In our contemporary society, north and south of the U.S.-Mexico border, Adelita's heroism has been commodified. For instance, Angel Martin's calendars, which exalt Adelita's beautiful face and body, continue to be very popular. Nationalism and sensualism merge as the glamorous femme fatale is pictured with two cartridge belts slung across her ample chest; she holds the Mexican flag in one hand, a cornet in the other. (See Figure 12.) Great numbers of these calendars are purchased year after year. Thus, the current popular representation of Adelita, a product of consumerism and the exploitation of the female body, preserves nothing of her feminist spirit. Instead the portrayal of Adelita in her revolutionary ensemble is sexualized and objectified. As an object of desire and erotic pleasure, Adelita is a commercial commodity.

Final Articulations: So Long My Dear Adelitas

> Ya me despido, querida Adelita,
> de ti un recuerdo quisiera llevar,
> tu retrato lo llevo en el pecho
> como escudo que me haga triunfar. (p. 39)

> [Farewell my beloved Adelita,
> from you a token I wish to take
> your picture I carry in my heart
> as a shield that will bring me victory]

"La Adelita" conveys a self-conscious performative space of gender and power relations. The protagonist is a revolutionary who foregrounds a model for representing the subject of history and popular consciousness. The name Adelita, then, becomes a symbol of trial and contestation. She is fiction, and she is reality. She bears witness to the subject of feminism in the U.S.-Mexico borderlands. She "traverses" the margins of nationalistic and patriarchal histories, constantly moving back and forth between the two. As Teresa de Lauretis puts it, proposing ways to characterize the subject of feminism as a phenomenon in constant motion (in its own context): "it is a movement back and forth between the representations of gender (in its male-centered frame of reference) and what that representation leaves out or, more pointedly, makes unrepresentable."[75] In this context of the "unrepresentable," La Adel-

FIG. 12. *"La Adelita," by Angel Martin. Reproduced from the popular calendars published annually in Mexico by Calendarios y Propaganda, S.A.*

ita's performative agency is an interplay between the reconstructed spaces inhabited by the texts which put her in evidence and that which has been centered by hegemonic discourses. In the popular imagination, she remains alive. Therefore, she becomes available as an alternative to patriarchy for women such as Josefina Niggli and La Chata, as they create new representations.

While Niggli dramatizes the heroism of La Adelita, striving to recover the historical subjecthood of women who fought in the revolution, La Chata's performing identity parallels the revolutionary ideals implicit in the legendary context of La Adelita. She *becomes* an Adelita, a revolutionary figure of the Mexican American stage. In their different ways, both Niggli and La Chata embody the spirit of this legendary figure, who remains accessible in the popular and cultural domain of Mexican people in the borderlands. And yet, there were real differences between these two artists. La Chata's artistic imagination was closely connected to the aspirations and experiences of the working-class people who comprised the largest segment of her public. Niggli's class position greatly favored her accomplishments as a dramatist and professional in academia. Nevertheless, both Beatriz Escalona—La Chata—and Josefina Niggli evoked in their theatricality the wondrous aesthetics of difference that mark the hybridity of the Mexican American experience in the U.S. In their very differences, artistic and socioeconomic, the two have helped to form a rich and diverse Mexican American identity.

Thanks to these women artists, and many others, the story of Adelita, the fighting soldier, lives on. Her revolutionary spirit inspires young Chicanas to challenge the exclusionary forces of American society in the 1990s. The song "La Adelita" continues to captivate people's imagination, and as a cultural site, helps to construct and deconstruct the contemporary Latina feminist subject.

Chicana Identity and Performance Art: *Beyond* Chicanismo

THREE

Performance art, with its focus on identity formation, enhances the cultural and political specificity of categories such as ethnicity, race, class, and sexuality. Many consider performance itself a contested designation where meaning is embedded in multiple levels of representation. This definition moves identity formation into the realm of indefinite processes unfolding in the bodily "acts" of the performer, the agency of production, and the spectator. It is this identity-forming and affirming aspect of performance art that is the focus of this chapter. The discussion has two aims. It underscores the cultural specificity of Chicana identity and its context in Chicano theater; and it examines the notion of performance as an autonomous system of production, separated from both the dramatic text and its representation. Questions of subjectivity, space, and politics are incorporated into the "performing bodies" of the two Chicana artists I examine here, Laura Esparza and Nao Busta-mante. Performance art becomes a vehicle through which the body is "exposed" and multiply delineated.

"The term performance, and specifically the verb performing," Diana Taylor writes, "allow for agency, which opens the way for resistance and oppositional spectacles."[1] It is precisely within such oppositional spectacles that the performance artists I focus on here "expose themselves" in order to subvert the enactment of power and representation. Laura Esparza, in *I DisMember the Alamo: A Long Poem for Performance*,

performs her identity and acknowledges its multiplicity by deconstructing the battle of the Alamo, a pivotal incident in Texas history.
Nao Bustamante explores her ethnic, female identity in *Indigurrito* by
mounting a hilarious critique of phallocentrism and whiteness. Both
performance artists deal with the political contestations that have defined their sense of history and shaped their personal stories. Their identity is not based in an essentialist sense of self; rather, it is constituted
through a performative sense embedded in their bodies, acts, and representation. For Chicanas, the performative consists of the materialization of "acts" which transgress normative epistemologies that affirm
and deny cultural and subcultural affiliations of the collective self. In
the larger context of the Chicano theater movement, Chicana performativity *must* be located in the realm of negotiations which transforms
silence into sound, invisibility into presence, and objecthood into subjecthood. This transformation must begin with the female body, giving
voice to a sense of self that will at last secure entry into the social and
discursive economy. In her book *Making Face, Making Soul/haciendo
caras*, Gloria Anzaldúa speaks passionately of the silence that invali-
dates the female body: "For silence to transform into speech, sounds
and words, it must first traverse through our female bodies. For the body
to give birth to utterance, the human entity must recognize itself as
carnal—skin, muscles, entrails, brain, belly. Because our bodies have
been stolen, brutalized or numbed, it is difficult to speak from/through
them."[2] For Anzaldúa, the metaphor implicit in the title of the book—
"making face/making soul"—corresponds in theory to a discursive level
of performativity embedded in *gestos subversivos* (subversive utterances). These utterances claim that the body, both as representation and
self-representation, is the object/subject of various epistemologies and
systems of production. Like Anzaldúa's position, my own stance in this
book is one that is typically marginalized in the dominant discourse.
Thus, I aim here to contribute to the larger, interconnected struggle in
which we, the long-silenced subjects, displace ourselves from the contours of marginality.

In examining Esparza's and Bustamante's work, this chapter highlights the role of the performer as a means for going beyond the stage to
appropriate mechanisms of control in the realms of culture and politics.[3] Performance art engages diverse cultural, personal, social, and
political systems of representation, but at the same time, it rebels against
basic modernist institutions. Many critics, including Jeanie Forte, have
explained this rebellion as in keeping with the continuing struggle of

twentieth century art against commodification. Performance art, Forte writes, "promised a radical departure from commercialism, assimilation, and triviality, deconstructing the commercial art network of galleries and museums while often using/abusing their spaces."[4] Esparza and Bustamante allude directly and indirectly to this "radical departure." They are, however, particularly concerned with the political implications of performance as a transgressive display of self, and one conducted within the space of their own personal narratives. Thus the relationship between self and representation enables the (im)possibility of identity as the subject of performance. *I DisMember the Alamo* and *Indigurrito* demonstrate the power of performance art; both are evidence of the way one-woman shows can succeed in undermining patriarchal society sufficiently to create a space for the performers, as women and as Chicanas.

A full appreciation of Esparza's and Bustamante's work demands some awareness of its historical, as well as its sociopolitical, context. El Teatro Campesino, which was organized around a collective system of production, brought the power of "group action" to the theater in the 1960s. In the 1970s and 1980s, the contributions of dramatists such as Estela Portillo Trambley and Cherríe Moraga created a broader space for Chicanas in theater.[5] Portillo's *The Day of the Swallows* (1976) and Moraga's *Giving up the Ghost* (1986),[6] precisely ten years apart, mark the end points of a distinct transitional phase in Chicano theater. This period saw the emergence of significantly new representational strategies. In Portillo's play, a misogynist lesbian, doña Josefa, feels trapped by her sexuality and prefers to die rather than accept her lesbian desire.[7] In Moraga's play, a groundbreaking work in Chicano theater generally and in the contemporary Latina stage specifically, the representations of lesbian and heterosexual desire define the paradoxes of culturally determined sexuality. Moraga's gendered sexual subjects—lesbian as well as heterosexual—expand the categories that have damaged the concepts of sexuality in Chicano/Latino culture. After studying the female desiring subjects in *Giving up the Ghost*, Yvonne Yarbro-Bejarano concluded that their representational subjectivity as sexual beings was "shaped in dialectical relationship to a collective way of imagining sexuality."[8] Indeed, Moraga's gendered subjectivities in theater and in the discursive configurations of her writing as a whole demonstrate that the constructions of nation, authority, history, and tradition are deeply sexualized and therefore depend upon a particular appropriation of space. Her recognition of this structure of everyday reality and her understanding of its implications are perhaps most clearly illustrated in her conceptualization of "queer Aztlán" (see Chapter 1).

The transition from *The Day of the Swallows* to *Giving up the Ghost* marks the emergence of a performativity beyond the confines of masculinist agendas and nationalist discourses.[9] In this context, discursive embodiments of female subjectivity and of identity politics have gained a new legitimacy. While Portillo's treatment of lesbianism was motivated simply by her desire for commercial success as a playwright, Moraga's attention to sexuality was rooted in her political awareness. She deliberately deconstructed and problematized the cultural forces that have shaped the roles assigned to men and women. Since the 1980s, as a result of Moraga's work, more emphasis has been given to the female body in this alternative space, and more direct questioning of sexuality has emerged.[10] In the 1990s, Chicana performance artists are using this alternative space in a manner that is at once amusing and radically innovative. They are generating their own stories as a means of gaining a fuller sense of themselves as Chicanas and as performers.

Chicano Theater: Cultural Nationalism and Beyond

> The nature of Chicanismo calls for a revolutionary turn in the arts as well as in society. Chicano theatre must be revolutionary in technique as well as content. It must be popular, subject to no other critics except the pueblo itself; but it must also educate the pueblo toward an appreciation of social change, on and off the stage.[11]

> The history of women's participation in theater history is of far-reaching significance in and of itself. Yet it is but one of the possible correctives to the monolithic great-man vision of human activity, which has obscured many aspects of history.[12]

The 1960s mark an important period of development in Chicano political life and culture. As a part of the civil rights movement, Chicano nationalism was the *grito* (cry, shout) that aroused Mexican Americans to assert control over their own cultural survival and determination.[13] As a political activity, the Chicano movement grew from several sources: a coalition of farm workers struggling to unionize in California and Texas; college and high school students who were part of the student movement developing across the country; and the urban working classes of the Midwest and the Southwest. Influenced by the black civil rights movement, the Chicano movement evolved into a defense of the rights of people of Mexican descent. César Chávez emerged as a national leader and as the central figure in the Chicano movement.[14] While black became a "beautiful" color in the affirmation of African American identity during the civil rights movement, for Chicanos, recognizing one another as "brown" constituted a way of asserting racial representation and rallying cultural resistance. Indeed, the conceptualization of *la raza*, literally translated as "the race," was used (and continues to be used) by Chicanos to accentuate the power of group identification. Initially, the term was popularly understood to mean "our people," but later it was broadened to include anyone from Spanish or Portuguese America. The notion of *raza* asserts a collectivity which affirms and defines identity in terms of one, shared culture among brown-skinned people.[15] The intertwining of collective identity, cultural pride, and the affirmation of color is succinctly captured in the following verses from a poem by Juanita Domínguez:

> Yo soy Chicano, tengo color
> Americano pero con honor
> Cuando me dicen que hay revolución
> Defiendo mi raza con mucho valor
>
> [I am a Chicano, brown skinned
> An American but with honor
> When they tell me the revolution has started
> I will defend my people with all my courage]
>
> Tengo mi orgullo, tengo mi fé
> Soy diferente, soy color café
> Tengo cultura, tengo corazón
> Y no me los quita, a mí ni un cabrón[16]
>
> [I have my pride, I have my faith
> I'm different, my skin is brown
> I have a culture, I have a heart
> And not any bastard can take that away from me]

The poetic subject expresses a militancy that was popular in discourses developed in the mid-1960s and early 1970s; the gender subject coupled with that aggressive stance, however, is the female subject's passive acceptance of the hegemonic representation of group identification associated with masculine markers of language inflection. An embodiment of cultural nationalism, the term Chicano symbolized the Mexican American community's efforts to actualize in political terms an ethnic impetus for self-definition, equal rights, and equal opportunities.

In theater, Chicano nationalism took the form of Luis Valdez's El Teatro Campesino. Spurred by the social and political upheavals of the civil rights and the United Farm Workers' movements, Valdez (and others) used theater to broadcast the call for unity and social change. El Teatro Campesino (which translates as the farm workers' theater) was oriented toward the cultural affirmation of working-class Mexicans. In conjunction with the political movement, the theater movement began with El Teatro Campesino's improvised performances in the fields of the Salinas Valley to support the striking farm workers. The company, which included members of the National Farm Workers Association (later the UFW), created satirical social skits, called "actos," that focused on issues related to the strikes and to Chicanos in general. The development of an active Chicano theater movement, along with the emergence of other cultural practices such as poetry and art, heightened the cultural awareness embedded in the Chicano movement at large.

Although Valdez's contributions to the development of Chicano theater are of great significance, his leadership had serious drawbacks for women in El Teatro Campesino and more generally for female representation in Chicano drama.[17] Recent critical evaluation of El Teatro Campesino's evolution reinterprets the company's history and analyzes the gender relations at work in its productions. Yolanda Broyles-González's and Yvonne Yarbro-Bejarano's contributions to this scholarship are especially important (see Chapter 1). Both decry Chicano nationalism's reinforcement of male supremacy or *machismo* as the symbolic rule of cultural representation. Broyles-González's and Yarbro-Bejarano's work informs the present discussion.

The combination of cultural nationalism and male domination that characterized the Chicano movement during the 1960s and 1970s repeatedly limited women's roles, activism, and creativity to self-objectification. A good example of this objectification is Juanita Domínguez's poem (quoted above), which displays the subject's alienation from those grammars of self-definition. As Angie Chabram has pointed out, Domínguez's poetic subject "marks the male gender by equating these features of Chicano identity with manliness."[18] From this perspective, the product of self-objectification becomes an instrument of male discourse and supremacy. Defined and dominated by men, Chicano nationalism silenced the voices of many women who participated in the Chicano movement, whether as activists or as theater workers. Yvonne Yarbro-Bejarano explains:

The prevalence of cultural nationalism also led to the reinscription of the heterosexual hierarchization of male/female relationships. In many organizations, male domination was the rule. Women were often excluded from the decision-making process. If their participation exceeded domestic tasks, they were often not credited for their ideas and labor. Chicanas' relationship to the leadership was at times in the form of sexual partners of the "heavies." Since "women's lib" was labeled a white, bourgeois invention, Chicana feminists who recognized gender as well as racial, cultural, and class oppression ran the risk of marginalization.[19]

In the theater, the implications of this kind of subordination in gender relations have been far-reaching. Yarbro-Bejarano has critiqued the "objecthood" that characterizes female roles in Chicano theater and culture.[20] She emphasizes how women who were attempting to "liberate" themselves were subjected to the liability of male dominance. Sue-Ellen Case puts it this way: "[for Yarbro-Bejarano,] the subject has become the specific conglomerate of one's oppressed object positions, negotiated with other oppressed, or 'different' positionalities within that field."[21] Yarbro-Bejarano reads the cultural images and subjectivity of Chicano theater within the frame of a conceptual opposition to its inscription of nationalism and patriarchy.

Broyles-Gonzáles takes a different position. With respect to El Teatro Campesino, she argues that the combined effects of male domination and Chicano nationalism shaped the company's productions and even affected the documentation of its history. "The history of the company," Broyles-González observes, "has been constructed as the history of the life and times of Luis Valdez. As such, El Teatro Campesino history has been shaped into a male-dominated hierarchical structure that replicates oppressive dominant tendencies within society."[22] Broyles-González examines the effects of that male-centeredness, beginning with El Teatro Campesino's early *actos*.[23] A feminist who situates her work in contempory cultural studies, Broyles-González draws attention to the gender politics that infused El Teatro Campesino's collective system of production. In play after play, the female roles amounted to no more than reductive characterizations: "Throughout the course of El Teatro Campesino's dramatic evolutionary process, the female roles have remained fairly constant in all the genres: variations of the same three or four types or categories. These characters are defined in a familial or age category: mother, grandmother, sister, or wife/girlfriend."[24] Interestingly, these variations are organized in a symbolic system which defines the worthiness of the female body in terms of its sexual functioning.

That is, the roles assigned to women cannot be fully comprehended without noting the specific historical and ideological articulations in which female sexuality is tied to reproductive ends. A woman is a grandmother, a mother, or a future wife, each of whom will follow the same path, but she is never a lesbian or a single mother enduring the hardships of society. In El Teatro Campesino, women were relegated to the roles of social reproduction within the organizational structures of the household and the traditional familial order.

The point here is not simply that these formulations highlight the construction of femininity attached to the traditional ideologies of domesticity and romantic idealization. More generally, the models perpetuated by El Teatro Campesino gave rise to a system of representation which simulated the unequal powers of the genders and exalted compulsory heterosexuality. Broyles-González does not distinguish between sexuality and gender. Her failure to do so is a major analytical drawback: Making such a distinction is critical for understanding women's roles in any cultural, historical, or political setting. It should be noted that the degree to which gender politics (of which Broyles-González's book is a mature example) is now established as a significant area of struggle in contemporary cultural studies is owed in great measure to the major contributions made by the discursive configuration of "body politics."

Though compromised by the failure to distinguish between gender and sexuality, Broyles-González's analysis is insightful in other ways. She notes that the standard designations—wife, sister, girlfriend, mother—are usually characterized by the "whore-virgin" dichotomy. The power and longevity of this conception may be traced directly to the entrenchment of Christian values and patriarchy in Chicano culture. The whore-virgin dichotomy can be fully understood only by examining the meaning of *marianismo* and *machismo*. The first represents the cult of the Virgin Mary and her subject position as mother of God; the second, the cult of male power and superiority. These interrelated concepts define powerful cultural values—ones that strengthen the subordination of the female subject in Chicano culture. By reinforcing the position of patriarchy, these "values" heighten the tension between culture and female subordination across national boundaries. Patriarchy is a sinfully real myth. Because its condition is established prior to its acts, it represents hegemonic power that "produces the world before it distorts it."[25] Patriarchal structures underlie the nature of knowledge itself, shaping notions of rights, rules, and responsibilities accordingly.

Patriarchy, Norma Alarcón contends, is the basis for the servile role of women in heterosexual relationships. Further, she argues that "when the wife or would-be-wife, the mother or would-be-mother questions out loud and in print the complex 'servitude/devotion/love,' she will be quickly seen as false to her 'obligation' and duty, hence a traitor."[26]

This "rebellious" outlook on the part of one who resists the traditional designation of gender roles has generated considerable debate among Chicanas and other Latinas. La Malinche, as a historical paradigm, has been placed at the center of this discussion: After the conquest of Mexico, in the gaze of the "new" *mejicanos*, she became "forever" a traitor (for other perspectives, see discussions of La Malinche in Chapters 1 and 4). La Malinche or Malintzin Tenepal was a young Tabascan woman given to Hernán Cortés by her tribe. She became his mistress, the mother of one of his children, and a translator. Many cultural critics and historians maintain that without her, the conquest of Mexico would have been difficult, perhaps even impossible.[27] For Chicana feminists, La Malinche is significant not only as an important historical subject, but also as a powerful symbol who represents the ethnic split between the indigenous people and the Spanish *conquistadores*. Alarcón, for example, explores the traitor paradigm in relation to the historical subjectivity of La Malinche. Cherríe Moraga sums up the importance of La Malinche this way:

> The sexual legacy passed down to the Mexicana/Chicana is the legacy of betrayal, pivoting around the historical/mythical female figure of Malintzin Tenepal. As translator and strategic advisor and mistress to the Spanish conqueror of México, Hernán Cortéz, Malintzin is considered the mother of the mestizo people. But unlike La Virgin de Guadalupe, she is not revered as the Virgin Mother, but rather slandered as La Chingada, meaning the "fucked one," or La Vendida, sell-out to the white race.[28]

La Malinche offers ethnic vindication within the context of cultural syncretism and political history. As a historical figure, she is a source of power for contemporary Chicanas who trace the *mestizaje* as a political act of resistance. The historicity implicit in La Malinche's story provides a paradigm for defining the contradictions that circumscribe Chicana performativity and cultural identity. As Moraga suggests, La Malinche, the mother of *mestizaje*, represents the binary opposite of the Virgin Mother. Together, the two symbolic paradigms capture the complexity of identity forged in the context of conquest, colonization, and Christianity. As cultural master tropes, both help to construct the terms for the formation of identity, defining the conditions for representation, self-representation, and transgression. Tey Diana Rebolledo and Eliana S. Rivero note in *Infinite Divisions* that La Malinche "lives on in every Chicana."[29] Rebolledo and Rivero point out major features which help explain Chicanas' connection and identification with La Malinche. They contend that the historical implications of her embodiment in Chicano culture are part of the same process which acknowledges the *mestizaje*, the hybrid nature of race. They position La Malinche as "the symbolic mother of a new race."[30] To use Gloria Anzaldúa's term, this "resuscitation" of La Malinche provides the tools for race consciousness and discursive militancy: "The work of *mestiza* consciousness is to break down the subject-object duality that keeps her [the Chicana feminist] a prisoner and to show in the flesh and through the images in her work how duality is transcended."[31] In Anzaldúa's terms, the binary oppositions which enable the deconstruction of subject/object are emblematic of the duality inscribed in "border" spaces. The border, therefore, is the site of both demarcation and obstruction, where the "inside" and the "outside" fuse in a performance of hybrid recuperation: Mexico/United States, heterosexual/queer, white/brown (black), first world/third world, and many other geopolitical and cultural negotiations. The prevalence and importance of such marked dualities in the lives of Latinas helped focus attention on another crucial border, the a/o split.

Discursive Hybridities

> The markers o/a, a/o announce the end of the nongendered Mexican American subject of cultural and political identity; they reinscribe the Chicana presence, which had been subsumed under the universal ethnic denomination *Chicano*. However, there are differences inscribed within these markers. Whereas *Chicano/a* consciously reinstates the Chicana subject within the ethnic discourse of Chicano, *Chicana/o* privileges the female subject within group characterizations that mark distinctions, giving the Chicana her own independent trajectory as well as a collective one.[32]

Scholars and feminists, such as Angie Chabram Dernersesian in the above text, have examined the ideological underpinnings of the "a/o" split in order to expose the hegemony inherent in group identity. These markers are an integral part of gender politics and they are crucial to an understanding of the symbolic representation of subjectivity in Chicano culture, including theater. Historically, the grammar of Spanish—and of most Romance languages—has subjected women to masculine constructions. The term "Chicano women," though it is often used by those inside as well as outside Chicano culture, is more than grammatically awkward. It sustains the gender hierarchy it is meant to bypass. The "a/o" split contextualizes ideological formations that challenge male hegemonic representations of group identity, and at the same time, "a/o" rejects assimilated grammars of identification. This distancing of the female subject from a male and Anglo-centered world is a constant marker in Chicana performance and in Latina theater generally.[33]

Chicana performance artists and writers have a social and political commitment to using cultural symbols in order both to explore the ramifications of being *mestizas* in occupied America and to reclaim their identity as women of Mexican descent in the United States. Although relegated to a subordinate position on the basis of ethnicity, Chicana identity cannot be subsumed by the simple ideological category of non-white. In Gloria Anzaldúa's conception of the new *mestiza*, the Chicana has a "plural personality," thus, "not only does she sustain contradictions, she turns the ambivalence into something else."[34] This ambivalence unravels the imperative characteristics which authorize the ideological grammars that historically have marked Chicana identity and thus, its performativity. Norma Alarcón sees identity formation around the term Chicana as signaling a "historically raced/gendered/class position," a product of two nation-states which proposes a subject-in-process.[35] Influenced by Julia Kristeva, Alarcón uses this notion to suggest that Chicana identity cannot be "unified without double-binds and contradictions."[36] In Chicana/o culture and identity, the border represents this contradictory "double-bind" state.[37] Anzaldúa's *mestiza* consciousness, in offering a paradigm that encompasses differences and contradictions, subverts the dominant culture. Performance art goes a step further. The work of Laura Esparza and Nao Bustamante involves not only recognizing and accommodating these double binds and contradictions, but exalting them as well. In their performances, the "double-bind" state of identity marks the hybridization of space. In turn, this space, hybrid and heterogeneous, reinforces the performativity of identity (de)formation.

Throughout Laura Esparza's and Nao Bustamante's performances, the process of performativity as a means of authorizing the subject is a key concern. With humor, these two artists invoke and then center that facet of their identity which makes them particularly aware of their

colonized and neocolonized conditional state. In this process of awareness, the subject of multiple determinations seeks the meaning of
decolonization. Such a process helps situate the act of the colonized
body seeking the site of the utopic, because decolonization remains a
metaphor of political effects and desire.

When Bustamante begins *Indigurrito*, part of her dialogue with the
audience affirms her identity as a *pocha*: "I don't know Spanish, I'm a
pocha. Soy una pocha. Eres una pocha también? (She asked a woman
in the audience, the woman answered no) Ay que lástima! Why am I
here? What am I doing?"[38] A *pocha* is neither Mexican nor "American."
Since its origin (in the aftermath of World War II), the term *pocha* has
been used primarily by native-born Mexicans, who apply it derisively to
U.S.-born Mexicans. Not surprisingly, many Mexican Americans and
Chicanos find the term offensive. The word refers to a person of Mexican descent who speaks little Spanish or who speaks Spanish "poorly,"
that is, not in accordance with the "high" standards of the academy of
the Spanish language. *Pochismos* (meaning, roughly, anglicisms) are
English words that have been made into Spanish nouns or verbs through
changes in spelling or pronunciation. These *pochismo* constructions
are typical in the U.S.-Mexican border states.

Bustamante's use of "camp," playing with *pocha*, is strategic. It allows
her to situate and define herself before anyone else can do so. Thus, she
immediately affirms her neocolonized subjectivity. In *I DisMember the
Alamo*, Esparza uses a similar technique to identify herself as *pocha*:

> The other day I was talking to a friend of mine, a prominent Chicana
> performance artist, and I told her that even though my father didn't like the
> word, there might be some honor in calling myself a pocha. And she said "A
> what?" and I said "A pocha." And she said, "A what?" and I said "A pocha."
> And she said "Oh that's funny. I thought you said a pork chop."[39] (p. 77)

This strategic process of identification as a way of "camping up" the
colonized self also gives Esparza a chance to involve her audience in the
process of decolonization. She makes the audience repeat the following
phrase with her: "What, you don't speak Spanish?" Once everyone is
repeating that phrase, she runs backstage and grabs a large pork chop.
Returning to her position on the stage, she hits herself with the pork
chop while the audience repeats "What, you don't speak Spanish?" The
irony involved in the performance is strategically connected to a larger
context in which the language of conquest becomes the object of the
subject's interpellation for identity contestation.

Plots of Subversion

For Esparza, born and raised on the west side of San Antonio, the history of Texas is an inevitable subject in performing her identity. In the opening scene of *I DisMember the Alamo*, she sings "Volver Volver," a traditional Mexican song about returning, going back. Her performance is a return; she is going back to claim "herstory," the history of the Alamo, which defines her identity in relation to her ancestors and reaffirms her subjectivity in an ethnic collectivity. By literally inscribing this history on her body, Esparza effectively indicates the representational levels of her identity:

> The history of Texas to me is a neighborhood I know by heart. The history of Texas is located here in my heart, in my blood. (*Lipstick X applied over heart.*) The history of Texas is never like a book or a movie. You can't put your hand on it. What happened can only be described one mirror at a time. (p. 73)

She appears on stage, sitting behind a white rectangular screen, "or in a white tent, or better yet a white 1950s refrigerator with two white wings, somewhat resembling the Alamo facade" (p. 74). Esparza's body is exposed as evidence of history and transgression. Her eyes can be seen through a hole cut in the white screen. Her widespread legs, clad in fishnet stockings, and her feet in high heels, project out through two more holes in the screen. The overall effect is seductive and revealing (see Figure 13). In the space between Esparza's legs, family pictures and newspaper clippings are projected on the screen. While her eyes stare with a piercing look that challenges the gaze of the spectator, her voice begins to narrate the story she believes best suits the Esparzas' genealogy. Her body is the result of that story. Consequently, it becomes the site where history is produced, transgressed, and altered.

During the "pre-show ritual," the theme music from the movie *The Alamo*, starring John Wayne, is played.[40] When Esparza starts her show, the movie itself begins on a television set that is placed on stage. Using both the historical event and Hollywood's version of it allows Esparza to emphasize the role Mexicans played in the battle. *The Alamo* and many other Hollywood productions have glorified the Anglo American settlers who wrested Texas from Mexico. Esparza's performance, by contrast, humorously subverts this romanticized view:

> It's a crock of shit. This Texas history lesson is a crock of shit. What do you remember about the Alamo, huh? *Viva Max*? John Wayne? It's all a pack of

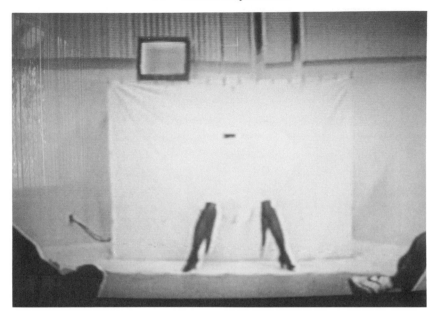

FIG. 13. *Laura Esparza's eyes and legs in* I DisMember the Alamo *are exposed in a performativity in which the bodily acts become discussable within the Alamo event in Texas history. Still taken from a video production of the performance at UC Irvine (1992). Courtesy of Marguerite Waller.*

lies. Epics. SAGAS. Truth and lies all done up to make each other look good. But I love a good story, don't you? You see, a lie can be kind of sexy. You know what I mean? Pow—instant intrigue. You can make any story a better one. And here I am, telling you my version, but there's another and another. (p. 72)

"Official" Texan history portrays men such as Jim Bowie and William Barret Travis as heroes who sacrificed their lives to defend their land and their comrades-in-arms. But these are myths. Bowie, for example, was actually a scoundrel, a wrangler who made a fortune running slaves and then went to Texas searching for lost mines and easy money. William Barret Travis was even more depraved. According to Rodolfo Acuña, Travis "had fled to Texas after killing a man, abandoning his [own] wife and two children."[41]

Esparza dismisses these so-called heroes and makes her great-great grandfather Gregorio the main protagonist of her story. His name is highlighted in newspaper clippings that she projects on the white screen. When she presents a slide of Jim Bowie, she says: "There are some who say Jim Bowie, hero of the Alamo, was protecting a hoard of gold he stole from the Apaches and hid in a well at the Alamo. Westward expansion, slaves, there was something for everyone, besides 'freedom.' And freedom for who? Did Gregorio know what he was fighting for?" (p. 73).

Esparza claims the history of Texas as the story of her family. The story of the Alamo, set within the history of Texas, is what validates her experience. The Alamo was a military defeat. However, it was a moral victory for Anglo and Mexican Texans who supported the state as a republic with a provisional government and called for its independence. San Antonio became the leading city of the newly formed Republic of Texas until the signing of the Treaty of Guadalupe Hidalgo, which in essence granted the whole Southwest to the United States. Esparza's story specifically deconstructs historical standards and re-affirms the existence of a competitive individualism within the collective sense of the "new" history she portrays. In addition to the newspaper clippings, she shows slides of family pictures as she narrates the story of *los* Esparzas:

> We have a family story
> A little familial history.
> A ritual secret of sorts.
> We tell it to each other,
> The family secret,
> Our creation story
> of how we discovered
> —ourselves. (pp. 67–68)

In departing from the official history of the 1836 confrontation at the Alamo to trace her family lineage, Esparza makes her individual and collective identity the subject of performance. The construction of Esparza's identity is based upon a collective whole which transcends the limitations of dominant discourses, which have declared history homogeneous. She insists that the personal is the "real" history, that the story of the Alamo is "herstory." She claims, "[m]y body is the battlefield of the colonized self. The land where conquests of Spanish, and Mexican, and American have occupied my cells" (p. 82).

Although Esparza deliberately introduces Gregorio Esparza, her great-great grandfather, as the star of "herstory," it is actually Ana, her great-great grandmother, who becomes pivotal. After all, she explains, it is only because Ana survived the battle that she, Laura Esparza, is alive today. It is precisely the denial of women as active subjects in the historical event of the Alamo that Esparza both foregrounds and subverts, creatively weaving transgression within transgression. The memory of Ana subverts official Anglo-centric history *and* undermines Gregorio's patriarchal story:

> 1,920 acres of land she could not claim as her right
>   as a hero of the Alamo.
> 1,920 acres she could have tilled to feed her family.
>   She fed her babies buggy meal to keep them alive.
> 1,920 acres she could not claim because her last
>   name was Esparza, Mexicana like the land she
>   stood on. An exile in her own land.
> Her cells are my cells.
> her grito is mine.
> She lived past the glory,
> the hype of history,
> And I am here simply
> because she survived. (p. 75)

The power of Esparza's performance lies in its emphasis on personal experience and emotional material such as family pictures. The slide projections of her loved ones contain a truth-effect which fundamentally enhances the relationship between the representational and the real. "The real is read through representation, and representation is read through the real."[42] For Esparza, the Alamo's intertextuality exists only as references that construct her family's historical background in San Antonio and deconstruct the legends of the Alamo. This linked constructing/deconstructing helps Esparza to perform her Chicana identity.

According to Marguerite Waller, Esparza's "dismemory/dismembering of patriarchal, nationalistic history leads not to an alienated (nation/ethnic/sexual) identity, but to accountable citizenship in a serious, but carnivalesque world whose energies flow with, rather than against, her multi-dimensional Chicana subjectivity."[43] By "dismembering" a nationalistic view of Texas history, Esparza's performative "I" explicitly becomes the site of creative intervention, and implicitly of political intervention, as well. She has a new story to tell:

> That's how I have this story to tell you now
> because it was never found in history books.

It was part of being my name, part of my body,
my locus,
my tierra,
family rooted in story. (p. 68)

Esparza invents a history as a way of performing her identity. In her version, only "herstory" is the "real" story. Esparza's body is a result of (and is presented as) a battlefield of "the profane war of lies." Her body "gives birth" to her story as she projects the family pictures and newspaper clippings. This pouring out of history functions as a discourse and metadiscourse of representation, and both narrate the dramatic story of *los* Esparzas: "That's how I have this story to tell you now because it was never found in history books." Reinforcing this discourse and metadiscourse with visual images, photographs, et cetera helps convey their meaning as an expression of performing identity.

Esparza ends her performance with a *rebozo* (shawl) around her waist, drawing diagrams with lipstick on her naked chest. She tells the audience:

I am this:
an india
inside a mestiza
inside a gringa
inside a Chicana
I am all of these
and my psyche is like a road map of Texas
traversed by borders
with never any peace at these borders. (p. 83)

Esparza enacts the reality of her multiple selves, acknowledging the many "borders" that crisscross her identity and give it its distinctive shape. Esparza's use of transgression within transgression allows the "I" performative subject to evolve in a continuous, multidimensional process of identity (de)formation. Her body—that of the performative subject present on stage—represents the ongoing exchange between colonization and decolonization. If decolonization holds out the capability of transformation in the realms of the subjected, then for Esparza and other Chicanas who affirm a neocolonized position, this negotiation remains a discursive strategy of representation and self-representation. In this constant negotiation, the metaphorical exchange of these categories—colonization and decolonization—responds symbolically to the site of performativity. Esparza's version of history comes to rest on the "relationship" between her subjectivity and the process of "decolonizing" the self from the dominant system of production. The disruption of the dominant (official) "history" constitutes a subversive strategy of intervention vis-à-vis Anglocentrism and patriarchal culture. In the process of decolonization, Esparza's body has the potential to "transmute" her subject position by authorizing an alternative way of knowing.

Decolonizing the Body: Indio *and* Burrito

This complex regenerative and symbolic process of decolonization also lies at the heart of Nao Bustamante's *Indigurrito*.[44] In her performances Bustamante, like Esparza, also delineates a particular space which subverts the order of traditional theatricality in Chicano culture (and in other contexts). A native of San Joaquin, California, Bustamante has been performing for more than fourteen years. Humor and irony are her trademarks. On her business card, she calls herself an "Assimilist/Protagonist." In the biographical notes section of the program for "Fierce Tongues: Women of Fire," a show that included a performance of *Indigurrito*,[45] she quipped, "I used to think I was the virgin Mary. Did you? I want more access." Humor, parody, seduction, and transgression are integral parts of her work and personal experience.

Indigurrito was Bustamante's response to the quincentennial celebration of the discovery of the Americas. In this piece, the performative subject exposes herself in a provocative game of parodic exaggeration and inversion. Even the title is a transgressive referential. A blend of two common Spanish words, Indian and burrito, *Indigurrito* manages to allude directly to the subject of colonization and decolonization and, amusingly, to a traditional Mexican dish. Most importantly, this hybrid referential captures the mobile, divided self, emphasizing that it can never be closed off from its cultural and political context.

In *Indigurrito*, Bustamante plays with words and with her body. Sometimes her improvised vocabulary makes no sense. Nevertheless, these absurd linguistic games produce suspense and hilarious repercussions as the audience reacts to, and sometimes participates in, her performance. Some of her stories are highly provocative: In one, for example, she describes an experience in which she masturbated while playing guitar. Bustamante's grammars generate an amusing spectacle where meaning is subverted and, of course, multiply interpreted. This type of transgression is what Mikhail Bakhtin calls *grammatica jocosa*. It provokes laughter, but in replacing the normal discursive pattern with a new order of words and images, it also "reveal[s] erotic and obscene or merely materially satisfying counter-meaning."[46]

During these word games, Bustamante occasionally touches her crotch, where a provocative-looking device hangs from a harness attached to her pelvis. This appendage appears to be either a dildo or a vibrator; its phallic resemblance is obvious. However, when Bustamante finally reveals the hidden device, she shows the audience that it is a burrito, wrapped in aluminum foil. Burritos are standard Mexican fare—they consist of a large flour tortilla, usually stuffed with beans, rice, salsa, and cooked meat or poultry. The bulging shape of the stuffed and folded tortilla is phallus-like. At one point in the performance, Bustamante holds this phallic device with one hand while she eats chips which she pulls out from between her breasts. There are two microphones on stage: Bustamante uses one to talk to the audience, while the other, much shorter, one stands near her lower body. With the burrito standing erect, she positions it against the shorter microphone to sustain the "erection" and free both of her hands for eating the chips that she continues to draw out from between her breasts. Suddenly, she also pulls out a small container of salsa. At this point, her performance becomes a complete comic event. Laughter (the audience's and her own) and the carnivalesque mood evoked by her actions become part of the transgression and subversion.

The mere presence of the "phallic" burrito attached to Bustamante's body introduces significant elements of the grotesque. It is an exceptionally radical and ruthless metaphor, with deliberate political implications. Her spectacle is an act of resistance and exaggeration which symbolically destabilizes the order of things, from food to the social body. Mary Russo's analysis of carnivalesque speech and spectacle suggests that they are heterogeneous in style and form, political in nature. She defines the carnival and the carnivalesque as an oppositional "redeployment or counter production of culture, knowledge, and pleasure."[47] Russo's theories of the carnivalesque are a critique of Bakhtin, who failed to incorporate gender analysis into his semiotic model of the body politic. For Russo, the mere definition of the female gender is transgressive: ". . . in the everyday indicative world, women and their bodies, certain bodies, in certain public framing, in certain public spaces, are always already transgressive—dangerous, and in danger."[48] Russo speaks of the dangers that women encounter in everyday situations; whether on or off the stage, female specificity subverts the order of the "space" in which men can safely "expose themselves."

In Bustamante's performance, the carnivalesque approach to the grotesque mocks phallocentricism and whiteness. Her voice is soft and sensuous as she interacts with the audience:

> I'm here to bring us together. I'm here to make amends. I'm here to absolve us from centuries of oppression. I'd like anyone here who feels the centuries of oppression to report to the stage now. I'd like to think of my performance not so much as audience participation, but more as audience salvation. I'd like any white men who feel like they want to take a bite of my burrito as a holy sacrament to relieve their guilt, to relieve that burden that they feel, to report to the stage now.

This passage discloses the central motive for Bustamante's performance. From here on, she repeats, in different ways, that members of the audience must participate in order for her to continue with her performance. She insists that the participant(s) must be white and male—"any white men" will do. She specifically identifies white men as the subject of her oppression and as the subject of colonialism. While she is inviting members of the audience to eat from her "edible device," a male spectator suddenly interrupts her to ask what type of burrito she is offering. Apologetically, she responds that it is vegetarian. Inevitably, her answer provokes laughter and furthers the interaction between the performer and her audience. According to Bakhtin, laughter "is an idiom never used by violence and authority."[49] I completely agree. Bakhtin proposed an image he found captivating—that of a body stretching its own confines and conceiving new bodies in order to generate amusement. Bustamante's body goes beyond the limits of conventional representation. The image she creates is not designed primarily to please either the "passive" or "active" spectator, but rather to challenge the social construction of an ideal type of "body" or "language." Her performance produces contested laughter, a spontaneous response based on differences and social subjectivity. Her audience grapples with the jumble of feelings, temptations, and provocations she inspires.

During her performance, Bustamante repeatedly states that "a taste of her burrito" will salve the white man's guilt. As the "holy sacrament," the burrito allegorizes several signifiers at the same time. It symbolizes the power of male subjectivity and patriarchal order, and it blasphemes the Roman Catholic sacrament of communion by subjecting it to farce and parody. Bustamante maintains that her burrito does not necessarily represent the phallus; it may be her enlarged clitoris. In either case, by her strategic use of the carnivalesque, she creates a powerful representation of knowledge, travesty, courage, and comedy.

After several attempts to recruit the targeted member of the audience—"any white man"—Bustamante decides to take the first bite of the burrito herself, as an apparent improvisation. Lying on the floor, she lifts her legs over her head and, in an amazingly acrobatic movement, reaches the burrito and bites off a portion of it. Standing up, she chews with obvious enjoyment. When she finishes eating that portion, she returns to the business of recruiting a white man from the audience. Closing her eyes, she begins counting, telling the audience that when she reaches ten, she expects to find someone on stage with her, kneeling down facing her lower body. When she is almost to ten, a man suddenly comes from the audience to the stage. She stops counting, but she keeps her eyes closed as she begins touching his face and hair. When she opens her eyes, Bustamante seems extremely surprised to find that the man kneeling at her side is Luis Alfaro, the person responsible for the program that weekend.[50] She reacts by questioning his decision to take responsibility for the culpability of others. Bustamante insists that she was expecting someone really "guilty," someone who represents the oppressor, not the oppressed. When she asks Alfaro why he decided to take the blame for centuries of oppression, he responds that he just wanted her to finish her act. Bustamante asks him to stand up, telling him (and the audience) that she prefers to close her performance without an "end" and without absolving any guilty white man from the audience. She invites Alfaro to leave the stage and suggests that they both go have a drink at a nearby bar. They exit, but Bustamante returns and throws the burrito directly into the audience. Beans, rice, and other ingredients fly out, hitting some members of the audience.

I have seen Bustamante performing *Indigurrito* on several occasions. Once, in San Francisco, she was able to finish her act. After recruiting more than five white men from the audience, she had them kneel down in a line and eat the entire burrito. One by one, each man took a bite, first admitting his guilt and remorse. After each had accepted his culpability, Bustamante absolved them all. The white heterosexual male is obviously Bustamante's targeted "ideal spectator." This is the same spectator Jill Dolan unseats and denaturalizes in her groundbreaking project, *The Feminist Spectator as Critic*.[51] Dolan problematizes the presence of that hegemonic spectator in order to construct a space for the marginal subject, which includes working-class women, feminists, women of color, and lesbians. It is precisely the monolithic space of the white male heterosexual—the dominant subject in power—that Bustamante subverts with innovation and wild humor. In *Indigurrito*, the process of decolonization, rendered suggestive and comic, again represents a metaphor inherent in the body's endless utterance. The body in its entirety, to allude to Hélène Cixous' notion, becomes an open-ended principle. Better yet, it is subsumed within multiple determinations in accordance with networks of representation. For Sue-Ellen Case, the body proposes "a certain type of textual space (that of no closure), which is a reading space, a writing space, and a social space, all at once."[52] It is that body that requires a spectator—for Bustamante, a white man—to participate. Present or absent in the "live" performance, as the perpetrator(s), the white male is inscribed as the necessary inquisitor of the performative. Ultimately, performativity in *Indigurrito* becomes the product of the search for the participant-spectator, which in turn helps to sustain the process of decolonization.

Both *Indigurrito* and *I DisMember the Alamo* are powerful works. Their success reflects the compelling overlap between the content and the form of their message(s). In the next section, I discuss some of the reasons why performance and performativity are uniquely suited to the radical agenda of many contemporary Latinas.

The Politics of Performance and Power

> Here I'm telling the family story as a performance art piece: that particular phenomenon in performance history driven by the economic requirements of American theater and the current government disposition on funding the arts; this particular chapter of performance history that clues us into the personal stories of every artist, actor, painter, poet or choreographer who has ever seriously considered the narcissistic requirements of art. I am giving away the family secrets, performing the family monologue, selling the family jewels, I'm colonizing myself! y La Equity: chinga tu madre![53]

> You can do with me what you want. I know it appears that I'm in control, but actually you're in control. One of the many wonderful paradoxes about performance is that actually you are controlling me right now so that if I give a bad performance, blame yourself.

These excerpts from *I DisMember the Alamo* and *Indigurrito* highlight some of the unique characteristics of performance art. In the first passage, Esparza sardonically defines the enactment of self-representation as a "narcissistic requirement of art"; in the second, Bustamante affirms the power and control the audience has over her. This necessary interaction with and participation of the audience is what gives her performance its distinctive power. Both Esparza and Bustamante evaluate the dynamics of power. Esparza specifically and ironically notes the political/economic power the government wields in its position as a primary funder of the arts. Since the early 1990s, many members of Congress have vowed to completely eliminate the National Endowment for the Arts; other legislators support bills that would deny NEA funding to individual artists.[54] This is the "disposition" Esparza refers to, and it is what compels her to give away the beloved secrets of her *familia*. Similarly, it is what motivates Bustamante to make the subject of her performance that monolithic white spectator. By telling the family story, Esparza gives away the "family jewels," the privacy of her own family, to recreate her multiple selves. Esparza and Bustamante think of their performances as a potential site of decolonization (and self-colonization, as Esparza puts it). They conceive of the act of performing as a means of breaking the silence and questioning the dominant structures of meaning and representation.

Performance art, and especially the one-woman show, is uniquely suited to this disruptive function. It is an exceptionally effective representational strategy because the subject explicitly articulates issues of identity and identification and openly struggles against coercive calls to cultural homogeneity. This system of production attacks universalizing agendas that have erased the subject's multiple determinations, as well as its agency. As a hybrid form of art, performance borrows not only from the fields of visual art, such as theater, painting, and video art, but also from dance and music. Jeanie Forte has noted the power of performance art as a postmodern genre, one that promotes a radical break with "patriarchal culture."[55] The one-woman show is aimed at bringing about just such a rupture with patriarchy and other dominant systems. Like most feminist performance artists, Esparza and Bustamante conceive of their performances as a means of enacting the world(s) of resistance. But even more importantly, they see performance art as a feminist vehicle for liberating the inner self from what Forte calls a "patriarchal text." Chicanas and other Latinas use this medium to represent and empower their own personal stories/histories. In performance art, Elin Diamond observes, the personal intersects with the "body's social text," to nourish discursive grammars of cultural differences, "of historical specificity, of sexual preference, of racial and gender boundaries and transgressions."[56] She suggests that performance is not necessarily a medium of absolute forms, but rather the site where contestation arises, "where meaning and desires are generated, occluded, and of course multiply interpreted."[57] This cross-referentiality of performance mirrors the referentiality of identity formation as a dynamic, ongoing process. Diamond is concerned with the representation of the self, questioning the production of cultural and subcultural affiliations which affect or cause the negotiations between discursive embodiments and reiterations of rules. I would add that these negotiations are possible because the positions of the subject's identification and circumstances are multiple and because the sites of gender, class, race, ethnicity, and sexuality complicate one another. Thus, performativity can neither separate out the grounds of multiple interpretations, nor subsume one under another.

Within the specificity of Chicano culture, the one-woman spectacle is a radical medium of expression. As the performative subject, the female gendered self seeks power by rejecting and subverting existing structures of power. As a representational strategy in Chicana/o theater, the one-woman show has contributed significantly to the visibility of Chicanas. For artists such as Laura Esparza and Nao Bustamante, performance art is the best medium for subverting and resisting structures of power embedded in our patriarchal society. Michel Foucault wrote that "[w]here there is power, there is resistance."[58] In his theoretical notion that all "I's" are sites where universalized operations of power always press on the subject, he demonstrates (unintentionally) that no one can avoid the realm of the "subjected." His own subject position as one of those in power clouded his understanding of the relations of subordination and led him to believe that the disempowered always remain marginal. In pondering modern society's monolithic power system, Foucault uncritically accepted power relations that subsumed the presence of the female subject into the objecthood of patriarchy, perpetuating the theoretical belief that the female "body" is more docile than the male.[59] From a Lacanian perspective, everyone is subjected to and colonized by patriarchal order, the law of the father. Again, in this view, the subject continues to be constrained by universalizing forces under which the symbolic order of decolonization remains a utopian illusion. In feminist performance, the gendered body ventures toward autonomy, becoming "decolonized," freed from the cultural depreciation implicit in socially defined gender and sexual relations. Therefore, it is important to suggest that just as there are diverse colonialisms or orders of domination operating in history, culture, and politics, there are various patriarchies, not a "universal" father.

Performance offers artists like Esparza and Bustamante a radical and effective medium for rejecting patriarchal definitions of the female gender. "Performing identity" is possible because of the constructed, illusionary nature of identity. The acceptance of identity as gendered and constructed focuses attention on the cultural politics that surround the Chicana question in particular, and women's autonomy more generally. The construction of a plural gendered identity problematizes the relationship between self and other(s). Esparza, for example, recognizes that she cannot hope to understand her own identity without acknowledging the historical and relational aspects of the self, the epistemology of her body. A gendered identity, Judith Butler claims, "is instituted through the stylization of the body and, hence, must be understood as the mundane way in which bodily gestures, movements, and enactments of various kinds constitute the illusion of an abiding gendered self."[60] Butler explains the "act" of gender this way:

> Significantly, if gender is instituted through acts which are internally discontinuous, then the *appearance of substance* is precisely that, a constructed identity, a performative accomplishment which the mundane social audience, including the actors themselves, come to believe and perform in the mode of belief.[61]

This insight into gender as a "performative accomplishment" leads Butler to speculate about the possibilities for constituting (performing) gender differently. Her discussion of performativity and gender situates the effect of difference in which genders are separated by regulatory systems. In contrast to theatrical or phenomenological models, which take the gendered self as existing prior to its actions, Butler understands these actions not only as constructing the performer's identity, but as "constituting that identity as a compelling illusion, an object of belief."[62] Her argument demolishes the theoretical grounds for forced gender identity and taboo. And, in practice, viewing the gendered self as a set of beliefs opens up sufficient space to construct and deconstruct the "illusion" of identity formation. Following Butler's theoretical perspectives, Diamond suggests that gender acts as both noun and verb: "Gender, then, is both a doing—a performance that puts conventional gender attributes into possibly disruptive play—and a thing done—a pre-existing oppressive category."[63] For both Butler and Diamond, these acts are possible through performativity, which indicates the power of discourse. For Esparza and Bustamante, performativity is a concern that constitutes who they are on the basis of what they perform. Beyond these theoretical models, Esparza and Bustamante conceive of identity as a narrative constructed to sustain a heterogeneous agent, one which is the product of *mestizaje* and colonization. The artists' internal struggles and multiple selves are the subject of representation. As Esparza observes, "The Indian in me will battle my Spaniard. My Spaniard will battle my Mexican and my American will have its own internal Alamo with my Chicana" (p. 89). Chicana identity and performativity 'render' the sense of self in relation to the paradoxes and contradictions caused by conquest and annexation. Understanding this as the political intermediary of a collective consciousness broadens the story of one's life, giving it greater possibilities for representation, as an identity constructed from other identities. Bustamante and Esparza recognize this interconnectedness and try to capture it in their performances. Esparza, for example, has acknowledged that "an important part of my myth is the heritage I have from the city. I feel the land and location of Texas in my blood and bones. I know that place as my body."[64] This is why her personal narrative cannot exist—why her identity cannot be performed and her body cannot be "exposed"—without Texas history and its transgression. The historical event of the Alamo is crucial to the philosophical "plotting" necessary for the politics of identity and its performance. Chicana identity thus configures a particular space where a gendered ethnic self is inscribed within multiple border crossings. In this construction, identity is hybrid and syncretic; and it is understood as a dynamic, performative accomplishment.

If Bustamante and Esparza show us how to articulate the borders that divide and unite us, how to make ourselves active, visible subjects through and in performance, other contemporary Latinas, in re-defining the stage and the role of text, give us another significant site for traversing those borders and contesting the status quo. The next chapter focuses on these topics in the context of Latina drama.

Cross-Border Subjectivity
and the Dramatic Text

FOUR

The definition of text has been substantially repositioned in the wake of performance art, as well as in performativity, where it now resides as an "utter-active" system of production. In "mainstream" Anglo American discourses, textual objectivity has been debated by a wide range of scholars, from Judith Butler to Eve Kosofsky Sedgwick and Sue-Ellen Case. For Latina and Latino intellectuals, ever since Gloria Anzaldúa published her groundbreaking piece, *Borderlands/La Frontera* (1987), the discursive configurations of hybridity have operated as models for inscribing the "border's" dynamics in a way that enables the fusion and convergence of contesting "textualities." With the publication of *Criticism in the Borderland* by Héctor Calderón and José David Saldívar (1991), a field of "border" studies, accurately recognized for its theoretical function and its practicality, was incorporated into institutional canons. Although recently the concept of "borders" has been posited as a cliché, the geopolitics of the U.S.-Mexico (Latin America) border space must be reconsidered continuously. As long as there is a dividing "wire" that separates peoples, worlds, and cultures, a border identity has to be constructed and deconstructed, in keeping with the act of "crossing" itself. As with any other cultural "site," a border space is in constant movement and commotion.

This chapter enacts the interface implicit in border identity, whereby geopolitics and cultural survival become paramount in the plays written by Latinas. I want to complicate the autonomy of performance by confronting the demands and traditions in the dramatic text which actualizes itself in the "performing" body of the act of reading. Beyond its concern with theatrical, dramatic, and performative activities, *Latina Performance* is about the spatial alliance of bodies, identity, commodities, and other fundamentals of culture that are at once the object of performance and the field in which it takes place.

Anzaldúa's discursive configuration does not directly delineate the grammars of the performative subject. Indirectly, however, the "border" is cast as the meeting ground of oppositional postures, the site where the third world joins the "authority" of the first world. The adjudication of such binary-opposed sites is a continual struggle among cross-border subjects, whose movements are aimed at securing economic survival and, as a consequence, cultural survival as well. For Latina dramatists and performance artists, the border itself is often a paradigm for theatrical and performative interventions. This is true for Milcha Sánchez-Scott's dramatic text, *Latina*, which is the main focus of this chapter.

As many have already suggested, texts are substantiated by various systems of production and reception. The prominence of this sense of "textuality" saturates more than the formulation of "print culture." As Case has commented, textuality "is posited as an after-effect of print."[1] Specifically, Case discusses the effect of "orality" (the public reading of academic research papers), noting that it is the institutions embedded in orality which define the medium of print implanted in the production of knowledge; thus, these institutions lead and demarcate the performative. The social function and desirability of performance in this instance supports the intellectual and virtual body by endowing it with presence, volume, visibility, and, sometimes, improvisation. In this kind of performance, the corporeality of text takes form through the resonance of multiple levels of representation and through authorial power. In the performance of a dramatic text, however, the power of representation is rooted in the many conventions of language, scene, meta-discursive figuration, character, and semiosis. Thus, I take a multilayered approach to the dramatic text. I examine it not only as a literary practice, but also as a heterogeneous artifact that integrates a series of representational subsystems. These subsystems correspond to the non-textual elements that produce the performative "state" of representation: Its pluralistic identity becomes an affirmative response to a reality and a language defined by openness and indeterminacy.

Although in this chapter I focus chiefly on Sánchez-Scott's *Latina*, I also make extended references to *Coser y cantar* by Dolores Prida and to *Simply María or the American Dream* by Josefina López. These discussions help demonstrate how all three playwrights use drama to reproduce their own polycultural, divided positionality as they construct personal and political identities. Sánchez-Scott's, Prida's, and López's dramatic contributions are also linked in that they each treat the discursive configurations of the cross-border subjectivity prevalent in contemporary Latina theater. That many Latina dramatists should be interested in the idea of cross-border subject formation is not surprising. As women of color, most Latina playwrights, artists, and intellectuals contend with the issue of identity in their private lives as well as in their work. Analyzing *Latina* and the other dramatic texts offers a way to explore the issue of identity in the context of migration. A close reading of these works (and related commentaries) reveals how identity becomes constructed and performed as subjects move across borders ("the barbed wire fence"). This "traversing" sense of identity and subjectivity is immediately apparent in *Latina*. In the opening scene, one of the protagonists, New Girl, abruptly crosses many geographical "spaces," from Peru to Mexico, and then from Mexico to Los Angeles, California. Her physical displacement is accompanied by a continuous revision of her identity. In Los Angeles, New Girl becomes one more "domestic"—and one more source of income for the Félix Sánchez Domestic Agency. She, like the other women who work for the agency, tries to survive her "American dream" by joining the ranks of the city's underpaid housekeepers, cleaners, and maids.

My reading of the "plays" in this chapter deconstructs the common charge that in the analysis of dramatic texts, the theatrical event remains simply an embodiment of the privileging text, as opposed to being treated as a theatrical intervention, the essence of a "live" performance. I conceive of drama and performance as moving, fluid aspects of the functionality of theater: As independent entities, the values and effects produced are dynamic and prolific, not exclusive and static. If I accept Case's arguments in her description of the after-effects of a "public performance" descending from a "community" of scholars, then my own analysis of dramatic textualities enters the space where the body of reception attempts to achieve the "performance" of an open(ed) book. As such, the full meaning of *Latina Performance* can only unfold in the interaction between the reader and the read, and thus my "performance" awaits additional interpretative expansions. There are no absolute parameters to describe what we know or what we want to imagine; imagination and knowledge are interrelated and complex. Neither is more decisive than the other. Together, they constitute a shared space in the production of culture, whether written, oral, or visual. As a "performative" accomplishment, this book makes me a potential presenter in a public forum where knowledge is necessarily disseminated as an interaction mutually perceived and/or challenged by a receptor. This dynamic function corresponds to the definitions which saturate the ways we know or the methods we use to know, or what we do not know but simply imagine. In "print culture," according to Case, the production of knowledge—be it in a public academic presentation, or through the discursive configuration of criticism, or in a stage production—"precedes and determines performance."[2] The transcendency of textuality and performance, then, allows me to accentuate the dynamic transactions within the uncertain, shifting, and contextual space of multiple determinants. As Diana Taylor explains, this transcendency is helpful when the goal is "to explore numerous manifestations of 'dramatic' behavior in the public sphere which tend to drop out of more traditional approaches to theatre."[3]

The Intersection of the Personal and the Dramatic in Latina

Milcha Sánchez-Scott's family background is diverse. Her father is Colombian, but he was raised in Mexico as well as in Colombia. Her mother is Indonesian, Chinese, and Dutch. Although Sánchez-Scott was born in Bali, she grew up in a variety of international settings. She learned English as a child when she attended a Catholic girls' school near London. Later, she moved to southern California, where she earned a degree in literature, philosophy, and theater at the University of San Diego, then an all-female Catholic college. After graduation, she moved to Los Angeles, where she currently resides. She wrote *Latina*, her first play, in 1980. In 1984, *Dog Lady* and *The Cuban Swimmer*, a pair of one-act plays, were produced by INTAR.[4] Both works were selected for the Theater Communications Group's "Plays in Process" series. *Dog Lady* was subsequently published in *Best Short Plays of 1986*. The play *Roosters* was included in *On New Ground: Contemporary Hispanic-American Plays* (1987). Other works include *City of Angels*, a trio of one-acts; *Evening Start*, produced in 1988 by New York's Theater for a New Audience; and *Stone Wedding*, written at Los Angeles Theater Center.[5]

Sánchez-Scott's conceptions of representational and theatrical space provide an opportunity to examine the U.S.-Mexican border as a cultural paradigm through which new kinds of identities are forged. In

Latina, the (re)construction of identity is shaped by economic and cultural factors operating within a specific physical—and theatrical—space. But, as I hope to make clear in this chapter, it is the *movement* of the play's subject(s) within those constraints that is crucial to the formation of identity. As border-crossers, the female protagonists define the marked heterogeneity among them, even as they share the same conditional (transitional) state. Each of the women characters hails from a different part of Latin America, and each comes to terms with her own separate identity as she recognizes the common context of the struggle for survival in the U.S. that links her to each of the other women. Thus, *Latina* helps us to view the notion of identity as a cross-border subjectivity, constructed and configured by the transitions of space. The barbed wire fence is the "object" through which the subject's venture is dramatically transformed: the act of crossing the border requires that the subject surrender her identity. Sánchez-Scott captures this aspect of border crossing in the passage below, which describes the protagonist New Girl's attempt to cross the U.S.-Mexican border with the help of a "coyote":[6]

> *It becomes night as* New Girl *starts her journey through the tunnel of light. The music changes to heart beating escape tempo. At one point we see* New Girl *paying off a policeman. Another moment a woman steals her shawl. Then a man accosts her at knife point and tries to rape her, but she escapes. Next, she is giving money to a slick city coyote, dressed in American type work clothes, who takes her to the end of the tunnel where it is night. There is only the moon and the sound and searchlight of an overhead helicopter. We see a large barbed wire fence. The coyote roughly holds* New Girl *by the wrist as the searchlight almost hits them. They both hit the ground and crawl on hands and knees to the barbed wire fence. She crawls through. He helps her. She stands up on the other side and looks back. There is triumph in the music with a moment of Peruvian flute. The coyote waves* New Girl *on. (p. 85)[7]*

In spite of all the difficulties New Girl faces, she finally succeeds in crossing the border. The border space as a "protagonist" in *Latina* is as dramatic as the subjects who risk their lives when crossing it. The complexity of the border space creates the potential for other spaces; these spaces in turn help address the problematic nature of identity. After New Girl successfully crosses the barbed wire fence, she is quickly transported to the chaotic city of Los Angeles, California, where she will be transformed. In turn, she will become someone else. In Los Angeles, she signs up with the Félix Sánchez Domestic Agency, a private firm that serves as a link between women (mostly undocumented workers) seeking employment and patrons (mostly upper-middle-class whites) seeking to hire maids. With humor and innovation, Milcha Sánchez-Scott explores the struggles of Latina women who come to this country as undocumented workers and seek employment as housekeepers. Her dramatization of subject formation as a process in which identity is an ongoing, personal (and group) performance is based on her own life experiences.

Latina was commissioned in 1980 by Susan Lowenberg, producing director of the New Works Division of Artists in Prison and Other Plays (AIPOP, later known as L.A. Theater Works). During a two-week tour of the state before its opening at the Pilot Theater in Los Angeles, the play's cast consisted of ten actresses of Latin American descent, including one undocumented woman who wouldn't perform in any place where she thought "La Migra" (the Border Patrol and agents of the Immigration and Naturalization Service) might show up.[8] In Los Angeles, the play was mounted by an all-female production/design staff, with choreography by Lynn Dally and sets and costumes by Janet Dodson. *Latina* was a great success, winning seven prestigious Drama-Logue awards later that year.[9]

The representational conflict performed in *Latina* is not dated, despite the passage of nearly two decades since it was written. The experience of Latina domestic workers in California has changed little over time. The play recalls the stories Sánchez-Scott heard while working as a counselor for a domestic employment agency in Beverly Hills. During the time she wrote *Latina*, Sánchez-Scott was working on a play with director Jeremy Blahnik at the California Institute for Women.[10] *Latina* evolved out of a conversation Blahnik and Sánchez-Scott had during a traffic jam on the way to a rehearsal: "I told Jeremy about a journal about domestics that I had kept while working as a counselor."[11] *Latina* is based on that journal and reflects the wide-ranging experiences of the women Sánchez-Scott met in the employment agency. As she has explained, "Many of the women who came into the agency were from tiny communities in South America and they were suddenly thrown into the middle of Beverly Hills and the whole California lifestyle."[12]

The agency was not simply a place to find jobs; it was a site for developing and preserving solidarity among the women. Coming into contact with one another at the agency provided an opportunity to reaffirm their individual ethnic identities. According to Sánchez-Scott, "In essence, they would gather at the agency not only to get jobs, but also to get bits of the cultures they had left behind. I had known a lot of women, including myself, who were going through an obvious denial of their latin roots, which they were trying to push into the background."[13] It was through her contact with these women that the dramatist learned to accept the richness of her own cultural background. "It was an interesting situation to me that these women, who have dignity, strength and big hearts, were so different [from me] in terms of what we were going through. These women made me realize that it is possible to come to terms with one's own Latinismo and to hold on to it in this society."[14] The need to "come to terms with [her] own Latinismo" seems to have been especially important to Sánchez-Scott at the time she wrote *Latina*.[15] Sarita, who is the receptionist at the Félix Sánchez Domestic Agency and one of the play's central characters, bears a striking resemblance to the dramatist. Sarita is an Anglicized Latina whose interests are portrayed as different from those of the other female characters. She dreams of becoming a movie star.

Sarita represents the *"vendida"* (sellout), the assimilated Latina who completely denies her ethnicity and cultural background. For Chicanas and other Latinas, the *vendida* paradigm is rooted in the cultural tyranny of the tradition of La Malinche, who has long been cast as a sellout, a traitor to her own race (see Chapters 1 and 3). In fact, a *vendida* is often referred to as a *malinchista*. Sometimes this question of "selling out" is further complicated by a confusion over the distinction between proximity and betrayal. For example, in separatist groups it is easy to become labeled as a sellout by maintaining existing (or forging new) alliances with white women, or by enjoying the comforts of a middle-class life. As I worked on my doctorate, some friends from my *barrio* in Arizona and some family members, envisioning the time when I would finish my studies and begin to work at a university, would say, "We hope you do not forget us and sell out to the white culture." In the eyes of some people, just being able to succeed in the "mainstream" economy can automatically make one a sellout.

For a Latina to succeed in the white, dominant structures of power requires more than overcoming class barriers. Racial differences raise an additional and major hurdle. In *Latina*, Sarita is working class (she's a struggling actress), but her internal oppression as an "ethnic other" is clearly a much greater problem for her than her class position. Sarita is an extension of the "sellout" prototype found in Mexican American theater at least since the early 1960s, when El Teatro Campesino first produced *Los Vendidos*. She is already assimilated to the "American" way. She speaks perfect English, even incorporating an "American" accent into her speech. Not only can she pass as white, she is a "white-wanna-be," obsessed with avoiding any identification with her Latin-ness.[16] Sarita vehemently denies her "Latin" self; she refuses to accept the reality and significance of that side of her. It is the poor domestic workers who eventually force her to deal with her true self.

Of *Latina*, Jorge Huerta has noted, "this play . . . centers around Sarita's personal identity crisis," but it also "encompasses the other women's problems—usually greater than hers—such as, 'How will I feed my children?' rather than 'Why wasn't I born an Anglo?'"[17] It is important to understand that both cultural and economic survival are central in the play. Huerta's articulation describes the basic motif of conflict. However, Sarita's identity crisis is also a pretext that allows the dramatist to explore how the experiences of migrant women, who must struggle to survive, shape their sense of identity. Women from Mexico, El Salvador, Colombia, Guatemala, and Peru are key characters in the play. All (except Margarita, La Cubana, and Sarita) live in constant fear of La Migra. In portraying both kinds of challenges, those facing Sarita and those facing the other women at the agency, Sánchez-Scott inter-weaves the problems of immigration with her focus on the complexity of identity as a social and cultural construction.

The "State" of Identity in Latina

> I am visible—see this Indian face—yet I am invisible. I both blind them with my beak nose and am their blind spot. But I exist, we exist. They'd like to think I have melted in the pot. But I haven't, we haven't.[18]

Gender construction is an identity "drawn" between the real and the fictitious. From Anglo feminist discourses to the perspectives of radical feminism, the in-between-ness of "the real" and "the imagined" allows the space of representation to contest the production of meaning. Here, theater embodies the space that lies in between the real and the imag-ined. In marking the relation of knowledge to imagination, theater is an ongoing negotiation between space, time, and the reiteration of discursive norms, some concrete and others abstract. Gloria Anzaldúa's discursive configurations in the above passage help to situate *Latina* in relation to the theatrical and real spaces of representation. Anzaldúa's politics of identity and visibility insist on the materiality of her body: her presence becomes a real effect of emotional, political, and discursive "truth." In *Latina*, the spatial transitions both produce and affirm a theatricality that embodies these relations.

The transition of space in *Latina* is abrupt, impulsive. Sánchez-Scott's description of the opening scene depicts New Girl in Peru, saying goodbye to the people in her village. In its projective, representational, and illusory character, this space corresponds to the symbolic status of theatricality. As the performance unfolds, "Peruvian flute music" can be heard and "village people" can be seen, creating both intimacy and a sense of imminent action. New Girl's mother, expressing sorrow and pain, lets her daughter go off in search of the "American dream":

> *The stage is dark. Then we hear Peruvian flute music coming from a distance. We see* New Girl *saying goodbye to a small group of* Peruvian Mountain Village People. *The time is dusk.* New Girl *is carrying a satchel. She has a Peruvian shawl around her shoulders. Her hair is in braids. She has on a peasant skirt and a work shirt and sandals on her feet. The* New Girl's *mother steps out and puts a St. Christopher medal around* New Girl's *neck. She embraces* New Girl. New Girl *tears herself away to leave.* New Girl's *mother falls to her knees[,] weeping. People around her help her up to wave at* New Girl. (p. 85)

The theatrical space shifts radically as New Girl successfully crosses the border and arrives in L.A. The abrupt changes in space are analogous with the transformations New Girl goes through. When she leaves her village people, she is typically dressed, wearing a "Peruvian shawl," a "peasant skirt," and a "work shirt." She has "sandals on her feet" and her hair is "in braids." Her dress, from head to foot, immediately establishes her identity, national origin, and class background. In order to cross the border, however, New Girl must change. Now she wears "American type work clothes" (p. 85). These are sufficient for getting across the border but not for getting a job. When New Girl is offered a position as a domestic worker, she must go through yet another transformation so that she will look more "Anglicized." New Girl's actions—leaving her village, crossing the border, arriving in L.A.—mark crucial moments in the play's theatricality and dramatic tension. However, the overriding importance of these moments lies in their role as an essential part of the metadiscourse, which focuses on the construction of a "fixed" identity and on the abrupt transitions of space.[19] Conventional and scenic, the play's spatial representations establish visual images that stress the actor's corporeal presence at the same time as they reveal the instability of identity: The young village woman from Peru becomes the border-crosser, who becomes the Latina immigrant, who becomes the undocumented worker. Each step marks a change—and each change reverberates across the performance as a whole. In a complex and contradictory process, the young Peruvian woman's many changes are constructed as a commodity of the geographical "space" they represent. Fashion becomes a defining statement in the constitution of meaning. New Girl's clothes simultaneously simulate and embody layers of defense against those who would dismiss her because of her indigenous look. Clothes also function as a metaphor for masking the undesired (or desired) body in settings where the economy of beauty is based on fleeting physical features. Once New Girl has arrived in the "city of the angels," she must become one of them: Her transformation is essential if she is to survive. To meet the demands of the employment agency, lipstick, a new hairstyle, and fashionable "American" clothes will suffice. Lastly, New Girl's "reconstructions" serve as a metaphor for identity problematized as a spectacle of unstable categories.

In addition to Sarita (the dramatist's alter-ego) and New Girl, other female characters in the play include the immigrants Alma, La Chata, Clara, Evita, Maria, and Lola; La Cubana (Margarita), the only worker with legal residency; and several wealthy white clients of the domestic agency. Although the women's national identity varies from one to another, it is clear that all share an awareness of their condition as marginal subjects in the U.S. All come to terms with their identity as Latinas in an attempt to define their cultural and economic condition. This is evident when the women discuss their nationalities.

> La Chata: No, she's only loca sometimes. She's from Cuba, those
> Cubans. Se creen mucho, like they are better than everybody.
> Evita: The ones from Colombia are the worst.
> Maria: No es cierto, I am from Colombia.
> Evita: You're the only person from Colombia I ever like.
> Clara: Los de Guatemala son los peores.
> Lola: I am de Guatemala.
> Clara: De veras, you are? I thought you was like me, from El Salvador.
> Lola: Poor people are the same everywhere. They are the ones that suffer.
> La Chata: Ay, sí, es la vida. (*Sounds of toilet flushing as* LA CUBANA *comes out of bathroom.*)
> La Cubana: Because you don't help yourself. You just have babies. You
> don't think how you will feed them. No, every year, plop,
> another baby and, plop, another baby. Then you come here
> and get on welfare. Help yourself, show some class, like me.

> (*She turns around and starts to walk out and there is a big piece
> of toilet paper stuck on the seat of her skirt. The women, seeing
> this, all point and howl with laughter.*) (pp. 107–108)

The protagonists perceive themselves as members of particular ethnic groups and humorously discuss the "good" and "bad" aspects of
their individual national identities. In the midst of their exchange, Lola
transcends the nationalist stereotypes and groups all of the women into
a single category, reminding them that "poor people are the same
everywhere." From Lola's point of view, identity is defined by the
economic and personal dimensions of one's present situation. These
women are all part of a disenfranchised minority, struggling to survive in
a foreign country. Sánchez-Scott deftly connects ideological assumptions regarding the women's condition with sardonic representations.
The toilet paper accidentally adorning the back of La Cubana's skirt
helps create a comic state.

Although *Latina* casts its protagonists in stereotypical roles, if the
play is read or produced properly, issues of identity emerge clearly as its
central motif.[20] Sarita makes it clear to the other women that the less
they "act like Latinas," the more successful they will become. When
New Girl is offered a job and Sarita tries to replace the young Peruvian's indigenous beauty with a more Americanized look, she is trying
to ensure that New Girl will be accepted by her future patron. Sarita
urges the other women to help her:

> SARITA: Okay, now we have to make her look like she's been here a
>   couple of years.
> LOLA: ¿Y por qué? Why we have to do that, because you say it?
> SARITA: Why? Because the client doesn't want someone who just fell
>   off the turnip truck, that's why!
> LA CHATA: (*To* CLARA.) Ay comadre, fíjate, they're using turnip trucks
>   to bring them in now. (*Radio volume gets louder with "Latin
>   Hustle."*)
> SARITA: Evita, you fix her hair. Margarita, get some lipstick. A ver, Elsa
>   quítale la falda y ponle la mía . . . (*The women all gather
>   around* NEW GIRL *and* SARITA. LOLA *sits disapprovingly to the
>   side.* LA CHATA *is too tipsy to stand, but yells instructions from
>   the side.*) (p. 132)

The implication is that the less "ethnic" New Girl looks, the more
successful she will be. Lola disapproves of the attempted transformation, but the other women are willing to lend a hand. Sarita not only
gives instructions about how New Girl must look, she exchanges clothes
with her.

The transformation of New Girl effected with the help of her peers marks the construction of identity as a constitutive act of theatricality. Moreover, it makes a definitive statement about identity as a process of ongoing transitions and transformations. With her stylized new look, New Girl seems to be an impersonation of Sarita. Meanwhile, Sarita, in donning New Girl's clothing, seems to have acquired the young Peruvian's image. This exchange symbolizes the beginning of Sarita's reorientation and eventual acceptance of her own *Latinidad*. This change makes her capable, later in the play, of taking a radical stand in support of the women and against the agency's exploitative clients.

Sánchez-Scott also underscores the relational aspect of identity construction through the character La Cubana (Margarita). Her unique position as the only domestic with legal documents (i.e., a green card) makes La Cubana arrogant. At one point in the play, when she accuses Sarita of giving her job to another woman in the group, Margarita flaunts her secure status:

> LA CUBANA: She didn't die! My old lady didn't die! You're just giving the job to Almita!
> SARITA: I swear to you the old lady is dead. And that's the truth.
> LA CUBANA: ¡Cerda! ¡Mentirosa! ¡Puñetera! ¡Bullshit!
> SARITA: Ay, Margarita, such language from a Lady's companion. Remember who you are.
> LA CUBANA: I know who I am. I am Cuban y I have a green card, ¿y tú? You are pocha. Mexican trying to be gringa. That's why the television people no want you, they know, they see, television is off, they watching you. They see how you lie, how you don't stand up for Almita, how you are afraid to speak up to the gringas. The television people no want you to be on the shows because you are dark face, pocha prieta, who don't tell the truth. (p. 120)

The power Margarita draws from her own identity lies in its contrast to that of the other women. Protected by her legal status, she is not hounded by fears of La Migra like the undocumented workers. Moreover, she is proud of being Cuban and feels superior to Sarita who, though legal, is unable to accept her Latina identity.

Another significant source of external/relational influence on the characters' sense of identity is the wealthy white women who hire the undocumented immigrants. All collude with don Félix, the owner of the agency, to exploit the women who work for them. In the dialogue quoted below, one such employer, Mrs. Camden, angrily demands a refund because Lola, her domestic helper, quit unexpectedly.

MRS. CAMDEN: That maid (*pointing to* LOLA) with no previous
warning, quit. It is customary to give two weeks' notice. She
didn't even call.

LOLA: You look at me like I'm a machine. So I act like machine.
Machine don't give notice.

MRS. CAMDEN: Oh, we treated you very well, you took advantage of it.
(*Addressing all the women, even* SARITA *on the phone.*)
Understand, please, that she had her own room and bath with
her own T.V. It is a very lovely room. I am sure she has never
seen anything like it before in Mexico. She had nothing, so
out of the goodness of my heart I bought her some nice
uniforms. She eats the same food we eat. I gave her the
advantages and protection of my home and this is the way she
thanks us?

LOLA: Why, no one in your house call me by my name. I hear you,
your husband, the children, all of you speak about me as your
Mexican maid. Always you say, "ask the maid, tell the maid."
Each day you make me more nobody, more dead. You put me
in nice white uniforms so I won't offend your good taste. You
take away my name, my country. You don't want a person, you
want a machine. My name is Lola. I am from Guatemala.

MRS. CAMDEN: She is an illegal. She is an alien. And if I wanted to I
could call immigration on her so fast it would . . . (pp. 138–
139)

Lola's rage is more than a reaction to economic exploitation; she is also
motivated by her desire to preserve some sense of her own identity. She
is angered by her employer's automatic—and incorrect—assumption
that she is Mexican: "You take away my name, my country. You don't
want a person, you want a machine. My name is Lola. I am from
Guatemala." The need to assert her individuality, to make herself real
("Each day you make me more nobody, more dead") is more important
to Lola than retaining her job.

The bitter exchange between Mrs. Camden and Lola brings into
focus a common tendency among Californians to identify all Latinos in
the state as Mexicans. The fact that Mexicans make up the majority of
the total Latino population in the U.S.[21] does not make it acceptable to
group all Latinos into a single, monolithic category. On the contrary, it
is important to recognize that the term subsumes a highly heterogeneous collectivity whose members differ from one another in class,
nationality, and culture. Sánchez-Scott captures this positionality both
directly and indirectly. In presenting her protagonists' identity as a
relational phenomenon, she is asserting the overarching importance of
these women's experience of displacement. They are national subjects

in a culture that is both alien and aggressive enough to present a constant threat of identity loss.

Another important aspect of identity construction treated in *Latina* concerns the role of language. The casual bilingualism used by La Cubana and other characters, who often intermingle Spanish and English in the same sentence, helps make Sánchez-Scott's dialogue original and authentic, an act of resistance. Language and its oral representation are potentially powerful resources because they rely on an exchange not only of linguistic signs but also of cultural markers which provide information about the position of the speaking subject. Sánchez-Scott's characters are positioned within two worlds; they move in and out of each through the use of their "border tongue." Although Gloria Anzaldúa coined this term to refer specifically to "Chicano Spanish," its ideological premise concerns bilingualism (or "Spanglish") as a characteristic of an ongoing performance of identity.[22] In *Latina*, language(s) become(s) a powerful tool of identification that dictates or necessitates certain cultural meanings. The bilingual experience embodies the dialectic between two cultures, two marked subjectivities, two "tongues." One represents the dominant language and culture that subordinates and marginalizes the subject, while the other is an affirmation of group identity intimately related to individual survival.

In society as a whole, language serves both to differentiate power from culture and to interweave the two. This dual function is clear in the "English-Only" campaign, for example, where rapid assimilation is supposed to result from the exclusive use of English in all official and public forums. As Diana Taylor has observed, "There is more than a little jingoism in the calls for cultural 'purity' underlying the 'English-Only' project."[23] In *Latina*, the construction of the subject is interwoven in a dialectical process in which language becomes a performed paradigm of the border space, theatrical and real. Beyond its geographic implications, the border marks movement between the self and the other. This kind of subject formation, with its divided positionality, allows Sánchez-Scott to reconcile two cultures within a single representation.

The Representation of Class and Racial Divisions in Latina

Wealthy white employers, as portrayed in the play, treat their domestic help as things, not as people. When Mrs. Homes comes to the agency to "return" Alma, she acts as if the young woman were a pair of ill-fitting shoes that needs to be exchanged:

> MRS. HOMES: I am returning Alma. (*She gestures, indicating* ALMA. SARITA *looks at* ALMA. ALMA *looks up and then bows her head.*)
> SARITA: Let me get your file. Would you like some coffee?
> MRS. HOMES: Oh, no, thank you, no Sara dear. (SARITA *walks to the file cabinet, opens drawer, stage right, near edge of stage, while* MRS. HOMES *takes a hanky out of her purse and dusts the seat before sitting.*)
> SARITA: (*To audience with the same gesture of the hand and voice that* MRS. HOMES *used earlier.*) I am returning Alma. What does she think this is, the May Company? (pp. 108–109)

Mrs. Homes finds Alma unsatisfactory because "she has no respect for my blue and white Chinese porcelain." In other words, Alma doesn't fit into the Homes' lifestyle. Mrs. Homes offers more money to employ what she terms a "proper person" (p.109), meaning someone who "understands antiques and fine things" (p. 109). She is willing to pay as "much" as $100 a week for someone who will live in, with Mondays off.

Mrs. Homes begins by asking for a black woman, but then changes her mind and requests an Asian.

> MRS. HOMES: Some of our friends have Orientals. I hear they are efficient. Oh, yes, indeed, and very clean, energetic, too . . . (SARITA *walks slowly to file cabinet area down stage right*) No grass growing under their feet, but they are moody, surly too, I hear. No, I can't have that, now, you Mexicans . . . (*at this* SARITA *turns her head with a start and looks directly at* MRS. HOMES) have the best dispositions. You people may not be the cleanest or the most energetic, but I'll say this for you . . . you know your place . . . (pp. 109–110)

Mrs. Homes doesn't request a white maid, of course. Without asking, she knows—as does the audience—that the agency would not have one. Race and class stratification ensure that the overwhelming majority of domestic laborers will be lower-class women of color. Mrs. Homes' actions, like those of the agency's other female clients, reflect stereotypes and misconceptions about the women they employ. The specific class, racial, and cultural divisions between the two groups underpin a hierarchy of power in which white females are always at the top; but these same divisions also contribute to a system of *interdependence* between employer and employee. Socially constructed assumptions and expectations on each side shape the experiences of both parties in an ongoing, reciprocal process.

In an essay on reproductive labor among African American, Mexican American, and Japanese American women, Evelyn Nakano Glenn makes a similar point. She proposes an analytical approach that integrates the cumulative effects of gender with those of race and emphasizes the relational nature of the two. Her case studies show that "race and gender emerge socially, as interlocking systems that shape the material conditions, identities, and consciousness of all women."[24] All women may engage in reproductive labor, but they do not necessarily perceive that experience in like terms. As domestics, women of color experience a "distinct exploitation" precisely because their employers/oppressors are female; meanwhile the employers gain a sense of superiority precisely because their maids are not white.

In addition to examining the economic and psychological exploitation inherent in the relationship between Latinas and their white employers, Sánchez-Scott also focuses attention on a hierarchy of power that exists exclusively among the Latina protagonists. Sarita, as the only U.S. citizen and a receptionist, is at the "top" of the group. La Cubana's status as the only one with a green card establishes her position as nearly equal to Sarita's. The rest of the characters are "inferior," merely undocumented workers who rely on Sarita to find them jobs. In between these hierarchies, the dramatist also addresses the issue of sexual subordination. One character, Evita, deliberately exchanges sexual favors for material goods. In the excerpt below, Evita is at the agency, excitedly recounting to don Félix and the women her latest experience with Mr. Hodges, her employer.

> EVITA: Ay sí . . . yesterday he took me to the May Co. and said, "Anything you want, Evita." (*The women "OOH" and AAH" and "Qué bueno."*) I got French blue jeans, the kind when you walk away they wish you was coming back.
> DON FELIX: Oh, honey, those are my favorite.
> EVITA: High, pero, real high-heeled shoes. Ay, I got so many clothes, I don't have enough days to wear them . . . and look . . . this Boluva watch he gave me. (p. 97)

Obsessed with the need to acquire material goods, Evita believes she is accomplishing the American dream. She seems unaware of the implications of the exchange she is making with her employer. Later, she is disgusted with him because she wants more "presents" than he gives her. She wants to get another job to make him jealous and get more money from him.

The sexual exchange between Evita and Mr. Hodges is presented as a kind of business deal. In real-life settings, however, the situation is often quite different. When I interviewed undocumented immigrants who worked as domestics in Los Angeles during the 1990s, I heard first-hand reports of the kind of sexual harassment some of these women endured. For example, Estela Ramírez, a Salvadoran woman in her early forties, explained that she quit her first job in order to avoid having to have sex with her employer's older brother. Recalling that job, she told me, "Tenía mucho miedo. El venía todos los días y me seguía a todas partes. Por eso fue que me fui y conseguí otro trabajo." [I was very afraid. He used to come to the house every day and follow me every-where. That is why I decided to go and look for another job.][25]

Expanding the Context of Dramatic Possibilities

In Latina theater, issues of cultural survival are a unifying concept in the struggle for recognition and the effort to project a public voice. Cuban Dolores Prida captures this sense as she describes her experiences as a struggling theater worker:

> In the theater, we have that saying—you know the one: "The show must go on." As I said before, soon Hispanics will be the largest minority in the U.S. Our presence here promises to be a long-running engagement—despite the bad reviews we get most of the time, despite the problems we may have with the lights, and the curtain and the costumes, and the enter and exit cues. Despite all that, this show will go on, and you might as well get your tickets now.[26]

Prida affirms the political economy implicit in Latina theater and also directly attests to the ongoing development of that theatrical tradition. Prida is confident that the presence of Latinos as a future "majority" will necessarily make them more visible as "minority" artists. She envisions a positive future—despite all the obstacles, "the show must go on," and the Latina/o stage, even if it is not fully recognized now, will soon be widely acclaimed.

Prida was born in Caibarién, Cuba, and currently resides in New York City. In addition to her numerous plays, collected in her *Beautiful Señoritas and Other Plays* (1991), she has also written two books of poetry, *Treinta y un poemas* and *Women of the Hour*. She is ranked among the most important playwrights of contemporary U.S. Latina theater. Prida is one of the few artists of Latin American descent to have been awarded an honorary degree from Mount Holyoke College. Considering herself a "theater worker," she stresses that her work is conducted in relation to others:

> Theater is people. Theater is team work. We need each other: playwright, director, designer, actors, choreographers, technicians, carpenters, composers, ticket takers, audience. We don't exist without each other.[27]

Prida conceives her own theater practice as a social forum where collaboration among directors, actors, and playwrights makes the performance a collective medium of expression. Her theater experience bears out her commitment to collaboration. When Prida began working with Teatro Orilla (a collective theater group in New York's Lower East Side), she swept floors and collected tickets. Then she progressed to running the sound equipment, designing the stage lighting, and "fill[ing] out endless forms for grant money."[28] Only after she had done all of that did Prida begin "to think I could write a play that would appeal to that particular audience: people who had never been to a theater before."[29] The specific audience she has in mind is Latinos. Prida believes that theater which addresses the needs and everyday realities of Latinos will draw this community into performance art. Theater is far more engrossing when audience members can readily relate to and identify with what they see on stage. She advocates an increasing cultural awareness in the Latino community.

Like Sánchez-Scott and many other dramatists of her generation, Prida is also concerned with the construction of the subject in process. In *Coser y cantar*,[30] she focuses directly on dualities and divisions inherent in hybrid spaces. In this play, Prida's protagonist "Ella" (the Spanish subject pronoun which translates as "she"), shares an apartment in New York City with her inner self, "She." The "Important Note from the Author" gives the reader this initial guidance:

> This piece is really one long monologue. The two women are one and are playing a verbal, emotional game of ping pong. Throughout the action, except in the final confrontation, ELLA and SHE never look at each other, acting independently, pretending the other one does not really exist, although each continuously trespasses on each other's thoughts, feelings and behavior. (p. 49)

The emotional game Ella and She play, which involves the "bouncing" of two distinct cultural selves, could only be conducted in a bicultural space. The struggle that Ella engages in while trying to deal with her inner self (She) literally gives voice to the paradoxical relation between her ethnic self and her assimilated side. Language, specifically the choice of one language over another, is an especially important way in which the protagonists declare their separate identities. In addition, the stage is divided into two different settings, two "ethnic territories."

Alberto Sandoval suggests that this subject in process—Ella versus She—shows how Latina subjectivity is always on the move. It is the product of and productive of dynamic cultural processes, never a static condition of self. Sandoval describes Ella's conflict as arising directly out of her bicultural status. She must learn "how to synthesize both cultures, how to survive and come to terms with the dilemma of a dual self that is demeaned, marginalized, and silenced by a monolingual-ethnocentric-white-Anglo-American system of power."[31] She must deal with her ethnic self, but she must also be able to meet her split subjectivity on common ground in order to incorporate the displaced materiality of her inner conflicts. Ella's body must learn to move without silencing She; she must retain a conscious recognition of duality and be able to alternate among the possibilities inherent in the movements, actions, and territories inscribed in her complex body. Ella must learn to speak with She, and She must learn to listen to Ella. This interactive mediation, discursive and dialectical, is crucial to any attempt at comprehending the subjectivity of Latinas in the U.S. In particular, understanding the process of transculturation and its potentially counter-hegemonic function is essential when dealing with the subject of Latina drama. This attempt to displace the dominant hegemony is crucial for comprehending the intercultural body in Latina drama. The process of transculturation embodied in the interaction between Ella and She is imperative, not only in Prida's dramatized subjectivity, but in the marked cultural interchange that provides multiple possibilities for understanding the subject formation in U.S. Latina/o drama.

Sandoval also remarks upon the close relationship between the dramatist's experiences and those of her protagonists. Like Sánchez-Scott, Prida draws from her personal experience as a dramatist and as a Latina to confront a limiting and problematic system of power. At the end of *Coser y cantar* Prida has Ella come to terms with her divided self by building a subjectivity that bridges the unstable territory between her two identities. She speaks with Ella, consolidating their alliance in such way that neither of them will silence the "other":

> SHE: I am as strong as you are! (*With each line, they throw something at each other—pillows, books, papers, etc.*)
> ELLA: ¡Soy la más fuerte!
> SHE: I am the strongest!
> ELLA: ¡Te robaste parte de mi!
> SHE: You wanted to be me once!
> ELLA: Estoy harta de ti!
> SHE: Now you are!

ELLA: ¡Ojalá no estuvieras!
SHE: You can't get rid of me!
ELLA: ¡Alguien tiene que ganar!
SHE: No one shall win! (p. 67)

In both plays, *Coser y cantar* and *Latina*, the conflict between cultural survival and acceptance is central. In *Coser y cantar*, Ella's main conflict deals with her self-affirmation as a Latina and her struggle with her assimilated self. In *Latina*, Sarita's cultural survival is dramatically juxtaposed with the social and economic context surrounding undocumented workers. However, as *Latina* progresses, the audience not only learns about the similarities and differences among the women who work for the agency, but also discovers why Sarita has difficulty accepting herself. Near the beginning of the play, when Sarita is on her way to work, she shows how repulsive and disgusting she finds her looks:

> I am tired of always feeling embarrassed! Embarrassed! Embarrassed! (*She is embarrassed.*) I'm embarrassed to be standing here on the street. I'm embarrassed to be standing here on the street in front of that place. I'm embarrassed to be working in that place, and I'm really embarrassed to be here waiting for Sleazy Sánchez to open up. And, I spent the better part of an hour deciding what to wear, because I don't want to be mistaken for a maid. I'm not a maid. You thought I was a maid . . . I am not a maid or a housekeeper. Housekeeper is what polite people call their maids. (*Pause.*) I don't want to look Latina. (*Loud sounds of car stopping, blare of radio with Disco sound and motor idling.*) That's embarrassing. (*Male whistle.*) (p. 86)

Sarita's embarrassment comes from being mistaken for a maid. She refuses to accept her own identity because she associates being Latina with being a maid. Her perception of her identity embodies the gap she experiences between who she is and who she wants to become.

As the play progresses, flashbacks provide glimpses of childhood experiences that triggered Sarita's present identity crisis. In one scene, a nun prohibits Sarita from praying for Mr. Amador, an undocumented worker:

> LITTLE SARITA: Hail Mary, full of grace, the lord is with thee, blessed art thou amongst women and blessed is the fruit of thy womb, Jesus. God bless grandma, Mommy and Daddy and please protect Mr. Amador, who works hard in the fields and don't let immigration catch him . . .
> SISTER AGNES: No, Sarita, you can't pray for something that's against the law. (p. 105)

Near the end of the play, a final flashback shows Sarita as an adolescent. She is again in conflict with a nun, but in this instance, the nun is sympathetic to Sarita's cultural background.

> SISTER: Is this your paper? (*Shows* SARITA *paper.*)
> SARITA: Yes, Sister.
> SISTER: It's a very good paper. Why did you sign it Donna Reed? And last week it was Gidget. Sara Gómez is a beautiful name.
> SARITA: It's a dumb name. It's Mexican.
> SISTER: Oh, Sarita.
> SARITA: Ah, Sister, you don't understand. I seen it on television.
> SISTER: You saw it on television.
> SARITA: Yes, I saw it on television on *Father Knows Best*. There's Kathy, Betty and Bud, and then there's Mr. Ed, the talking horse, David and Ricky Nelson. Even on *Leave It to Beaver* the people have names like June and Ward Cleaver, Eddie Haskell . . . I never saw anybody named Jesusita, Rubén or Sara Gómez.
> SISTER: A rose by any other name would smell as sweet. Can't you see that Sara Gómez is a special name? (p. 135)

By this point, Sarita's negative impressions of her culture have already shaped her attitude. She wants to substitute an Anglo name for her own, and she rejects the sympathetic nun's estimation of her culture as beautiful. Sarita associates Latino culture with gangs and Cholos.

> SISTER: Father Juniperro Serra . . . Ramona.
> SARITA: Cholo wagons . . . Graffiti . . . Gangs.
> SISTER: El Camino Real, San Luis Obispo.
> SARITA: Homeboys, Low Riders, Chebbies. (p. 136)[32]

In addition to the flashbacks that explain why Sarita acts as she does, mannequins (representing Sarita's thoughts) give voice to her inner conflict:

> DUMMY IN WHITE: I will teach her. I will teach her not to be ashamed. I will show her the statues of Francisco Zúñiga and she will see how it is to be a strong, proud Latina.
> DUMMY IN BLACK: ¡Ayyyyy, qué vivan las Latinas! (p. 111)

The mannequins help the audience understand the evolving state of Sarita's consciousness. Changes in her self-understanding over the course of the play, reinforced by the complaints and insensitivity of the agency's wealthy women clients, account for Sarita's metamorphosis at the end. As the play's dramatic action unfolds, it becomes obvious that

Sarita has always favored the customers and has had no sympathy for the women workers, who often were abused and exploited by their employers. Lola, the rebel of the group, angrily demands better treatment: "Oyes, Sarita, why didn't you defend Alma? You always take the gringas' side. First me, now Alma. Why don't you stand [up] for us?" (p. 112).

When Sarita does finally accept her own identity, she reacts violently:

> MRS. CAMDEN: I am glad to see someone take pride in their work. (*Turns and starts to walk to front door.*)
> SARITA: Pride! Pride? (*Sarita goes after* MRS. CAMDEN *ready to tear her apart. As* SARITA *takes a swing at* MRS. CAMDEN's *back,* LOLA *grabs* SARITA's *arm, throwing her off balance, which causes* MRS. CAMDEN *to turn around.*) Let me go, let me go, I say. You pink, colorless pig!
> MARIA: Hurry, lady, hurry. You must leave. (*Fast exit,* MRS. CAMDEN.)
> LOLA: Sarita, I only wanted you to stand up for us, not to kill the woman. Andale, un abrazo. (SARITA *collapses into* LOLA's *arms.*) Ahora sí, eres una latina completamente latina.
> (p. 140)

"Now you are really one of us," Lola tells Sarita, acknowledging that she has finally stood up for them. This incident provides a happy resolution for Sarita's personal conflicts, but it is not the end of the play.

In the next scene, La Migra raids the agency. Most of the women are taken prisoner temporarily, pending their deportation and forced movement back across the barbed wire fence. The final scene represents a critical climax in the play's theatricality and its mimetic correspondence with reality.

> EVITA: ¿Quiénes son? ¡Don Félix! ¡La migra!
> DON FELIX: (*Looking up from phone.*) No. No puede ser. I fixed it. I fixed it. (*To telephone.*) Carlos, hombre, call my lawyers. (DON FELIX *drops the phone and runs to the window and looks.*) ¡Sarita! ¡Viene la migra! Immigration! (*General commotion as lights start to dim.* LOLA *is torn out of* SARITA's *embrace by* LA CHATA. *All women run towards back room exit. Except* LA CUBANA *who stands still holding green card.* DON FELIX *is at file cabinet putting paper into briefcase.* SARITA *walks slowly to stage apron. As lights get dimmer we hear voices of immigration officers herding the women. Women's screams and protests are heard. Some women call* SARITA *with requests to call relatives.* LA CHATA *singing "Mexico lindo."* DON FELIX, *carrying briefcase, and* LA CUBANA *run after* SARITA *onto stage apron as curtain falls behind them.* SARITA *has back to them as she faces audience.*) (pp. 140–141)

In its realism, the commotion and turmoil caused by the appearance of La Migra provides an ending that reinforces the power of the play's theatricality. Margarita (La Cubana), Sarita, and don Félix are not included in the general roundup, since they are "legal." As the curtain falls, and La Cubana and don Félix continue their conversation, the ending becomes the beginning—another young woman crosses the barbed wire fence with the help of a coyote.

> DON FELIX: (*Speaking to* SARITA.) Don't worry, honey. They can't touch you. You're free to go and my lawyer says they can't hold me. I didn't break the law. I didn't bring them up here.
> LA CUBANA: And me, what about me, Sarita?
> DON FELIX: Honey, you got a green card. You got no problems. I'll see you tomorrow, Sarita. Sarita! They'll all be back. They just put them on the bus and drop them on the other side. When they get the money, they will be back. You'll see. (*Putting his arm around* MARGARITA, *they walk off the stage.*) Listen, Margarita, tomorrow there's this job with an old lady . . . (SARITA *walks over and sits on the bus bench. Flute music, helicopter lights and sounds, barbed wire fence as we see creeping towards the fence another new girl and her coyote.*) (p. 141)

The barbed wire fence and another new girl and her coyote are central images that represent a cyclic vision, one of an endless process in which undocumented workers go back and forth, forever negotiating a border space. The implied mimetism suggests how the theatrical space conveys the real space of representation. The space upon which *Latina* focuses, including the physical setting described in the annotations, is simultaneously factitious and real. Its representational character corresponds to the metadramatic discourse that is grounded in the text as a literary artifact. Its mimetism is tied to the real-life struggle of those who cross the border. The play's cyclic vision of space (both factitious and real) suggests that nothing will stop the flow of undocumented immigrants across the country's borders. The validity of that vision has not been challenged by the passage of time, nor by the increasing number and severity of measures taken by state and federal agencies in an attempt to stem immigration.

In Search of the American Dream

Don Félix, the only male character in *Latina*, is the owner of the domestic agency. He represents the Latino small businessman, always in search of new enterprises. Although Guatemalan himself, don Félix treats the women who work for him with indifference. He views them as the merchandise he sells. Some women have a greater value than others, and he will do anything to get a higher price. When he interviews New Girl, he sums up her potential dispassionately.

> DON FELIX: No English, no references . . . . another $60 girl, if we're lucky. Ah, don't waste time with her. Just work with the $100 and up girls. Wait a minute, wait a minute. Why don't you teach her to count to ten in English? Yeah, just to ten. That's all she'll need. (p. 92)

New Girl learns to count to ten in English. She gets a job with Ms. Harris, a divorced woman who works in public relations and needs someone to look after her two children. As Ms. Harris negotiates for a domestic, she bargains over salary. Cynically, she says: "I really can't afford anybody, but Silvia said most of your women were . . . well, you know, illegal" (p. 131), As used by Ms. Harris, "illegal" becomes a visible marker that consolidates theatricality with reality. As a concept, "illegal" is completed when it is followed by the term "alien." Thus, in the U.S., it marks a real space in which the continual degradation of undocumented workers symbolizes an ongoing relationship of subordination and power. On the other side of the barbed wire fence, the "border-crossers" are seen as *desperados*, persecuted subjects, chased by La Migra day and night. In his reflections on the prevalence and importance of border culture, Guillermo Gómez-Peña observes that in the space between two cultures, distorted views of "the other" are commonplace. Fear is "everywhere." To Anglo-Americans, Gómez-Peña notes, "'we' are a whole package that includes an indistinct Spanish language, weird art, a sexual threat, gang activity, drugs, and 'illegal aliens.'"[33] These distorted views influence how others see the border crossers, their place and their rights, including those who have the power to affect that site and those rights. For Latino immigrants and undocumented workers in this country, the way they are perceived dictates in part how they are treated. These perceptions come from representations of their subservient position. In the play *Latina*, the protagonists' subordinate position as domestic workers and as undocumented employees suggests a frame of representation that has material and emotional consequences beyond the level of theatricality. This space constitutes a subjectivity across cultures where the Third World and First World intersect, one dominant and powerful and the other *alien*. In theory and in practice, the borderlands are emblematic of this intersection. The border space *is* the very site of regulatory separation and obstruction.

During a visit to the domestic agency "Meet My Maids" in West Los Angeles, I learned from the receptionist that customers openly and unapologetically request undocumented workers as a way of getting "cheap labor." Most of the time, women without papers are willing (forced) to work more than 40 hours per week for less than $150. Even wealthy families offer wages that only undocumented immigrants will accept.[34] Eva Meszaros, owner of a domestic agency in Van Nuys, reports regularly turning down requests from customers demanding "starving girls who are willing to work for $100 a week."[35]

The quest for the American dream and the "problem" of immigration frequently appear in Latina dramatic and performance art as symbolic paradigms in representations of cultural identity and subject formation. In addition to *Latina* and *Coser y cantar*, *Simply María or the American Dream*, a play by Josefina López, addresses these topics.[36] The drama opens in an unspecified town in Mexico and then shifts rapidly to downtown Los Angeles as it follows the dreams and aspirations of María, a young Mexican immigrant in the U.S. As in *Latina*, the protagonist moves across the barbed wire fence to contend with life in a border space. The action takes place during a dream María has after failing to convince her parents that she should be allowed to go to college. In the theatrical space, the voices of three young women represent María's inner conflicts; they embody the conflicting roles that confront her as a woman caught between two cultures. The first voice represents the myth of the American dream.

> MYTH: (*Shaking* MARIA *lightly.*) María get up and come see.
> MARIA: Who are you?
> MYTH: I'm Myth. María, come see what can be.
> MARIA: What do you mean? What's going on?
> MYTH: María, you are dreaming the American dream. You can be
> anything you want to be. Follow me. (*The sound of a horse is
> heard.*) (p. 130)

The American dream, with its dual emphasis on individualism and productivity, defines one of the roles María must contend with. Also competing for attention in María's consciousness is her potential role as wife and mother. The myth of the American dream helps the protagonist to break with traditions that require her to be a subservient wife and mother. In a dream within a dream, María asserts her independence and rebels against the cultural impositions that dictate what roles she must play as a Mexican woman. She refuses to accept these limitations and decides to go her own way, in search of the American dream. After she overhears her parents arguing and finds out about her father's extramarital affair, she decides to leave home. She writes the following letter to her parents:

> MARIA: "Dear Mamá and Papá. Last night I heard everything. Now I know that your idea of life is not for me—so I am leaving. I want to create a world of my own. One that combines the best of me. I won't forget the values of my roots, but I want to get the best from this land of opportunities. I am going to college and I will go struggle to do something with my life. You taught me everything I needed to know. Goodbye."
>
> GIRL 1: Los quiero mucho. Nunca los olvidaré.
> GIRL 2: Mexico is in my blood . . .
> GIRL 3: And America is in my heart.
> MARIA: "Adiós." (*Fade out.*) (p. 141)

María, like Sarita in *Latina* and Ella in *Coser y cantar*, confronts her inner self as a way of surviving the physical and metaphysical dilemma of being caught between cultures. María declares her "Mexican-ness" to be an integral part of her identity, but she also accepts her "American-ness" as part of her inner self, her "heart," she says. Girl 1, Girl 2, and Girl 3 represent María's inner struggle. She expresses her love for her parents and for her cultural background, but she decides to go in search of her American dream (Figure 14). That is, she vows to pursue her own liberation and independence. As in the other plays, the protagonist's identity emerges from the context of the dramatist's personal experience. The subject formation involves a construction in which understanding one's self in relation to the other is central; the other represents the dominant culture which forces the self to assimilate. In the three plays, the protagonists learn to deal with their divided subjectivity, moving in and out of an unstable space. It is an ongoing process; the characters never fully assimilate into the dominant system. Lastly, in *Simply María*, as in *Latina* and *Coser y cantar*, the subject of immigration is self-referential. The struggles of López's protagonist reflect the real-life experiences of the dramatist. Born in San Luis Potosí, Mexico, López moved to Los Angeles with her parents at the age of five. She and her family resided in East Los Angeles "illegally" for almost thirteen years, until they obtained their legal residency (green cards) through an amnesty program.

In all of these plays, the immigrant-subject must contend with the

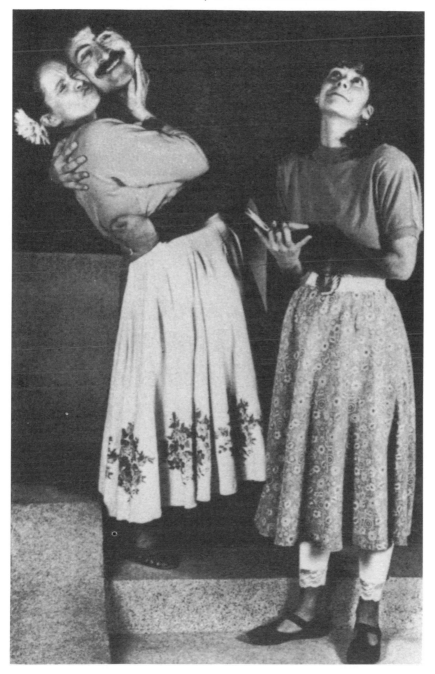

FIG. 14. *Scene from* Simply María: *María and her parents. 1992 National Tour directed by Socorro Valdez, March 3–8 at the Japan American Theatre, Los Angeles, California. Courtesy of Teatro Campesino.*

dual burden of economic hardship and psychological/cultural assault. Whole, integrated identities seem to be luxuries of the prosperous and the dominant. The border-crosser must be prepared to move as swiftly between identities as she did between countries. In each case, it is "traversing" the open space, the in-between ground, that holds both the most promise and the most danger. I close this chapter by examining some of the implications of this border space for identity formation, and in particular for sexual identity formation, among Latinas.

Nepantla *and Final Articulations*

In California, proponents of the "Save our State" initiative created Proposition 187, which California voters approved on November 8, 1994. This law denies social services and non-emergency health care to anyone suspected of being an undocumented immigrant. The impetus behind Proposition 187 is an anti-immigrant hysteria with deep histori- cal roots. At the turn of the century, this kind of extremism helped consolidate support for segregation laws aimed at African Americans and Mexicans; during the Great Depression, it fed nativist efforts to exclude Mexicans from the U.S. It is the same old story today. On one hand, proponents and supporters of Prop. 187 are against undocu- mented immigrants receiving social services, but on the other hand, they join those who exploit them. Those who employ undocumented immigrants may publicly proclaim, "We don't want you here," but in private, they say, "We can use you." An especially visible example of this hypocrisy involved Senate candidate Mike Huffington. In response to intense media pressure, Huffington, a strong supporter of Prop. 187, acknowledged that for five years he employed an undocumented immi- grant to take care of his children.

Renato Rosaldo notes how anti-immigrant hysteria "obscures the cultural identities" of those who make it across U.S. borders. As he puts it, these individuals "become anonymous brown hordes about to engulf Los Angeles and a number of other North American metropolitan centers."[37] The successful border-crossers become part of an exploited group that typically works for less than the minimum wage. "Illegal aliens," "the brown invaders," Rosaldo suggests, "speak with a measure of irony as they simultaneously accede to and resist their cultural homogenization."[38]

Rosaldo's critical perspective on the immigrant subject also func- tions as a metaphor for speaking about Latinos generally. He views positions of domination and subordination as linked directly to the mastery and control of arbitrary knowledge. The reproduction of meaning proceeds, he argues, "because culture and power are always at play with one another."[39] Who comes to this country and who is able to "assimilate" the American dream are fundamental components of a politics geared to reproducing capitalist society. Economic deprivation, the struggle for survival, leads people to cross the border in search of the American dream on the other side, *el norte*. But the border that divides people, Gloria Anzaldúa stresses, "is a vague and undetermined place created by the emotional residue of an unnatural boundary. It is in a constant state of transition."[40] Thus, crossing the barbed wire fence can be dangerously disorienting. In *el norte*, the struggle to survive entails greater risks than many people realize. It involves hidden hardships of a psychological and metaphysical nature. Latina dramatists, by examining the transitions and transformations that occur in border spaces, have contributed to a much clearer understanding of the challenges to identity implicit in immigration.

The construction of identity in the plays discussed in this chapter implies movement—particular notions of subjectivity and reason exist in transitional space. Anzaldúa calls this state "*nepantla*, el lugar de la frontera."[41] She explains that "to be disoriented in space is to be *en nepantla*, to experience bouts of disassociation of identity, identity breakdowns and buildups."[42] Her particular focus is the Mexican immigrant. The U.S.-Mexican borderlands can be defined roughly as the territory centered on an international boundary line that stretches from the Gulf of Mexico to the Pacific Ocean. The borders at the Mexican cities of Tijuana (adjacent to San Diego, California) and Juárez (adjacent to El Paso, Texas) are among the most frequently crossed, both legally and illegally. Anzaldúa describes the border as an uncertain space which induces a state of *nepantla* in the immigrants who cross it:

> *Nepantla* is the Nahuatl word for an in-between state, that uncertain terrain one crosses when moving from one place to another, when changing from one class, race, or gender position to another, when traveling from the present identity into a new identity. The Mexican immigrant at the moment of crossing the barbed-wire fence into the hostile "paradise" of *el norte*, the United States, is caught in a state of *nepantla*.[43]

For her, the state of *nepantla* is not limited to the disorientation implicit in the geopolitics of space, but extends to the alterations involved in race, class, gender, and sexuality. From *Borderlands* to the discursive configuration of *nepantla* as the land in the middle, Anzaldúa's politics of space demonstrate the constant struggle for cultural recuperation and resistance. If sexuality is included as one of the categories of the nepantla state, heterosexuality, as the prevailing division, would dismiss the "chaos" Anzaldúa proposes in her conceptualization of *nepantla*. "Disorder" is necessary for the representation of the excessive symbolism which marks the very site of binary oppositions. Without such disruption, heterosexuality will remain in the order of categories that society presupposes as unchanging. This persistence is evident in the plays analyzed here. Heterosexuality is assumed in the theatricalization of events that make the female gender asexual, or conventionally involved in a sexual relationship where her body is being used as merchandise. In *Latina*, Evita voluntarily exchanges sexual favors with her male "patron." For economic reasons, she is "willing" to serve not only as her employer's maid, but also as his mistress. If there are any implications in the passive condition of identity in *Latina*, they fall precisely within the contours of an unchallenged heterosexuality. At the very site of the unspoken, the body is understood as in equilibrium with the social embodiment of the world. In Evita's case, the body is being exploited, and thus the representation of sexuality is violent, if not vain.

Heterosexuality is also a presupposed category in *Simply María*. Although in this instance, María is able to break the cycle that supports the entitlement of this institution, the category's principle is clear in the protagonist's dream, which explores the many possibilities of her gender roles. Mary, the holy virgin mother, appears to her with the other Marías (the alter egos), who present to the protagonist all the alternatives she has in life as a woman:

> Mary: (*Barely able to speak.*) María, before you are a wife, before you are a mother, first you are a woman! I'll be back. (*She's dragged out.* MARIA 2, *who won the fight, acknowledges the cheers of the crowd, then gestures for* MARIA *to kneel and pray.* MARIA 2 *puts a wedding veil on* MARIA.)
> MARIA 2: A woman's only purpose in life is to serve three men. Her father, her husband and her son. Her father. (*Ricardo appears. He picks up* MARIA *and escorts her to the church. The bell and the wedding march are heard. The following title is displayed:* WHITE WEDDING.) (p. 132)

The dream is a conventional strategy which allows López to critique the presupposed roles that are socially constructed in Latino culture. Although the dramatist orients her protagonist to refuse these roles (wife and mother) and makes her go in search of other possibilities, the synthesis of the heterosexual model is constructed and presupposed in the protagonist's decision to "create a world of her own" (p. 140). Even in refusing these roles, the protagonist consciously and unconsciously presupposes heterosexuality; what she critiques is its compulsory function. At the end of the play, María and her mother go their own ways, breaking the culturally determined pattern of their lives. But heterosexuality remains presupposed as an unquestioned (unquestionable) "normal" category throughout the dramatic events. Indeed, María is not concerned with exploring her sexuality per se. Her goal is to obtain "the best from this land of opportunities" (p. 140). She is more concerned with her "American dream," which for her means getting an education and becoming financially independent. The implicit suggestion is that the protagonist is challenging the traditional conception of female roles in Latino culture. That is, some parents would not allow their daughters to go to college because they believe marriage is the ultimate goal for women. I remember hearing remarks such as "Why do you want to attend college if you are going to end up marrying," from the parents of some of my friends who were beginning to make plans to go to college. Some of these young women obediently followed their parents' instructions and abandoned their dreams of college; others, like the protagonist in *Simply María*, followed their own impulses.

In Prida's play, on the other hand, sexuality is depicted simply in terms of the protagonist's erotic fantasies. Ella sees herself as a savior of the world, "a superwoman," a leader followed by multitudes. She sees herself as very attached to her body and to sexual desires. She touches herself without inhibition:

> SHE: (*Sensually mischievous.*) I am lying naked. Totally, fully, wonderfully naked. Feeling good and relaxed. Suddenly, I feel something warm and moist between my toes. It is a tongue! A huge, wide, live tongue! The most extraordinary thing about this tongue is that it changes. It takes different shapes. . . .It wraps itself around my big toe . . . then goes in between and around each toe . . . then it moves up my leg, up my thigh . . . and into my . . . (p. 58)

Ella stops She, seemingly to prevent her from finishing the sentence with the word vagina. Ella is politically correct, unlike She, whose language and movements are characterized by lust and sensuality; Ella claims to be uninterested in the pleasures of her body. While Ella's fantasies are connected to her commitment to help others, She's erotic motivation represents the notion of sexual stasis saturated by the kind of contradictions and misgivings that Ella voices. After discussing another fantasy, in which She expresses the desire to become "a great dancer . . . like Fred Astaire and Ginger Rogers!" Ella asks, "Será que eres bisexual?" (p. 59). Desire becomes a paradigm for representing sexuality as an unstable category, in transition, perhaps. As opposed to the presupposed heterosexuality in the other plays, Prida's dramatic tension firmly embraces the bordering implicit in queer desire, the lure of what is and what could be. Unlike Ella, She can easily enter what Gloria Anzaldúa has labeled "el mundo surdo" (the left-handed world), a place—both with and without sexual orientations—for those who don't fit within "straight" parameters.[44] In the concept "el mundo surdo," Anzaldúa foreshadows the duality embedded in *nepantla*. Both sites mix affinities and orientations in order to shed light on the forces acting upon non-static identities. I take up this topic again in the next chapter, where I bring into my argument of non-static sexuality the Latina-lesbian body and queer performativity.

For Anzaldúa, the border-crosser image draws attention to the transitory sense that is part of the complexity of identity and space, and which plays an important role in the formation of community. Like Cherríe Moraga, she calls for changing a universe in which "[t]he rational, the patriarchal, and the heterosexual have held sway and legal tender for too long."[45] Both would fashion a substantial discourse in which the border-crosser would find a place, where "I with my own affinities, and my own people with theirs, can live together and transform the planet."[46] In principle, the border space and those who cross it constitute the formation of this "planet," one full of contradictory encounters but also great expectations. Contradictions are common "disorders" across all humanity; they are paramount for the border-crosser. In Moraga's theater, these issues are at center stage. Her latest dramatic work, *Heroes and Saints and Other Plays*, brings together the results of ten years of producing theater and writing plays. The collection showcases Moraga's priorities as a writer and producer of Latina theater—lesbian desire, AIDS, religion, pesticide poisoning, family, and community.[47] Her protagonists, real or surreal, move in and out of the instability Anzaldúa calls *nepantla*: from the butch in the raw to a head with no body, Moraga's "border-crossers" represent the many possibilities of hybrid cultures.

Border-crossing is not limited to Mexicans. Many Latin Americans traverse border spaces. For Cuban immigrants, it is usually the ocean that is the "dividing line," and the sea-crosser is a transitory subject of her/his own venture. As Anzaldúa emphasizes, being caught in a state of *nepantla* not only represents the continuous process of immigration, but is also synonymous with poverty and the struggle for cultural survival. This state is clear in the conflictive situations in which Sarita, Ella (She), and María are caught as they repeatedly strive to find a cultural whole. For the other women in *Latina*—whose struggles go beyond cultural survival and reflect more their political and economic condition as "illegal" workers—their mark of subsistence is the mark of internal resistance. Sánchez-Scott's protagonists remain wandering in that fundamental duality which constitutes *nepantla* or border spaces. Overall, however, Sánchez-Scott, Prida, and López, in creating protagonists who portray a Latina subjectivity that is dynamic and vibrant, offer positive and realistic models for negotiating identity inside and outside the theater.

Self-Representation: Race, Ethnicity, and Queer Identity

FIVE

Representation and self-representation are compatible with identity politics and queer performativity. In the Anglo American canon, the concept of "queer performativity" has become synonymous with an oppositional discourse which resists essentialist definitions of identity politics and performance. For Sue-Ellen Case, the charge to correct these categories' "essentialist practices" has served as an invitation to contest sexuality and the "virtual" capacity of the body and technology.[1] For Elin Diamond, performativity takes root in the corporeality and the established density of performance, its historicity and cultural politics.[2] By debating Judith Butler's theoretical configurations, the "constraints which impel and sustain performativity,"[3] both Case and Diamond expand the categories that constitute the ritualization of cultural production and the site of non-static "acts" which determine it. Performativity, then, is perceived as the very site of the subversive "spoken" world, where the "sexed" body is understood as not consonant with its existing, presupposed characterization. Clearly, for Butler, Case, and Diamond, performativity is not a definitive or unique act, "for it is always a reiteration of a norm or set of norms, and to the extent that it acquires an act-like status in the present, it conceals or dissimulates the conventions of which it is a repetition."[4] From the non-singularity of "performative" acts to the utter-active discursive practices that produce performativity, the enactment of conflicting structures is (paradoxically) dissimulated and conditioned in the process of reiteration.

In "adopting" the implicated grammars of "queer" and "performativity," I often find myself within complicated discursive spaces. Homogeneity and homophobia have shaped the system of knowledge and the meaning of categories such as race, ethnicity, and sexuality, leaving me in a kind of *nepantla*. I am in the middle, between poststructuralist rationality in the name of "difference" and the margins of Latina sensibility. From Anzaldúa's "el mundo surdo" and Moraga's "queer Aztlán," to the discursive configurations of Anglo American discourses, "queer performativity" subverts the dominant order of pre-established epistemologies of cultural production. For Anzaldúa and Moraga, I believe, the performative or performativity are "absent" articulations; but the site of confluences in which non-static identities and political agency dwell demarcates shared grammars and ideologies. For Latinas, the "queerness" in cultural productions develops in such different areas as texts, performances, and productions by self-identified gays and lesbians. More than a movement, then, the queer constitutes ways of reading and understanding the "unnatural" body untethered from the legislative institutions embedded in heterosexuality and patriarchal cultures. Latina queer activists, artists, and intellectuals have a connection with all social protest that shouts for freedom of expression. Like many diverse (queer) communities in the U.S., they may not have the last word on how life *should* be lived, but they can express how it *shouldn't*. This scenario supports the struggle against racism, sexism, and homophobia in which the agenda of repressive regimes is counteracted by the radical context inhabiting the word "queer" and its functionality.

In this chapter, I use the notion of queer identity, i.e., the conscious recognition of oneself as "different" and the deliberate rejection of a heterosexist world view, to refer specifically to lesbian sexuality.[5] I want to emphasize the way lesbian identity is infused with the sense of queerness, rather than constructing "queer" as a category that replaces lesbian identity. I want to maintain the integrity of the lesbian body and its agency. I want to preserve its historical, cultural, and political meaning. Specifically, I want to center the lesbian body, whose performing identities demarcate the site of queer representation. By claiming the integrity of the lesbian body, I am not necessarily supporting essentialist definitions; instead, I want to distinguish one of the "bodies" implicit in queer politics. I argue for the disruption of the lesbian body as part of a larger project in the assertion of queer identities. In my analysis of the queer-lesbian body, feminist epistemologies are fundamental in critical relation to hegemonic structures of cultural formation. Both queer politics and feminism have become, as many have argued, interdisciplinary areas of investigation.

In analyzing the work of Monica Palacios *(Latin Lezbo Comic: A Performance about Happiness, Challenges and Tacos)* and Alina Troyano/Carmelita Tropicana *(Milk of Amnesia/Leche de Amnesia* and *Carmelita Tropicana: Your Kunst Is Your Waffen)*, I wish to establish a discourse that questions "queer theory." Moreover, I intend my analysis to challenge the implications of other signifiers that mark the power structures of self-representation, performance, and the politics of lesbian identity. We need to think more carefully about exactly where our sexuality comes from: it can arise from body, soul, or mind. It can be a combination of all three; it can be the product of our social conditioning; or it can be the result of cultural taboos. "Like any other identity formation," Lynda Hart reminds us, "lesbian identities are constructed from a history of identifications, not only identifications *as*, but also identifications *with*; and not only *between* the signs heterosexual/homosexual, but also *within* the sign lesbian, which is all too often presumed to be a unified, coherent strategy."[6] Identity politics demands a space for representation across diverse social categories to ensure that the lesbian body within queer studies will include multiple specificities.

As a Chicana lesbian, I am committed to drawing attention to the effects of race and ethnicity, to critically examining the ways in which they compound the issue of identity for Latina lesbians. We are constrained by two different systems of repression: the Anglo American dominant society and our confining Latino culture. Carla Trujillo, the editor of *Chicana Lesbians*, suggests that, as lesbians, "we refuse to *need* a man to form our own identities as women. This constitutes a rebellion many Chicanas/os cannot handle."[7] The layering of oppression implicit in an identity that includes being female, lesbian, and Latina makes coming out a highly charged act, potentially isolating and always a threat to the dominant society. I grew up learning the many contradictions and boundaries that my female sexuality implied within the context of cultural repression and censorship. In spite of the fact that sexuality traditionally has been a taboo subject in Latino culture ("La palabra que no se dice"), it is important to recognize that we are constantly surrounded by sensuality, often portrayed in the popular media and other systems of communication as a violent type of erotics. Lesbian sexuality, however, remains outlawed in Latino culture; it is literally "unspeakable." Consequently, the decision to "say the unsaid," while highly personal, is also by definition highly public and political. It is a challenge to a whole system of patriarchal, heterosexual conformity.

Lesbian Identity: Coming Out as a Political Act

> Writing, like sex, is a scary and exciting process of self-discovery, full of contradictions and mixed feelings, but well worth it. We change ourselves, we change those around us, until nothing is ever the same.[8]

As Adela Alonso suggests in the passage above, identifying one's self is a complex process—scary, contradictory, and, above all, social. Identity is interactive; it requires the presence of an "other" in order to convey meaning and movement. When the personal becomes the subject of representation, it must also promise the presence of other "subjects." Yvonne Yarbro-Bejarano argues that securing this pivotal sense of self will help us to assemble a crucial element in the destabilization and reconfiguring of "regulatory categories" which focus on problems of subjectivity. This mechanism, she suggests, "will help us to produce more complex imagining of ourselves in the world and the place of race in our lived realities as gendered sexual subjects."[9] Yarbro-Bejarano cannot conceive of the sexualized body without its race, "even in the absence of people of color." Although Yarbro-Bejarano's assertion about the sexualized and racialized body requires a degree of essentialism, it is politically effective in the struggle against homophobia and racism. This is a fundamentally important perspective since in dominant discourses, whiteness is frequently an absent paradigm. The identity of whites is usually deficient in the epistemologies of race analysis because, like heterosexism, its blankness presupposes an established order based on existing structures of power. An identity predicated on power, even unconsciously, lacks a sense of consciousness and accountability.

Representation and self-representation are powerful acts of queer performativity because they evoke a sense of being located historically and socially. This positioning provides the basis for a sense of belonging and participating in the creative processes of a particular culture. Latinas and other women of color "act" upon the racialized subordination and discrimination that has been designed to silence them. When the performance artist functions as the representor of "her-self," she is simultaneously placed in a position of power as she articulates her "identities" through a process of self-definition. The technology of self-representation allows the artist to create and sustain a metaphorical resonance of reality, "a metaphor that functions as a trope of truth beyond argument, of identity beyond proof, of what simply is."[10] In this sense, the gendered self is understood within a representational subjectivity in which the "real" person becomes a metaphor. Clearly, this approach involves a total rethinking of the gendered self as an autobiographical subject: the performative subject cannot be constructed separately from her sexuality, race, and ethnicity. I join Yvonne Yarbro-Bejarano in affirming that "Everyone's sex has a race and vice versa."[11] By showcasing the narratives of Monica Palacios and Alina Troyano/ Carmelita Tropicana in this chapter, I hope to further our understanding of the complex process of "self-discovery" and thus contribute to the critically important process of forging community without surrendering or denigrating differences.

Lizbeth Goodman has noted that the technology of self-identification is an emerging practice in feminist performances, where the act of coming out is understood as both political and representational.[12] It is precisely this aspect of performance art—the opportunity it makes available to "women of color" to use their racialized and sexualized bodies as a metaphor to disrupt and challenge the dominant system of representation—that makes this medium so attractive to Latinas and others. Coming/being out is an ongoing process of de-identification, a setting aside of the normative demands of heterosexuality. These rules of dominant society—what Judith Butler calls "the normative phantasm of a compulsory heterosexuality"—are altered in lesbian self-representation.[13] Indeed, lesbian identity formation is a continuous process which involves constructing a practical sense of identification and, at the same time, disputing fragmented grammars of domination implicated within heterosexuality. Lesbian identity rests upon the notion that knowledge is at play within the radical alterations of scholarly research and identity politics.

I agree with Shane Phelan's description of lesbian specificity as "an open field for politics, a politics that knows itself to be such and so empowers its practitioner more democratically than do academic and popular discourses of 'truth.'"[14] Phelan examines lesbian political theory and considers the problems of a feminist theory which has ignored the specificities of race and class as important variables. She criticizes identity politics for theorizing the notion of difference from the inside out, rather than from the outside in. Both personal and political, Phelan's work recognizes the ways in which the theorization of difference has been appropriated by white feminists, with new forms of racism as the inevitable result. She calls for a new approach, one that could provide a solid basis for coalitions and take the place of "a theory that tries to unite by overlooking differences or simply celebrating them in the name of 'diversity.'" Phelan proposes a lesbian specificity that "requires both that we recognize differences and that we share a community; that we value both relationality and individuality. This is an ideal worth striving for."[15] Although this suggestion is very familiar to both Anglo feminists and women of color, the ideological premises of contemporary feminism, especially insofar as they reflect the influence of psychoanalysis, are rooted in a lingering romanticism. Thus, the traditional indifference to racial, class, and cultural differences continues to legitimate the power of the social body in constituting the multiple subjects of feminism. For lesbians, contemporary feminism's continuing failure to address the full reality of the "social body," including the technologies that govern desire and the roles of race and class in a diversified construction of subjectivity, is a serious problem. Attempts to widen the forum continue, however. For example, in Chela Sandoval's discursive notion of "oppositional consciousness," a new community based on the power of contrasts is proposed as the source for political gesticulation.[16] The goal of a community based on the strengths of difference, as in Moraga's and Anzaldúa's dialectics, is generated again in Sandoval's framework.

The need to create a forum that recognizes and rejects the tyranny of heterosexism, that acknowledges and exalts the importance of race and ethnicity in shaping the self, is a pressing *political* as well as social problem. "The absence of names for our feelings is a deprivation of power," Adrienne Rich asserted when talking about coming-out narratives.[17] In declaring the tellers' sexualized bodies, these accounts of coming out represent a process of self-discovery and disclosure, "an acknowledgment of a previously hidden truth."[18] But this "previously hidden truth" is not, and never can be, a benign secret. The tyranny of heterosexual norms, their explicit definition of lesbianism as "abnormal," requires hiding same-sex desire. Likewise, this same tyranny makes coming-out narratives into political acts, since those who tell their stories are deliberately subverting and transgressing the dominant social body's normative standards of truth.

An important first step in understanding lesbian identity and politics, then, is to recognize heterosexuality as problematic. The French feminist Simone de Beauvoir did so in 1949, becoming one of the first feminists to challenge the Freudian definition of same-sex love as a form of arrested development. In his theory of "inverts," Freud described homosexuality as a sexual aberration and proposed ways to "prevent" the perversion implicit in its development.[19] Even in neo-Freudian psychoanalysis, same-sex desire is frequently and fallaciously explained as an illness.

Simone de Beauvoir's work broke new ground by redefining certain mechanisms underlying contemporary discourses on sexuality. For her, lesbianism was an act of resistance to male dominance. In describing the lesbian as one who tries to reconcile her autonomy from patriarchy, she suggested that lesbianism is "an attitude *chosen in a certain situation.*"[20] She believed that one can be responsible for one's sexual orientation. It is this point that has led many contemporary feminists to criticize her for misapprehending lesbian subjectivity. For example, Claudia Card sees Beauvoir's "fantastic failure" to approach the lesbian subject as a "great paradox": "Beauvoir seemed not to see that if 'homosexuality' is a choice, heterosexuality is likewise a choice. To put it in her more specific language, it is an attitude which is not physiologically, psychologically, or economically determined and which can likewise be evaluated according to its authenticity."[21] Card problematizes the notion of "choice," which in Beauvoir's text represents and misrepresents lesbian desire and the implications of heterosexuality.

Although I agree with most of Card's observations, I think that the significance of Simone de Beauvoir's contribution—her early recognition that lesbian identity represents a radical distinction of sexual difference—should not be overshadowed by the limitations of her admittedly essentialist and ahistorical approach. It is important to keep in mind that the arguments *The Second Sex* formulated decades ago remain very influential in contemporary feminist criticism and in queer theory; moreover, Beauvoir's ideas have successfully crossed national boundaries and encompassed multiple discourses.

A second step in understanding lesbian identity and politics is to recognize the ways in which the tyranny of heterosexuality disempowers all women by silencing some. This is a message that threads through Adrienne Rich's work. In her essay "Compulsory Heterosexuality and Lesbian Existence,"[22] Rich calls for women, and particularly heterosexual women, to confront the forces of patriarchy in general and of compulsory heterosexuality in particular. In the foreword to the 1982 version of her essay, Rich explains the purpose of her writing:

> [I did not write] to widen divisions but to encourage heterosexual feminists to examine heterosexuality as a political institution which disempowers women—and to change it. I also hoped that other lesbians would feel the depth and breadth of women identification and women bonding that has

run like a continuous though stifled theme through the heterosexual experience, and that this would become increasingly a politically activating impulse, not simply a validation of personal lives.[23]

Rich's examination of what she calls "unexamined heterocentricity" critiques the effects of the institution of heterosexuality on both lesbians and heterosexuals. Rich's essay is considered a masterpiece in lesbian academic circles, but the greatest power of her ideological formulations lies precisely in their ability to reach other identified feminists who are not necessarily lesbians. Written more than a decade ago, Rich's feminist discourse problematizes heterosexuality as the assumed "natural space" which perpetuates "compulsory" notions of homogeneous sexuality as an innate and unquestioned "given" for most women. These questions are central to most coming-out stories. For Latina lesbians, the performing (or narrative) aspects of coming-out acts balance their sexualized bodies with other important categories, such as race and ethnicity, providing the opportunity to democratically mark the evolution of the gendered subject. This process is especially important in Monica Palacios' *Latin Lezbo Comic: A Performance about Happiness, Challenges and Tacos.*[24]

Monica Palacios: Coming Out as a Latin Lezbo Comic

> MONICA: In the 8th grade I was this jock? [*EMPHASIZES PRESENT POSE, EXAGGERATES TWO MORE POSES AND STOPS*] I loved getting sweaty with a bunch of girls—but I didn't know why! I felt frightened—yet HORNY! (p. 84)

Palacios begins her performance by narrating events from her adolescence and early adulthood. Her stories juxtapose a description of her self-consciousness about "exposing" her sexuality with an ongoing performance of that same sexuality. In one story, she tells how, in the eighth grade, she began to have sexual desires for other young women. Those feelings confused and frightened her, but, at the same time, they oriented her toward examining the first signs of her lesbian identity. In *Latin Lezbo* she broadens this youthful reaction to her own sexual feelings to encompass general reactions to lesbianism:

> I've noticed the word LESBIAN makes some people cringe. And I think this is happening because the word LESBIAN makes people think of some yucky activity that has to do with a TRACTOR! [*MIMES DRIVING A TRACTOR, THEN RAISES RIGHT HAND AND WAVES*] (p. 85)[25]

For many years, still haunted by that image of lesbianism as involving a "yucky sexual" venture, Palacios preferred to call herself "gay" rather than lesbian. "The word lesbian was soooo upsetting to me!" she confesses (p. 93). In re-viewing the different situations which made her accept her lesbian identity, she recalls her experience as a "young college coed":

> YOUNG COLLEGE COED: I mean, like, why do we have to use that word? It's so gross! Why can't there be a different word like — PRECIOUS! If men are GAY, I WANT TO BE PRECIOUS! (p. 85)

Palacios' amusing technique allows her to present crucial interrogations concerning homosexuality and related subject constructions of queer identity: gay versus lesbian. While she represents herself growing up as a "gay" woman, she becomes more aware of her positionality as a feminist as an adult. At that stage, she is finally able to identify herself as a lesbian. That gender-specific construction gives Palacios the opportunity to separate her queer desire from those patriarchal grammars implicit in the historical condition of the term "gay." Palacios' story is one of accepting herself as a lesbian. "The American thing to do," she claims, would be to annul the distinctiveness of that term, dismiss its exclusively female application. Instead, she now embraces — celebrates — the word and all that it connotes. She continues her coming-out story this way:

> MONICA: I'm so glad I've matured. And as I became more involved in the gay and lesbian community, I started using the word more. And one day I said the word a bunch of times [*REPEATS THE WORD LESBIAN 7 TIMES*], and I got over it! Because folks, it's just a word. I was making a big deal out of nothing. It seems to be the American thing to do! (p. 85)

Palacios' conceptualization of her own sexuality is intertwined with her politics as a woman. Her acceptance becomes crucial in her coming-out story: It goes from the early stages of self-identification to a later, broader examination and demystification of the hierarchical order implied in the gender distinction of homosexuality. This acceptance is also a crucial element in Palacios' personal commitment to the gay and lesbian community. An active member of VIVA, a queer-oriented organization which promotes the arts in the Los Angeles area, Palacios has been the project coordinator for Teatro VIVA. As part of this organization, she has been involved with Dyan Garza in the production of

Chicks & Salsa, a yearly event that features only women artists (e.g., poets, musicians, performance artists). Most importantly, Palacios has helped produce AIDS-prevention materials and events designed to educate Latino communities.

Palacios validates her lesbian identity in a story of self-identification that is at the same time a critique of the entire matrix of homogeneous representation. Those (like myself) who knew Palacios before the first production of *Latin Lezbo* were already aware of her sexual orientation. Thus, this performance piece is a coming-out story not as a public announcement of a previously hidden fact, but as a revelation of the *process* of finding her self. *Latin Lezbo* presents self-examination as a metaphor for visibility and empowerment. Palacios is determined to make a statement, and within that statement to "invent" the meaning of her sexual identity. Her narrative, at once revealing and subversive, embodies a critique of homophobia and compulsory heterosexuality. As a comic, she is determined to accomplish this radical agenda with humor. That she is successful is clear in Antonia Villaseñor's comment: "Always generous, and always quick-tongued, Palacios not only breaks ground, but also cracks you up."[26]

Latin Lezbo attacks and subverts the notion of hegemonic sexuality which affected Palacios' own experience as a Chicana performance artist. She points out in her piece: "And everybody I met was either homophobic, racist or sexist—usually, all three. But I had to give the biz a good shot. I was a fighter—sort of" (p. 109). Palacios refuses to accept that heterosexist world that denies her a space in show business. Narrating a crucial event in her career, she describes trying to fit into what she calls "generic comic: straight, white, male" mainstream clubs. Changing the mood from a comic to a serious tone, Palacios recalls, "And every time I'd tell male comics I was from San Francisco, they would respond with a stupid homophobic comment. I wanted to smack them in their abdomens with an oar! Instead, I walked away angry, confused, my tummy ached. So you can imagine how I felt on stage" (p. 109).

Palacios' aggressive approach in *Latin Lezbo* attacks the power dynamics in stand-up comedy, in which males are powerful and women are disempowered by male humor:

> I just hated how comedy was and still is a boy's game. Club owners don't like to book women because, quote, " . . . They talk about women things and their periods." End of quote. Yet guys would get on stage, grab their dicks, talk about shit, talk about farts and the audience was on the floor! I wanted to make them stick their tongues on ice trays! Bitter?! I'm not bitter. I'M A WAITRESS! (p. 101)

FIG. 15. *Monica Palacios poses on the cover page of the performance program for* Latin Lezbo Comic (1990). *Photo at top by Ed Krieger. Photo at bottom by Becky Villaseñor. Courtesy of Monica Palacios.*

After several attempts to make it in the mainstream clubs, Palacios re-evaluated her situation:

> I had a chat with my creative guru—you know, my higher self. And after a pack of M&M's and a wheel of brie, I decided: FUCK THIS SHIT, MAN! I HAVE TO BE WHAT I'M ABOUT!
> Wow! I am so profound!
> I stopped going to these clubs and those stupid auditions! I couldn't put my LATIN LEZBO COMIC self into those Hollywood molds.
> I figured it out, I now only did and got involved with projects that had to do with me: gays and lesbians, Chicanos, Latinos, women, poli-tics—PANTY FASHION SHOWS! (p. 102)

Palacios' comedy is aimed to go beyond enjoyment and humor. Her performance uses comedy as a tool to construct new ways of displaying and making visible the queer self in opposition to the heterosexism, patriarchy, racism, and sexism of our society. Her narrative, with its different, amusing situations, unfolds as an oppositional act, rejecting the dominant order which oppresses not only her, but other women as well. Consider the following example. Presenting herself as a waitress, Palacios critiques the passivity of women and the domineering role of men.

> WAITRESS: Good afternoon. My name is Monica, what can I get for
>   you?
> MAN: Well, the little lady—
> WAITRESS: Sir, the little lady has a mind of her own and she will order
>   for herself.
>   Ma'am, what can I get you?
> WIFE: An ah, ah, ah baked potato!
> WAITRESS: Ok, a baked potato. Much more assertive. Let it out. Let it
>   out!
> WIFE: And a salad!
> WAITRESS: Ok, a salad. You were fantastic! [*TO Man*] Wasn't she
>   great? [*TO Wife*] Don't you feel much better? Now turn to
>   your husband and demand ORAL SEX!
> [*BLACK OUT*] (p. 104)

Palacios' narrative events decenter the social order that she finds bur-densome. Her sardonic stories highlight points of resistance within existing power relations, sexual practices, and gender rules. Using nar-rative within narrative, *Latin Lezbo* deliberately constructs a space for evaluating the oppression of women in the heterosexual order.

Palacios identifies oral sex as a fundamental right for women's sexual pleasure (and liberation). Positing this type of sexual activity—representative of lesbian erotics—as the true source of pleasure repudiates the conventional view of sexual intercourse in terms of (male) penetration. Palacios uses this framework of sexual pleasure in order to question in a more direct context some implications of heterosexual relations. Oral sex, she suggests, is what a woman needs in order to obtain maximum fulfillment. Heterosexual activity is based on an act of penetration which, in itself, creates a hierarchical relationship between a superior, the one who penetrates, and a subordinate, the one being penetrated. From the vantage point of her own queer sexuality, Palacios interrogates these hierarchies of superiority and inferiority: They reflect the dictates of "nature" she directly attacks.

Palacios uses humor to sardonically censure repression and transgress the traditional social order. She challenges audience members to participate in a dialogue, one that asks them either to identify with her or to take responsibility for addressing the oppression, racism, and homophobia of their own lives. As Yarbro-Bejarano has pointed out, "Centering the Chicana lesbian subject also means decentering the traditionally privileged spectator, and Palacios' show raises the same issues of audience reception as Moraga's work for the theater."[27] Indeed, Palacios' lesbian representation "denaturalizes" the conventional and heterosexual spectator. Her didactic spectacle is intended to break through heterosexist misconceptions about lesbians: "Most important for me, the show is out there—hopefully—educating people. I make it really funny, but I hope I'm out there making my point."[28]

Latin Lezbo also addresses the struggle to come out in the private sphere, with family members. Palacios uses different voices as a way of sardonically presenting the queer side of her family story, what she calls the "double dyke familia":

> MONICA: But what a big burn on my family because my other older
>   sister is also a LESBIAN! You know my family thinks—
> FAMILY: Did you guys eat the same thing? How does this
>   happen?
> FILM ANNOUNCER: [*COMMERCIAL VOICE*] Just when the Mexican
>   Catholic family thought they had one lesbian daughter, they
>   actually have two! Experience their confusion in: DOUBLE
>   DYKE FAMILIA!
> Every year the familia had the same holiday wish: "Por favor, let them
> bring men home to dinner. We don't want to march in that gay
> parade!"
> DOUBLE DYKE FAMILIA! (p. 108)

Palacios recalls the first time she brought the woman she loves to a family reunion. She performs the reactions of each member of her family. Her precocious niece calls her "Lezbo"; her older sister muses: "I'm not sure I understand it. Her girlfriend is nice—I GUESS THAT'S WHAT SHE CALLS HER! HER LOVER-PERSON?!" (p. 116).

Palacios' personal narrative humorously affirms her individual self as well as her collective sense of identity, making the audience "crack up." The comic approach balances Palacios' annoyance as she challenges the sources of her oppression. The comedy breaks the tension automatically and helps liberate the intolerant spectator she is directly addressing. *Latin Lezbo*'s comic tone does not deny the seriousness of the issues raised; instead, it helps to prevent fear and intimidation in the audience.

Throughout her performance, Palacios tells and retells her coming-out story in various situations, with the result that lesbian subjectivity is increasingly centered, placed with ever greater determination in both the public (show business) and the private (family) spheres. Palacios' individual journey provides a critical space which systematically exposes the self, demystifying the heterosexual orders that exist in each sphere. Both the public and the private are important to her, as it is the "interweaving" of the two that has shaped her identity. In this sense, the technology of self-representation is a form of identity politics, one based upon a notion of the self which moves toward integrating specifically sexual and ethnic components of identity. As Yvonne Yarbro-Bejarano notes, Palacios not only exposes her coming-out narrative and the homophobia of her "people," she also "Mexicanizes the signifiers of European-American history and popular culture to negotiate complex relations of power and race."[29] Palacios refuses to accept one facet of her identity without the other. The two are equally important in her process of self-definition. Her "racialized" sexuality is a distinctive part of her coming-out story. She puts it this way:

> You see, I figure artists are going to save this planet. So I must continue with my plan. Weaving the lesbian side of me with the Mexican side of me. And writing about it. And talking about it. And pushing for and demanding change! BECAUSE, HEY FOLKS, IT'S TIME! (p. 109)

Her performance of assumed ethnic and sexual identities transgresses patriarchal and heterosexual privileges and indicates that it is not an "accident" that lesbians and Latinas are often marginalized. Defiantly, *Latin Lezbo* couples the politics of identity with those of visibility. In theory, Palacios' performing identity attempts an articulation of that which is excluded from the phallic order, providing an ontological account of coalitional identity politics that is materially needed. Sue-Ellen Case also addresses the issues of "performing lesbian" head-on. Case's insistence on the validity of the conjunction "performing lesbian" challenges the essentialist charge that identity claims position the formation of the subject prior to other social constructions.[30] In confronting the charge that lesbian identity invokes an "ontological claim," Case's arguments address the politics of space "within the regime of the visible." Her stance on performing lesbian is rooted in her "technocriticism" of the embodiment of representation as "a screening device that somehow retains the body, the flesh, the 'live' in tandem with technology, and claims visibility through its unique operations."[31] Case's project is conflictive, but it also enables autonomous representations of the lesbian body which exceed the normative system of sexuality and articulate the staging of presence as a potential political site. Thus, the notion of "performing lesbian," in practice (Palacios) and in theory (Case), is a body that produces an uncanny effect while inscribing it as performance.

Overall, Palacios' strategic system of representation involves narrative within narrative. But in between the stories that expose her early sexual desires and the eventual acceptance of her lesbian identity, she denounces the stifling effects of mainstream homophobia and racism on her as a lesbian and as a woman of color. Palacios casts her divided positionality, and the heterosexism, homophobia, racism, sexism, and internal oppression it evokes, in ironic and humorous terms:

> Look, folks, I didn't come all the way from LA to trash my people. It's just that, I am walking a very fine line.
> And what has troubled me for so many years is that, Latinos and gays and lesbians are very oppressed groups. Why can't we come together, discuss our similar problems, go forth AND KICK ASS! And then—go get a beer. But as I struggle with Latino homophobia, I see so much discrimination and racism get thrust into Latino faces. Especially Mexicans—especially in Southern California.
> ARE WE INVISIBLE?!
> [BLACK OUT]
> [SPEAKS IN THE DARK]
> Ok, alright. [PAUSE] Do I sound angry? Are you sitting there thinking, "O brother. We came here for comedy, but she is just another angry Latina lesbian! STOP TRIPPING AND MAKE US LAUGH, BITCH." (p. 103)

To address the specifics of lesbian sexuality, Palacios assumes the role of instructor. She farcically performs the "mechanics" of lesbian sex as an educational aid for the audience. She knows such didactic lessons are needed, since "society cannot fathom two women having sex because there is no man" (p. 107). Palacios' approach to the grammars of lesbian sexuality spoofs common misconceptions about same-sex desire. Playfully acknowledging that "lesbians reach orgasms through— GIGGLING!" (p. 99), she shows some diagrams of women "giggling." At the same time, she critiques popular media for misrepresenting the corporeality of lesbian erotics:

> [*SHOWS SECOND DIAGRAM OF TWO FUNNY LOOKING BEE-HIVE WOMEN GIGGLING*]
> Bee-Hive Women: Oh, Hilary! Oh, Claire! Oh, Hilary! Oh, Claire!
> [*STAGEHAND STRIKES DIAGRAMS AND EASEL*]
> Monica: And lesbian sex scenes—in videos and films—are so misrepresented. It's not sex. It's more like a folk song! [*SINGS*] How about an orgasm lesbian woman. [*STOPS SINGING*] (pp. 99– 100)

She continues to perform this humorous "erotics" of lesbian sexuality until she approaches the subject of safer sex. Then she declares: "FOLKS, REMEMBER WHEN SAFER SEX FOR LESBIANS WAS JUST KEEPING YOUR FINGERNAILS SHORT!" (p. 100). This articulation is followed by a shift in topic and a return to her personal narrative.

In the last segment of the piece, Palacios doubles back to the grammars of sexuality. Her closing number is composed of a mixture of popular songs in which the word "vagina" is sung in place of certain key words in the original lyrics. She dedicates the song to her parents, "for going all the way." She ends *Latin Lezbo Comic* with the parody below.

> [*SINGS TO THE TUNE OF "LULLABY OF BROADWAY"*]
> C'mon along and listen to
> My Lullaby of Vagina
> The hit parade and belly-hoo
> My Lullaby of Vagina.
> [*SINGS THE NEXT LINES LIKE A TRADITIONAL MEDLEY BUT REPLACES THE KEY WORD WITH VAGINA*]
> . . . I left my vagina in San Francisco . . .
> . . . Vagina Cathedral. . . .
> . . . The days of wine and vagina . . .
> . . . I want to hold your vagina . . .
> . . . I'm a little vagina short and stout. Here is my handle. Here is my spout . . .
> . . . The shadow of your vagina . . .
> . . . La vagina. La vagina. Ya no quiere caminar . . . (p. 110)

The song's playful substitution of "vagina" highlights the grammars of sexuality in a unique way that humorously honors womanhood while also challenging social and cultural taboos and breaking the silence of sexual oppression. The transgressive signifiers in this fabulous interpretation move the desiring subject away from the material condition of these taboos and representation. The subversion in Palacios' musical composition lies in its embodiment of the vagina not only as an object of desire but also as a transgressive site for gender-based structures of power. Furthermore, this transgression captures Palacios' queer sexuality and the pleasure she feels in the process of inscription, self-enactment, and mimetic correspondence. The performance centers the lesbian body, whose desires flow through subversion, while at the same time the inscribed erotics becomes a celebratory inversion: a strategic performance of resistance, pleasure, and comedy. This allegory of the vagina challenges the site of the unspoken, the locus of female sexuality. Palacios' strategy for contesting identity does not stage the fetishization of the female libido but rather contests the body as the ground for queer self-representation and resistance. If the phallus is the ideal value in the context of heterosexual practices and cultural imperatives, then the vagina becomes the spoken body in consonance with lesbian desire and enactment. This desiring subject recalls Moraga's protagonists in *Giving up the Ghost*[32] (see also Chapter 3). The dynamic representation of sexuality in Moraga's play brings together the lesbian body and the heterosexual counterpart as a duo in a conflicting "dance," altered by the tyranny of patriarchy and heterosexism.[33]

Yet a third way of examining Latina lesbian identity is apparent in Alina Troyano's work. She creates a wholly separate self—the outrageous Carmelita Tropicana—to provide the freedom and space she needs to fully explore and accept both her ethnic self and her sexuality.

Carmelita Tropicana: Tête-à-Tête *with Alina Troyano*

> WRITER: Years ago when I wasn't yet American I had a green card.
> [*Darkness*] On my first trip abroad the customs official
> stamped on my papers "stateless." When I became a citizen, I
> had to throw my green card into a bin along with everybody
> else's green cards. I didn't want to. I was born on an island. I
> came here when I was seven. I didn't like it here at first.
> Everything was so different. I had to change. Acquire a taste
> for peanut butter and jelly. It was hard. I liked tuna fish and
> jelly.[34]

FIG. 16. *Postcard announcing the performance of* Milk of Amnesia *at Highways Performance Space (Santa Monica, Calif., October 2–5, 1997), directed by Ela Troyano. Photo by Uzi Parnes.*

Like Palacios' approach, Carmelita Tropicana's strategy for contesting identity stages a reflective humor which destabilizes the order of marked signifiers. *Milk of Amnesia/Leche de Amnesia* is a performance of resistance to a forced assimilation into "American-ness." It brings together Alina Troyano, the Cuban writer/artist, and Carmelita Tropicana, the scandalous queer performance artist. The latter is a wholly invented identity; Tropicana is a cultural icon of discursive oppositions forged through the interstices of two American nationalities, each distinct from the other, culturally and geographically.[35] Carmelita Tropicana and Alina Troyano engage in a *tête-à-tête* where memory, humor, and autobiography become integrated. The narrative base is Tropicana's loss of memory, an amnesia she attributes to the process of acculturation. The voice of the artist/writer (Troyano) at the beginning of *Milk* (quoted above) marks the space of self-representation as the intersection between memory and that system of power that forces the subject to change—to alter even her taste for food.

As a performative, multiethnicized subject, Carmelita is outrageous and scandalous; Alina is her antithesis. Tropicana is confident and never afraid to speak. During her performances, she frequently remarks, "Carmelita Tropicana no tiene pelos en la lengua." This expression is commonly used among Latinos to allude to someone who speaks more than necessary. Indeed, Tropicana converses freely; she has no inhibitions. She turns Troyano's life into a performance masquerade—her tactical interventions call for a redefinition of identity to include a double-bind subject, a discursive hybrid that merges both culture and imagination. In an interview conducted by David Román, Tropicana explained how Alina became bound to Carmelita as the autobiographical voice in *Milk*. Attempting to separate Carmelita from Alina, Román asks who he is interviewing. Tropicana responds:

> TROPICANA: Carmelita. Yes. But now when I put on my glasses, it's Alina. (Laughter) Before it was much easier to separate the two. Now that I started doing *Milk of Amnesia* the boundaries are blurred. This is what identity is all about. We try to separate ourselves and put ourselves in little compartments. We don't even realize we are doing it, it's second nature. We are forced by society to create an identity with very defined boundaries. My new work explores this process and one of the results is that *Milk of Amnesia* is more explicitly autobiographical, more Alina. But Carmelita also deals with these issues.[36]

Tropicana clearly recognizes the boundaries implicit in the process of identity formation, but she just as clearly rejects the hegemonic structures of containment in our society. Tropicana's identity is fluid. It is the result of a creative process, crisscrossed by a multiplicity of intentions and experiences. In *Milk*, Tropicana consciously transforms herself into different characters, some of whom are familiar parts of her artistic repertoire, including Pingalito Betancourt (a bus driver), Arriero (Columbus' horse), and Cochinito mamón (a little pig). The voice of the writer, Alina, as opposed to the voice(s) of Carmelita, is the stage equivalent of the self in writing; one is an extension of the other.

The inscription of identity is a dialectical process involving contradiction and resistance. According to Peggy Phelan, this type of inscription "is a leap into a narrative that employs seeing as a way of knowing."[37] The voice of the writer in *Milk* emphasizes the speaking subject as constituting autobiographical identity and memory because, as suggested by Phelan, "Mimetic representation requires that the writer/speaker employs pronouns, invents characters, records conversations, examines the words and images of others, so the spectator can secure a coherent belief in self-authority, assurance, presence. Memory. Sight. Love. All require a witness, imagined or real."[38] Carmelita Tropicana, with her thick Cuban accent, is an invention of mimetic correspondence, parody, and cultural resistance. She is the witness the spectator needs. She embodies behaviors and emotions through sardonic action, memory of both the unconscious and collective mythic kinds. Carmelita (along with Alina and other protagonists she portrays) performs consciously for the intercultural spectator, the one capable of embracing the politics of her (their) performing identity. Thus interculturalism as it is negotiated in Tropicana's performing identity regulates the claims of diverse orders of being, various sexualities, historicities, etc.

Pingalito Betancourt (Tropicana in drag) welcomes everyone to the show. Pingalito introduces himself to the audience as the driver of the M15 bus route.[39] Having learned of Tropicana's accident (she lost her memory during a chocolate pudding wrestling match), Pingalito decides to visit her in the hospital. He intends to help her recover, as he tells the audience: "You see, people, the doctors have their methodologies for curing amnesia and I have mine" (p. 95). His approach is to tell Carmelita some facts about Cuba as a way of helping her remember. The recitation of these facts constitutes his performance. He assures Carmelita that she is 150 percent Cuban and 150 percent artist. Then he extols the natural beauty of the island, proudly declaring, "Cuba is known as the 'Pearl of the Antilles'" (p. 96) After describing the beautiful country, he glamorizes the women, objectifying their beauty as commodities of pleasure and commercialism:

> But ladies and gentlemen, none can compare with the beauty of the
> human landscape. Esas coristas de Tropicana [those show girls in
> Tropicana]. With the big breasts, thick legs. In Cuba we call girls
> carros and we mean your big American cars. Your Cadillac, no Toyota
> or Honda. Like the dancer, Tongolele. (p. 96)

He explains that Tongolele, a famous Cuban actress and dancer, is the
prototype of the beauty he pictures. Pingalito continues his lesson on
Cuban culture, turning now to the beauty of the language: "You talk
with your hands, you talk with your mouth" (p. 96). Within this context,
he makes some remarks about race, tracing his own heritage to Africa.

Lillian Manzor discusses the role of Pingalito, analyzing the cultural
implications of his entrance on stage, walking to the rhythm and singing the lyrics of a *mambo* by Dámaso Pérez Prado. According to Manzor,
the music signals the African tradition embedded in the Cuban cultural
experience.[40] Music is intimately tied to the intercultural project embedded across the multiple significations that the performing body
suggests. Pingalito finishes his performance by reciting a poem, "Ode to
the Cuban Man," which he dedicates to Carmelita. The poem lam-
poons the Cuban male prototype:

> The Cuban man has a head for business
> He combines the Jewish bubbula with the Afro babalu
> That's why they call him the Caribbean Jew
> Above all the Cuban man is sensitive, sentimental
> With sex appeal for days
> And this is where our problem comes
> Our hubris, our Achilles tendon
> It is our passionate and romantic side
> We love women too much
> Too many women, too many kids. (p. 97)

As Pingalito, Tropicana goes beyond stereotypes. Pingalito represents
the *macho* prototype of Latino culture, but his captivating and charm-
ing characteristics force the spectator, male or female, to like him. He
seems inoffensive and harmless. His presence on stage reinforces the
performative multiethnicized subject. He is confident that everything
he says, every description he recounts, will help Carmelita to recover
her memory. Nevertheless, his approach fails to help her; Carmelita
must go to Cuba to find her cure.

Speaking of the cultural amnesia that began precisely at the moment
Tropicana became an American citizen, Manzor has suggested that
"Carmelita's body is the locus of a dissociated self, of a self in process of
creation amidst cultural alienation, of a self whose cultural and discur-

sive creation lead to self-alienation."[41] In *Milk*, the corporeality of memory is central. Narratives of the self and identity unfold in the stories within stories about who Carmelita Tropicana is in relation to Alina Troyano, where she was born and who she has become. Tropicana proclaims, "Carmelita has chutzpah. Alina, on the other hand, has a lot of fears."[42]

The technologies of self-representation in *Milk* raise important questions: who speaks for and as the autobiographical subject? How does identity surpass its enactment? Tropicana herself has suggested that the central issues in her piece focus attention on the corporeality of this loss of memory and its recovery:

> I am playing with different issues in *Milk of Amnesia*. It's about a parallel journey, Carmelita and Alina both go back to Cuba. One is more theatrical and more humorous; Carmelita lost her memory when she hurt her head while chocolate pudding wrestling. That's why she has to go back. Alina goes back to Cuba to cure her cultural amnesia. Basically both of them are telling a story from two different points of view.[43]

At stake in *Milk of Amnesia* is the relationship between the real signifier of identity, Alina Troyano, and the performative simulation of real experience, Carmelita Tropicana, the performance artist. Tropicana has the courage necessary to confront her lost memory; Alina does not. Tropicana is Alina's invention: she is a metaphor, providing proof of the underlying split of the self into two tropes. As one speaks, the other fears; however, the existence of both makes possible both separation and memory, essential for the fictional union of identity.

In the performance, the prerecorded voice of the artist/writer offers a range of figures that compose the space of acculturation in which the "American way" becomes the product of Tropicana's amnesia. As a potential marker, milk is instrumental in the narrative when the act of remembering is emphasized as a point of resistance in self-representation. The voice of the artist/writer, the autobiographical body, is crucially present in the "I":

> In the morning I went to school. Our Lady Queen of Martyrs. That's when it happened.
> In the lunchroom. I never drank my milk. I always threw it out.
> Except this time when I went to throw it out, the container fell and milk spilled on the floor. The nun came over. Looked at me and the milk. Her beady eyes screamed: You didn't drink your milk, Grade A pasteurized, homogenized, you Cuban refugee.
> After that day I changed. I knew from my science class that all senses acted together. If I took off my glasses, I couldn't hear as well. Same

> thing happened with my tastebuds. If I closed my eyes and held my
> breath I could suppress a lot of flavor I didn't like. This is how I
> learned to drink milk. It was my resolve to embrace America as I
> chewed on my peanut butter and jelly sandwich and gulped down my
> milk. This new milk that had replaced the sweet condensed milk of
> Cuba. My amnesia had begun. (p. 95)

The voice of the artist/writer, introducing the cause of the memory loss,
positions the speaking subject by generating the space which stimulated
the amnesia. The subject's wounding loss of her homeland, Cuba,
triggers a cultural amnesia. The only way to find out what others mean
when they tell her that she is Cuban is for her to return to the island.

The far-reaching effects of the artist/writer's deliberate efforts to
assimilate underscore the importance of everyday lived experience in
shaping identity. The removal of mundane reference points creates in
her not only a sense of loss, but also a feeling of displacement. José
Esteban Muñoz sees this displacement as the source of the "exilic" state
in Tropicana's loss of memory. He points out that when the "exilic
subject" occupies a space which is not "home," the production of
meaning "unravels a life world of singular cohabitation and dual tem-
porality."[44] Tropicana's sense of displacement and exile marks a self-
divided space. The subjectivity that is the product of that two-nation
state cannot be consolidated without contradictions. As Norma Alarcón
has argued, what ultimately unifies the subject is the recognition of her
differences vis-à-vis the dominant culture: "The contradictions between
subject positions move the subject to recognize, reorganize, reconstruct, and exploit difference through political resistance and cultural
productions, and to see herself 'in process.'"[45]

In *Milk*, the artist/writer's discursive fashion reveals significant frag-
ments of the past. She recreates memories of experiences that undercut
her Cuban identity, thus reinforcing the space of cultural amnesia that
is being explained in the performance. For example, she recalls that in
high school, when she was asked to write an essay on the American
character, she wanted to write about Cuban tropical fruits, such as
mangoes. Standing in front of a mirror, she decides not to write about
mangoes. She is afraid, worried that others will think she is crazy. The
voice of reason intervenes, "A shadow appeared and whispered: Mango
stains never come off" (p. 98). This and other accounts emphasize the
protagonist's sense of displacement. Questions about belonging—finding characteristics you share with others or recognizing what differenti-
ates you from them—are part of the process of creating a sense of
location. For the artist/writer, the need to belong somewhere poses

major political questions about individualism and collectivity. As a member of diverse communities, she must balance the demands of each. She also recognizes that these multiple affiliations shape her own sense of becoming:

> As if by accident, the pieces were falling into place when I entered the WOW theatre and a comedy workshop was to take place. The teacher would not give it unless four people took it. There were three signed up for it, and with me the body count would be four. I said no. No. No. But the teacher she was cute. So I took it. But it wasn't me. I couldn't stand in front of an audience, wear sequined gowns, tell jokes. But she could. She who penciled in her beauty mark, she who was baptized in the fountain of Havana's legendary nightclub, the Tropicana, she could. She was a fruit and wasn't afraid to admit it. She was the past I'd left behind. She was Cuba. Mi Cuba querida, El Son Montuno . . . (p. 99)

Here is the story of the "birth" of Carmelita Tropicana. The grammar of the speaking subject, I, splits into "myself" and "herself." Through the creation of Tropicana, Troyano, the reasonable and inhibited writer, is at last able to find Cuba, "the past she had left behind." On one hand, this split is crucial because it gives the artist/writer the sense of belonging that she craves. On the other hand, since the space Tropicana constructs assumes the underlying pervasiveness of ethnicity, the lost memory functions as a marker of the absent space, Cuba. As the pretext of the text, this conventional rhetoric then becomes consonant with the representation of the ethnic self.

The performance of *Milk* involves slide projections, video, a soundtrack of popular Latino music, and songs performed by Tropicana. The stage set is minimal. It is divided into two compartments; one is the artist/writer's space, and the other is where the microphone stands. All the props used by Tropicana, including the music stand, make-up, hats, etc., are located in the artist/writer's space. At one point, the artist/writer reads into the microphone as slides are being projected. Images include the Plaza, with a Cuban flag flying; the countryside; and the cemetery Tropicana visited when she was looking for her dead relatives. As Tropicana pointed out in the interview with David Román, this is the only time Alina is seen on stage.[46] The rest of the time, the artist/writer interacts only through her voice, which is prerecorded. The slides show Alina's former house, depicting its different sections. Alina, now on stage, narrating live, shows a picture of herself when she enters the house: "I couldn't wait to go inside," she recalls. "Those are the stairs, the stairs I fell from when I was six months old. I bolted upstairs to my bedroom" (p. 106). The discourse implicit in this process of representation validates the autobiography. Most important, this metadiscourse, as the projection of meaning, reinforces the mechanism of self-representation using multiple signifiers. As Tropicana explained to Román, this type of staging "forces the audience to confront the issue of multiple identities and perspectives. I think this mixture of writing, performing, and staging styles works well to bring forth the issues I am addressing throughout *Milk of Amnesia*."[47] The acknowledgment of that staging system in Tropicana's work is crucial in contemporary art. This system of production has become a self-conscious convention with a developing theory of its own. In practice, it has influenced an evolving performativity as an awareness of the political referentiality of various representational alternatives presented by the multiethnicized body.

The artist/writer and her alter ego present different stories related to "their" recuperation of memory. Each version complements the other to form a unified process of self-representation. The artist/writer focuses attention on the substantial corporeal nature of her identity; Tropicana's theatrical interventions, through metaphorical resonance and humorous situations, mark the same functionality. The artist/writer's interactions with her past, at once personal and material, spur the recovery of her memory. In contrast, the return of Tropicana's memory results from her absurd encounter, while eating a pork sandwich, with the pig Cochinito mamón:

> CARMELITA: My vocal cords, my tonsils. The pig and I, we had our operations at the same clinic. The clinic with the blue tiles. I remember. We are all connected, not through AT&T, E-mail, Internet, or the information superhighway, but through memory, history, herstory, horsetory. [*She shadowboxes as she recites the poem*]
> I REMEMBER
> QUE SOY DE ALLÁ
> QUE SOY DE AQUÍ
> UN PIE EN NUEVA YORK (A FOOT IN NEW YORK)
> UN PIE EN LA HABANA (A FOOT IN LA HAVANA)
> AND WHEN I PUT A FOOT IN BERLIN (CUANDO
>   PONGO PATA EN BERLIN)
> I AM CALLED
> A LESBISCHE CUBANERIN
> A WOMAN OF COLOR AQUÍ. . . . (pp. 108–109)

Tropicana remembers happily, acknowledging without hesitation her identity and its multiplicity. Race, sexuality, and ethnicity become dominant markers of the ideological space she consciously performs.

The trip to Cuba helped both Tropicana and the artist/writer to "heal" their amnesia. As cultural markers, food and taste, sights and sounds are crucial components in both the loss of memory and its recuperation. In this sense, the recovery breaks through the constructed and collective nature of memory itself. After Tropicana finishes reciting the poem, she greets the audience, acting as if the show was just beginning:

> Hello people, you know me. I know you. I don't need no American Express card. I am Carmelita Tropicana, famous nightclub enter-tainer, superintendent, performance artist. And I am so happy to be here with you today, because ever since I was a little girl I ask my mami, "When can I do a show called *Milk of Amnesia* at P.S. 122?" And here I am. I am so lucky. Lucky I can dance un danzón, cantar un son, tener tremendo vacilón. Thanks to El Cochinito mamón, sandwich de lechón. I got to exit with a song, sabrosón like a sandwich de lechón. (p. 109)

Carmelita exits dancing and singing a celebratory melody of accom-plishment. She thanks the pig for having helped her to recover. After Tropicana exits, the artist/writer's voice is heard. In a reflective tone, she describes the theater festival she attended during her stay in Cuba. She mentions seeing plays that were very critical of the present situation in Cuba. She sounds disillusioned; her voice expresses her disappoint-ment over the lack of answers to the many problems she encountered. "Instead," she observes sadly, "I have more questions" (p. 109). She wonders whether she is looking at these conflicts from an American point of view. Pondering Cuba's many contradictions, she muses:

> No one is homeless in Cuba, although homes are falling apart. Everyone gets health care, but there is no medicine. There is only one newspaper, but everyone is educated. No conspicuous consumerism. The dollar is legal, but there's the U.S. embargo. The clothes are threadbare, vivid colors now turned pastel. So much food for the soul, none for the belly. (p. 109)

The artist/writer speaks dramatically about Cuba's many problems. She uses the expression "no es fácil" (it's not easy) here and on many other occasions during the performance. As a cultural marker, this remark stresses the dilemma presented by Cuba's contradictions, but most critically, it is a reference to the U.S. embargo. Lillian Manzor, who was also in Cuba in 1993, attending the same theater conference, believes that this expression was used to imply that the U.S. embargo had affected both Cubans in the United States and those on the island.[48]

Closing her final monologue, the artist/writer continues to wrestle

with her positionality as a Cuban American. She feels she must choose
between her Cuban-ness and her American-ness: "Is Cuba my wife and
America my lover or the other way around? Or is Cuba my biological
mami and the U.S. my adopted mom?" (p. 109). When the voice of the
artist/writer ceases, the lights go up and Carmelita, in her "beauty
queen" ensemble, enters the stage. Telling the audience about her
recuperation, she divulges the fact that now she is able to drink two
kinds of milk: "The sweet condensed milk of Cuba and the pasteurized
homo kind from America" (p. 110).

While Tropicana's Cuban accent marks specific grammars of ethnic
representation, her extravagant masquerade and its many transformations construct and deconstruct both Anglo and Latino stereotypes of
femininity and masculinity. Lillian Manzor notes that Tropicana, from
her multicolored costumes and five-inch platform shoes to her linguistic malapropisms, embodies a Carmen Miranda–like excessive materiality. Indeed, the staging transition of Tropicana's trip to Cuba is
marked by a recording of Carmen Miranda singing a cut from the
soundtrack of the film "Weekend in Havana." Characterizing Tropicana's excesses as "indigenized" and recast "self-reflexively," Manzor
concludes, "As a gay self-parody of Carmen Miranda, then, Tropicana's
performances open up the space for a different kind of self-representation, one that constructs female bodies which resist fetishization while
undermining traditional ethnic *and* gender representations."[49] As recurrent subtexts in Tropicana's representational system, these components
of identity are glamorized in a distinctive fashion.

In performing identities in which sexuality and nationality intersect,
Tropicana inscribes these categories as constants of self-representation.
This, in turn, allows us to understand them as critiques of homogeneity.
Tropicana's closing segment underscores her quest for the heteroge-
neous subject with music by Pedro Luis Ferrer. This song casts the
collective sense of belonging into a single act of resistance:

> EVERYBODY FOR THE SAME THING
> BETWEEN THE PAGES OF COLONIALISM
> CAPITALISTS, HOMOSEXUALS, ATHEISTS, SPIRITUAL-
> ISTS
> MORALISTS
> EVERYBODY FOR THE SAME THING
> [*The tape plays several choruses until the end.*] (pp. 110–111)

Tropicana ends *Milk* affirming herself as a performance lesbian
artist, "a lesbische cubanerin" (p. 109) who embodies an extravagant

sense of queerness. As Carmelita Tropicana, the nightclub entertainer, Alina Troyano's identity is queerly reconfigured in a multidimensional fashion. Tropicana comes to have a life of her own, existing according to her own creative impulses, actions, movements, and excessive mimicry of ethnic and sexual embodiment. She is always acting; she models the use of queer reflection as a form of resistance to the demands of the social and sexual roles assigned to Alina. Bombshell Tropicana's exotic and multicolored presence is the product of mimesis: she amusingly destabilizes both a theoretical practice and a specific female body image constructed by Hollywood to reflect the "exoticism" of Latinas. Tropicana's sardonic power of presence at the site of the inscription of the queer is also the site of resistance which marks the possibility of self-representation in alternative ways.

Palacios, too, uses ethnicity and sexuality to critique homogeneity. In her inscription of the queer, the grammars of the erotic subvert the very terms of desire. With her parodic interpretation of the vagina, Palacios enters the territory of sexual pleasure most appropriate for and typically derived from men's perspectives in cultural production. Her erotic language thus achieves two goals. It subverts the dominant discourse associated with heterosexual models; and most importantly, it accomplishes this subversion from the perspective of male-oriented terms.

Queering the Performative: Using Camp as a Weapon

> *Employing the subversive power of the unnatural to unseat the Platonic world view, the queer, unlike the rather polite categories of gay and lesbian, revels in the discourse of the loathsome, the outcast, the idiomatically-proscribed position of same-sex desire.*[50]

The goal of the queer "activist," whether theorist or artist, is to provide an oppositional structure that attacks the grammars of compulsory homogenization. In the film *Carmelita Tropicana: Your Kunst Is Your Waffen* (1993),[51] directed by Tropicana's sister, Ela Troyano, Tropicana unseats what Sue-Ellen Case calls "the Platonic world view." Tropicana's parodic system of representation takes aim at the homogenization inherent in the Platonic world, rejecting this enforced conformity which leaves her no space to be queer, female, and Latina. The movie develops technically through a series of stories that the protagonists tell in a theatrical mode. Most of the action takes place inside a prison, representing both symbolically and physically the confined space the protagonists confront as women, queers, and Latinas.

In the movie's initial story line, Tropicana and Orchidia (Livia Daza Paris), both members of GIA (an anti-racist, anti-sexist queer organization) are arrested when they battle an oppositional group of right-wingers during a demonstration in front of an abortion clinic. As the demonstrators are being rounded up by the police, Tropicana's sister, Sophia (Sophia Ramos), who is trying to succeed in the corporate business world, suddenly finds herself at the scene. She too is taken to prison. Once in jail, the women find Dee (Anne Lobst), an Anglo by ancestry but Puerto Rican by soul. Dee, who is HIV positive, tells them the story of how she was adopted by a Puerto Rican women's gang and how she became a "sandunguera." As the women become acquainted, they promptly identify Dee as one of them, as another Latina in the group.

The film's plot moves ahead through stories the women tell each other. Tropicana recounts to Sophia and the rest of the group the life history of Cukita, their great-aunt. Cukita's tragic tale is depicted without dialogue, unfolding metatheatrically in a black-and-white flashback. The use of subtitles and a dramatic musical score in this segment of the movie sharply increases the tension. Cukita's life has all the makings of a *telenovela* (a Latino soap opera); hers is a story of melodrama, tragedy, and love set in prerevolutionary Cuba. She is the widow of a man who committed suicide after he killed the woman he loved. Cukita suffers a similar death. She is murdered by a young man who seduces her and then kills her (after dancing a tango) when he realizes that she cannot reciprocate his love completely because of class differences.

The brutality of these events is mitigated by the way Tropicana chooses to tell the story. Her version is full of parody and burlesque romanticism. The women prisoners play the female roles in the great-aunt's life story, but it is Carmelita Tropicana in drag who impersonates the young man who kills Cukita. Overall, the humor and irony that infuse the narrative suggest a camp performativity reflecting the particular kinds of parodic exaggeration and excess that are the trademarks of Tropicana's discursive mode. The *ranchera* interpretation breaks the tension among the protagonists and brings them together in a serenade of solidarity and liberation. With Orchidia, Dee, and Sophia dressed in matching army camouflage, and Carmelita Tropicana wearing one of her distinctive dresses and a pair of tacky shoes, the women perform Tropicana's original interpretation of the song "Prisioneras del amor" in their cell.

As the following verses show, the song's lyrics capture the breadth and depth of constraints on all women's lives while simultaneously parodying the protagonists' actual imprisonment.

> Luchando siempre unidas
> abriéndonos las puertas
> para no ser más
> prisioneras del amor
> prisioneras de la vida
> prisioneras de una historia
> que nos borra y que nos quita
> el valor de ser mujer
> Rompiéndonos los hábitos
> de monjas enclaustradas
> haciendo que la liberación
> sea nuestra religión

> [Always struggling united
> opening doors to each other
> to stop being
> prisoners of love
> prisoners of life
> prisoners of a history
> that erases us and takes away from us
> the value of being a woman
> Ripping off our habits
> of cloistered nuns
> making from liberation
> our religion]

The stricken intonation of the women's voices as they sing is eerily reminiscent of the style of the Mexican singer Chavela Vargas.[52] The cast sings with a passionate sarcasm—expressing musically the tyranny and oppression they face as women. They are prisoners of history and of love, marooned in a life that wipes out the treasure of being a woman. In the song, and in the prison cell, they all become the same. The two queer activists, the businesswoman, and the Anglo–Puerto Rican woman all are striving for transformation.

I agree with José Esteban Muños that the ideological discourse implicit in the performance of the song represents more than just campy humor.[53] The song is an act of resistance marking the oppositional space of its own representation. It is a challenge to the established order of domination, a rejection of patriarchal power over women and a condemnation of cultural alienation vis-à-vis Latina identity. Muñoz maintains that the call for emancipation in the song must be taken as a "political call for liberation from a dominant culture that reduces such identities to hollowed-out stereotypes."[54] Muñoz's specific concern is with the notion of "camp" in the film. He sees a difference between Troyano's use of camp and that notion conceived merely as a white middle- and upper-class gay male sensibility. For Muñoz, Troyano's approach represents a counter-system employed to attack stereotypical notions of identity:

> *Carmelita Tropicana* is a film that refigures camp and rescues it from a position as fetishized white queer sensibility. Camp is a form of artificial respiration; it breathes new life into old situations. Camp is, then, more than a world view; it [is] a strategic response to the breakdown of representation that occur[s] when a queer, ethnically marked, or other subject encounters her inability to fit within the majoritarian representational regime. (pp. 139–140)

Troyano's version of camp takes seriously the effect of ethnicity. That perception of camp which, in queer studies, has been characterized as a gay-male-identified modality, is quite different in *Carmelita Tropicana*. Tropicana's camp plays on powerful signifiers specifically encoded by the two levels of her identity—broadly as a Latina, and narrowly as a Cuban.

Tropicana's camp sensibility stages a heterogeneous aesthetic similar to the stylistic conventions of "rascuachismo." The rascuache aesthetic evolved over the first four decades of this century in popular performances rooted in the *Carpa* tradition. The spectacles presented in the *Carpas* combine diverse artistic forms such as dance, music, theater, and clowning. To be rascuache, Tomás Ybarra-Frausto suggests, "is to posit a bawdy, spunky consciousness, to seek to subvert and to turn ruling paradigms upside down."[55] As a form of vernacular practice, the notion of rascuachismo encodes a comprehensive worldview: It is "a way of putting yourself together or creating an environment replete with color, texture, and pattern; a rampant decorative sense whose basic axiom might be 'too much is not enough.'"[56] Ybarra-Frausto finds this sensibility rooted in Chicano structures of thinking. As an aesthetic of self-parody and representation, excess and camp performativity, rascuachismo is a keen, insolent attitude that first codifies and then moves beyond the established order. Of course, just as not all queers are activists, not all queers are rascuache, or vice versa.

In Monica Palacios' work, camp performativity is enacted in allegory that directly addresses the notion of same-sex desire. This use of inverted grammars to articulate queer desire, Sue-Ellen Case suggests, represents de-identification with that "natural" specificity of the hetero-sexual world.[57] For Case, the "unnatural-ness" in queer desire rein-scribes sexual difference in a way that dissolves the idealistic conven-tionalism implicit in its discursive oppositional structures of knowledge and truth. In this sense, the subversive force of the "unnatural" repre-sented by the queer unseats the Platonic essence of the world. In comparing the discourses implicit in queer "activism" with those under-lying civil rights activism, Case explains, "Unlike petitions for civil rights, queer revels constitute a kind of activism that attacks the domi-nant notion of the natural. The queer is the taboo-breaker, the mon-strous, the uncanny."[58] Palacios uses this type of "activism" as a perform-ative device to embody the multiple signifiers of her identity. She strives to balance her ethnic self and her lesbian identity, while simultaneous-ly contesting the homogenizing mechanisms of the dominant system of representation and/or of cultural norms.

"Camping up" the multiplicity of identity is crucial to both Palacios and Tropicana. Each uses her representational system to highlight the sardonic powers of transgressive imagination. For Tropicana, fruits rep-resent her Cuban identity; for Palacios, tortillas mark her much ac-claimed Mexican-ness.[59] This parodic redeployment of food within the intersection of sexuality and nationality is an important signifier of queer space for both women. What their work demonstrates, as Case reminds us, is how significantly the development of a theoretical notion of queer has been shaped by the process of self-representation. Case's construction of the queer, like the construction of her social identity, "is historically and materially specific to [her] personal, social, and educa-tional experience."[60] I join Case (and others, such as Judith Butler, Gloria Anzaldúa, and Teresa de Lauretis) in defining queerness as an attitude, a way of reacting against homogeneity and dominant dis-courses. Both Palacios and Tropicana put homogeneity on trial as a way of contesting identity. Both use performance to literally embody cul-tural resistance. While insisting on their own specificities as Latina lesbians, both women perform new inscriptions of subjecthood, coun-teracting dominant discourses.

Each artist, however, approaches and inscribes queer space in her own distinct way. Palacios exposes the erotics of same-sex desire in order to mark a militant sense of difference, in opposition to heterosexism and homophobia. Palacios centers her sexuality in a fashion that performs the grammars of the erotically marginal. Within the queerness embed-ded in *Latin Lezbo*, the adjective "lesbian" makes visible and outspoken what has been for the most part publicly unseen and silent. Tropicana's inscription of queerness resides in her own constructed identity as a performance artist who theatricalizes and embodies a permanent masquerade of ethnic exaggeration and parody. By inventing an identity, she makes it possible to enact her lesbian subjectivity in the realm of the visible.

For Latina lesbians, particularly, the desire to codify lesbian sexuality is quite significant. Queer identity politics and performativity within politics of visibility reside in the commitment to 'perform' our lived experience as Latina lesbians. By definition, this commitment is political as well as artistic. Coming out as a Latina lesbian means publicly laying claim to an identity that is simultaneously ethnic and sexual, subversive and strong.

Final Utter-Acts

Throughout this book, my reading of the Latina body has perceived it as being in constant movement. From the late 1920s to our contemporary period, Latinas' theatrical and performative accomplishments provide living proof of a cultural tradition that has evolved as the product of such diverse factors as land annexation, revolution, migration, and exile. The configuration of "Latina" depends on a recognition of her body (identity) as discursively constructed within different hierarchies of power. Thus, the notion of her presence on and off the stage is figured as fluid—she is necessarily continuously engaged in forging unforeseen, coalitional, and even contradictory identities. In *Latina Performance*, the use of "Latina" as an embracing category enables a discussion of multiple projections which claim a cultural whole.

The term "Latina" is understood as one body—against essentialism—a body in process, transculturally and transhistorically, marked and unmarked by the conscious politicization of collective and individual identity. This process is evident in the first chapter, where the historical trajectory follows the subject in question as a way to reinscribe the cosmology that shapes the process of identity construction and its deconstruction. If there is a historical perspective in *Latina Performance*, it is only tangible in that first chapter; the rest of the book does not follow a historical chronology in the traditional sense. I trace a chronology of the subject formation in the first chapter in order to anticipate the setting in which she *must* move and perform her body. As a "traversing" history of Latinas, this framework helps to locate later articulations which move the subject transhistorically from Mexican

American aesthetics to the Chicano movement, and consecutively to Chicana identity and performance art, Latina survival and subjectivity, and queer representation.

To write a chronological history of Latina theater in the U.S., the subject of performance should be located right after land annexation. In Texas and in California, for example, the origins of the Spanish-language professional theater are to be found in the mid-nineteenth century. But, there is also evidence that plays were being performed as early as 1789 in California. Other historical antecedents that should be incorporated into this yet-to-be-written history of Latina theater would include the impact of Puerto Ricans after U.S. intervention on the Island in the late nineteenth century. A good place to begin to trace the history of women of Latin American descent on the U.S. stage would be archival collections. Major institutions such as the University of California, Berkeley and the University of Texas at Austin have gathered important historical documents in archival collections that are open to serious researchers.

I chose to examine a group of theater practitioners who have been overlooked in theater criticism and performance studies. With the exception of Carmelita Tropicana, who has received a little more attention in both Latina/o and Anglo American contexts, the performing artists and dramatists I have included in my book need to be recognized as a capable "body" of women who have managed to innovatively expand the boundaries imposed by the political economy of institutionalized systems and cultures. Embodied in the discursive notions of hybrid sensibilities, all of the women I have discussed defied the dominant power structures to begin conceptualizing an aesthetics against regulatory practices, homogeneity, heterosexuality, and patriarchal domination.

Latina Performance centers performance artists and dramatists as determining figures of an emerging field that has many possibilities, and therefore is open for further analysis. Typically, both insiders and outsiders, when referring to a Latina theatrical tradition, restrict their discussions to the works of Cherríe Moraga and María Irene Fornes. Because these women's contributions have been well-covered by many critics, both Anglo Americans and Latinas, I chose not to include them in my study. However, their presence can be felt throughout these pages. A mentor for many Latinas in theater, Fornes has earned six Obie Awards and her achievements include more than thirty plays. She has produced and directed numerous stage productions of both her own and others' work. Born in 1930 in Havana, Cuba, Fornes came to the U.S. when she was only fifteen. Chronologically, she follows the generation after La Chata and Josefina Niggli. She was a major influence on Cherríe Moraga.

Cherríe Moraga's impact on Latina theater is by now almost literally legendary. More than a gifted dramatist, she is the transgressor, the taboo breaker in Chicano culture. Her theoretical work is an important foundation for my own cultural criticism. Along with Gloria Anzaldúa, Moraga inscribes the merger and convergence of discursive configurations which bring together the subject of feminism and the lesbian body in Latina cultural criticism and theory. Moraga's and Anzaldúa's critical and creative perspectives have had tremendous influence on Latina/o studies and on various aspects of Anglo American feminist politics. Both Moraga and Anzaldúa have helped me to broaden my position, extending *Latina Performance* beyond theatrical and performative discourses. Within the necessary articulations which have become part of a growing, increasingly self-concious body of radical feminist criticism, their groundbreaking theories intersect in the performance of the female body who seeks to dismantle the shackles of colonialism and neocolonialism. Their beliefs, in concert with the views of many non-Latina feminist scholars, have helped me to situate the grammars of in-between-ness in which both Third World thinkers and First World theorists coalesce in a *tête-à-tête* of political affiliations. The mediation of these two positionalities is crucial for grasping the body of my book: The way this adjudication was traced saturates the utter-active site which borders discursive articulations among theatricality, performance, and performativity. It is precisely this action which "traversing" *must perform*. It moves around these grammars in order to cross over the epistemologies that divide knowledge from the creative domain, and vice versa. Thus, this constant "traversing" also moves into its analysis the specificities of race, nationality, class, and ethnicity, making it clear that lesbian sexuality is a liberating modality in queer representation, that the negotiating of space aims to move the subject from the "margins" of the stage to its center.

Latina Performance focuses on the less-studied Latina theater practitioners. By selecting them and their works, I wanted to draw attention to a significant body that deals with issues I consider relevant to performing the heterogeneous character of group identity. In defining the field of Latina theater and performance, it is essential to address the heterogeneity that makes up the body of the subject in question; it cannot be simply ignored. My approach to theatrical and performative activities is not absolute, but comprises particular gesticulations that locate the Latina body as a site of discursive contestation. How might we best think of her position as a gendered subject? Certainly, the material condition goes beyond metaphysical inquiries. Any invocation of the Latina body cannot sidestep, but must continually foreground, discursive configurations and issues of representation. As representative of a cultural space, the Latina body continually signals a corporeality that surpasses mechanisms of domination within and beyond the Latino community. The Latina body is caught between spaces whose movements constitute the intervention of the powerless Third World inscribed in the vitality of the First World, or vice versa. It is in this interactive "scenario" that the Latina body performs her life. There, in between two worlds (and possibly more), she emerges as neither self-determined nor fully determined, but forever exchanging and subverting oppositional transactions in which tradition is directly transgressed and re-imagined. Like any other body, the Latina body is an incomplete, ongoing process which is constitutive of a specific history, political affiliations, and cultural processes. Thus the Latina's future prevails as a question of finding the right tone or grammars with which to express the "intercultural" space mirrored in her own genealogy.

My analysis ranges from the foundational and transgressive/innovative roles played by Latina performance artists and dramatists, to the discursive configurations that epitomize the intersection of Third World feminist politics and Anglo American discourses. *Latina Performance* has attempted to "negotiate" a confluential referent mediated by the binary correlation of these grammars. The performative sense of Latina subjectivity is embedded in the task of cultural production from the figures by which it is conveyed in the sites of resistance and historical negotiation. The demarcation of identity or the epistemology of the Latina body—How do we know she exists?—is the defining political concern of my book. Indeed, as much as it is necessary to produce that knowledge, to continue the future of this debate and, hence, of performativity, it will be calling into question the cultural formations of individual subjectivity and social negotiations of the collective self. My position has taken into account gender oppression as it interacts with the effects of political and cultural dependency and as it shapes the contestation of identity (de)formation. Thus, this book can be placed as part of a scholarly discussion on feminist performance and critical theory, as well as being a study of a limited number of "bodies" (texts and performances) by U.S. Latinas. My voice, as the "utter-active" mediation of cultural and feminist analysis, also becomes a performance of multiple interactions, imbued with my own lesbian desire, which responds to the demands of a radical oppositional politics.

Notes

1. In Quest of *Latinidad*

1. Chandra Talpade Mohanty, "Under Western Eyes: Feminist Scholarship and Colonial Discourses," *Boundary* 2, no. 12 (1984), p. 336.

2. Diana Taylor, "Opening Remarks," in *Negotiating Performance: Gender, Sexuality, and Theatricality in Latin/o America*, ed. Diana Taylor and Juan Villegas (Durham: Duke University Press, 1994), p. 9.

3. One serious omission in *Negotiating Performance* is co-editor Juan Villegas' failure to acknowledge the importance of race and queer theory in his conclusion to the volume.

4. David Román and Alberto Sandoval, "Caught in the Web: Latinidad, AIDS, and Allegory in *Kiss of the Spider Woman, the Musical*," *American Literature* 67, no. 3 (September 1995), pp. 553–585.

5. José Cuello, "Latinos and Hispanics: A Primer on Terminology," Nov. 19, 1996, in *Midwest Consortium for Latino Research* ("MCLR-L@msu.edu"). Note that these references were posted as a service to MCLR subscribers. José Cuello is an Associate Professor of History and Director of the Center for Chicano-Boricua Studies at Wayne State University in Detroit.

6. Judith Butler, *Excitable Speech: A Politics of the Performative* (New York: Routledge, 1997), p. 74.

7. John O'Sullivan, quoted in Albert K. Weinberg, *Manifest Destiny: A Study of Nationalist Expansionism in American History* (Baltimore: John Hopkins University Press, 1935), p. 145.

8. Rodolfo Acuña, *Occupied America: A History of Chicanos*, 3rd ed. (New York: Harper Collins, 1988), p. 20.

9. Lothrop Stoddard, *The Rising Tide of Color: Against White World-Supremacy* (New York: Scribner's, 1920).

10. Acuña, *Occupied America*, p. 240.

11. Cherríe Moraga, *The Last Generation: Prose and Poetry* (Boston: South End, 1993), p. 156.

12. Ibid., p. 157.

13. Suzanne Pharr, *Homophobia: A Weapon of Sexism* (Little Rock: Women's Project, 1988), pp. 16–17.

14. Cherríe Moraga, *Loving in the War Years: Lo que nunca pasó por sus labios* (Boston: South End, 1983), pp. 139–140.

15. Moraga, *The Last Generation*, p. 148.

16. Ibid., p. 159.

17. Sue-Ellen Case, *The Domain-Matrix: Performing Lesbian at the End of Print Culture* (Bloomington: Indiana University Press, 1996), p. 164.

18. Moraga, *The Last Generation*, p. 150.

19. Ibid., p. 164.

20. Juan Flores, *Divided Borders: Essays on Puerto Rican Identity* (Houston: Arte Público, 1993), p. 14.

21. Ibid., p. 189.

22. Sandra María Esteves, *Yerba Buena* (New York: Greenfield Review, 1980).

23. Puerto Rican feminists and other Latinas look to Julia de Burgos (1914–1953) as an important precursor. Burgos' poetry has been reprinted in political and educational pamphlets distributed both on the mainland and in Puerto Rico. The first shelter for battered women on the Island was named after Burgos. In *Yerba Buena*, Esteves includes a poem dedicated to Burgos. Some of the lines are:

> For you, Julia, it will be too late
> but not for me
> I live!

24. Boricua is a term that expresses the vernacular signification of Puerto Rican identity. Being a "boricua" or "borinqueño" involves those elements which are constitutive of *mestizaje* and hybridity. A boricua identifies mostly with the African and/or indigenous heritage, counteracting the standardization and the estrangement of dominant culture.

25. Sandra María Esteves, *Bluestown Mockingbird Mambo* (Houston: Arte Público, p. 43). One other collection of Esteves' poetry has been published: *Tropical Rain: A Bilingual Downpour* (New York: African Caribbean Poetry Theater, 1984).

26. *Bluestown Mockingbird Mambo*, p. 43.

27. Juan Flores, *Divided Borders*, p. 187.

28. Gloria Anzaldúa, "Chicana Artists: Exploring *Nepantla*, el lugar de la frontera," *NACLA: Report on the Americas* 27, no. 1 (1993), p. 39. This number was a special issue entitled *Latin American Women: The Gendering of Politics and Culture.*

29. Norma Alarcón, "Latina Writers in the United States," in *Spanish American Women Writers: A Bio-Bibliographical Source Book*, ed. Diane E. Martin (Westport: Greenwood, 1990), p. 557.

30. Seymour Hersh, "Censored Matter in Book about CIA Said to Have Related Chile Activities," *New York Times*, September 11, 1974.

31. Writer-director Gregory Nava deals with these issues in his film *El Norte* (1984). In this film, a brother and sister leave troubled Guatemala for the U.S., "the land of many opportunities." They cross borders illegally from Guatemala to

Mexico, then from Mexico to California. With the help of a *coyote*, they reach Los Angeles. Once they have made it to the "promised land," their problems are not over; they simply begin to take a different shape.

32. Coco Fusco, "Norte: Sur—A Performance-Radio Script by Coco Fusco and Guillermo Gómez-Peña," in Fusco's *English Is Broken Here: Notes on Cultural Fusion in the Americas* (New York: New Press, 1995), p. 170.

33. Martha E. Gimenez, "Latinos/Hispanics . . . What Next! Some Reflections on the Politics of Identity in the U.S.," *Heresies* 27 (1993), p. 40.

34. Ibid., p. 42.

35. Gladys M. Jiménez-Muñoz, a Puerto Rican of African descent, notes that the denial of an African heritage is more noticeable among black Latinas/os and people of darker-skinned pigmentation, "where the emphasis is on non-African identifications: either toward the non-existent 'Indian' element among mulattoes and blacks in the Caribbean or toward the 'whiter' element among the mestizo and mulatto populations of Mexico, Central America, and South America." Jiménez-Muñoz, "The Elusive Signs of African-ness: Race and Representation Among Latinas in the United States," *Border/Lines* 29, no. 30 (1993), 11.

36. Failure to acknowledge African roots, Jiménez-Muñoz argues, makes it impossible for U.S. Latinos to fully comprehend their contemporary experience: "like our slave ancestors—particularly the captive women—today in the United States we continue to live in multiple ways the experience of exclusion, deportation, refusal, repudiation, erasure, ignorance, and attack." Ibid., p 15.

37. Diana Taylor, *Negotiating Performance*, p. 8.

38. Ibid.

39. Chandra Talpade Mohanty, Ann Russo, and Lourdes Torres, eds., *Third World Women and the Politics of Feminism* (Bloomington: Indiana University Press, 1991), p. 7.

40. Ibid.

41. Chiqui Vicioso, "An Oral History," in *Breaking Boundaries: Latina Writing and Critical Readings*, ed. Asunción Horno-Delgado, Eliana Ortega, Nina M. Scott, and Nancy Saporta Sternbach (Amherst: University of Massachusetts Press, 1989), p. 231.

42. For example, consult Angela Davis, *Women, Race and Class* (London: Women's Press, 1982). Davis writes that black women suffer a double threat in economic production when racism and sexism merge to assign black women to low-paid jobs. However, she points out that a black woman's consciousness of oppression and her activism contest white feminist theory. Davis has criticized the concept of a culturally homogeneous black woman, addressing the historical subject who, in her own (Davis') discoveries, has resisted white domination.

43. Gloria Anzaldúa and Cherríe Moraga, *This Bridge Called My Back: Writings by Radical Women of Color* (New York: Kitchen Table, 1981), p. xxiv.

44. Norma Alarcón, "The Theoretical Subject(s) of *This Bridge Called My Back* and Anglo-American Feminism," in *Making Face, Making Soul/haciendo caras: Creative and Critical Perspectives by Women of Color*, ed. Gloria Anzaldúa (San Francisco: Aunt Lute, 1990), p. 366.

45. Vicioso, "An Oral History," in Horno-Delgado, Ortega, Scott, and Sternbach, eds., *Breaking Boundaries*, p. 231.

46. Carmen Tafolla, "La Malinche," in *Infinite Divisions: An Anthology of Chicana Literature*, ed. Tey Diana Rebolledo and Eliana S. Rivero (Tucson: University of Arizona Press, 1993), p. 198.

47. *Loving in the War Years*, p. 108.

48. Bertolt Brecht, ed. John Willet, *Brecht on Theatre: The Development of an Aesthetic* (New York: Hill and Wang, 1964), p. 23.

49. Griselda Gambaro, "¿Es posible y deseable una dramaturgia específicamente femenina?" *Latin American Theatre Review* 13, no. 2 (1980), p. 19.

50. I am responsible for this translation and others, unless otherwise noted.

51. Charles Driskell, "An Interview with Augusto Boal," *Latin American Theatre Review* 9, no. 1 (1975), p. 72.

52. Manuel Galich, an excellent critic and playwright, was originally from Guatemala but was forced into exile and spent some time in Argentina. Later he became a citizen of Cuba, where he founded, and directed until his death in 1985, *Conjunto*, a theater journal of the Departamento de Teatro Latinoamericano of Casa de las Américas. This journal plays a major role in propagating theater produced under oppressive conditions and provides a space for discussing the issues these productions raise. Consult Manuel Galich, "Las ideologías en la dramaturgia y la crítica en América Latina," *Conjunto* 38 (1978), p. 6.

53. Diana Taylor, *Theatre of Crisis: Drama and Politics in Latin America* (Lexington: University Press of Kentucky, 1991).

54. Ibid., p. 43.

55. Beatriz Rizk points out that this new theater movement originated in 1955 in the western city of Cali (Colombia), with the creation of the "Escuela Departamental de Teatro," which later became the "Teatro Experimental de Calí" (TEC). Beatriz J. Rizk, "The Colombian New Theater and Bertolt Brecht: A Dialectical Approach," *Theater Research International* 14 (1989), p. 132.

56. Valdez and Teatro Campesino received international attention. In 1973, Peter Brook brought his group from the International Center of Theater Research in London to work with Valdez and his company.

57. Yolanda Broyles-Gonzales, *El Teatro Campesino: Theater in the Chicano Movement* (Austin: University of Texas Press, 1994), p. 163.

58. Ibid., p. 144.

59. Elin Diamond, ed., *Performance and Cultural Politics* (New York: Routledge, 1996), p. 5.

60. Gambaro, "¿Es posible y deseable una dramaturgia específicamente femenina?" p. 21.

2. The Mexican American Stage

1. Tomás Ybarra-Frausto, "La Figura del Donaire," in *Mexican American Theatre: Then and Now*, ed. Nicolás Kanellos (Houston: Arte Público, 1983), p. 43.

2. Tomás Ybarra-Frausto, "I Can Still Hear the Applause. La Farándula Chicana: Carpas y Tandas de Variedad," in *Hispanic Theatre in the United States*, ed. Nicolás Kanellos (Houston: Arte Público, 1984), p. 54.

3. Ibid., p. 47.

4. These are popular verses. They were not taken exactly from any particular

written text. Their oral character corresponds to the nature of the song itself. For more information about some of the collected verses of "La Adelita," consult Baltasar Dromundo, *Francisco Villa y La Adelita* (Durango: Victoria de Durango, 1936) and María Herrera-Sobek, *The Mexican Corrido: A Feminist Analysis* (Bloomington: Indiana University Press, 1990).

5. I am responsible for this and all other translations, unless otherwise noted.

6. Shirlene Soto, *The Emergence of the Modern Mexican Woman: Her Participation in Revolution and Struggle for Equality 1910–1940* (Denver: Arden, 1990), p. 44.

7. The Maderistas were the followers of Francisco I. Madero, the educated son of a wealthy mining family. Madero was an outspoken critic of Porfirio Díaz's autocrat government and is widely credited with having started the Mexican Revolution. The Maderistas defeated Díaz and made Madero president of Mexico in 1912. Unfortunately, Madero's government was chaotic and short-lived. Counter-revolutions broke out in the north, led by Generals Venustiano Carranza, Francisco "Pancho" Villa, and Alvaro Obregon. Villa gained control in the northern state of Chihuahua. He demanded agrarian reform, calling for confiscation of large haciendas in 1913. While Villa created powerful troops—often leading them into battle—his flamboyance earned him a dubious reputation north and south of the border.

In the south, Emiliano Zapata led a peasant movement aimed at securing land and liberty for the poor. The *zapatistas*, as his troops became known, saw the struggle as a chance to control their lands. In the 1990s, the *zapatistas* continue the struggle for social change as the Mexican government isolates and harasses the country's indigenous communities.

8. Dromundo, *Francisco Villa*, p. 40.

9. Soto, *Modern Mexican Women*, p. 44. Verses of "La Valentina" express a representative stoicism similar to that in "La Adelita":

> Valentina, Valentina,
> rendido estoy a tus pies,
> si me han de matar mañana,
> que me maten de una vez.
>
> (Valentina, Valentina,
> I surrender at your feet.
> If they're going to kill me tomorrow,
> let them kill me now.)

10. Nicolás Kanellos, *A History of Hispanic Theatre in the United States: Origins to 1940* (Austin: University of Texas Press, 1990), p. 18.

11. Nicolás Kanellos, "An Overview of Hispanic Theatre in the United States," in Kanellos, ed., *Hispanic Theatre*, p. 9.

12. Ybarra-Frausto, "I Can Still Hear the Applause," in Kanellos, ed., *Hispanic Theatre*, p. 55.

13. An aristocrat, del Rio is alleged to have been presented at the Spanish royal court when she was 14 years old. Ibid., p. 30.

14. Ibid.

15. *La carpa* (1993), screenplay by Carlos Avila and Edit Villareal; produced by Michael Zapata and Carlos Avila. In this film, the story of *los carperos* (*carpa* performers) is juxtaposed to the story of a farm worker who has been killed by an Okie. The performers bring the case to the stage, recreating the event in a comical way but denouncing the injustice of those in power.

16. Antonio Ríos-Bustamante, "Latino Participation in the Hollywood Film Industry, 1911–1945," in *Chicanos and Film: Representation and Resistance*, ed. Chon Noriega (Minneapolis: University of Minnesota Press, 1992), p. 21.

17. Ibid., p. 20.

18. George Hadley-García, *Hispanic Hollywood: The Latins in Motion Pictures* (New York: Citadel), p. 29.

19. Reported in Ríos-Bustamante, op. cit., p. 22.

20. Ybarra-Frausto, "La Figura del Donaire," in Kanellos, ed., *Mexican American Theatre*, pp. 50–51.

21. Ibid., p. 47.

22. Frank Trejo, "Vaudeville Back on the West Side," in *The San Antonio Light* (March 24, 1976), p. 7B.

23. Ybarra-Frausto, "La Figura del Donaire," in Kanellos, ed., *Mexican American Theatre*, pp. 41–51.

24. Ybarra-Frausto describes these events as follows: "[La Chata's] beauty, energy and vivacity charmed one of the Areu Brothers, who fell in love with her, married her and took her away as a part of his troupe." Ibid., p. 44.

25. Ybarra-Frausto notes, "the same daring and outré routines with which the American Negro entertainer had scandalized Paris were presented by Dorita Ceprano in San Antonio in late evening shows, *sólo para adults*" (adults only). Ibid.

26. Kanellos, *A History of Hispanic Theatre*, p. 94. It was during this period that she won a contest sponsored by Kaiser Stockings for the most beautiful legs.

27. María Teresa Marrero, "In the Limelight: The Insertion of Latina Theater Entrepreneurs, Playwrights and Directors into the Historical Record," in a special issue on Chicano theater, eds. Carlos Morton and Lee A. Daniel, *Ollantay: Theater Magazine* 4, no. 1 (1996), p. 80.

28. Kanellos, *A History of Hispanic Theatre*, p. 94.

29. Ibid., p. 95.

30. Ybarra-Frausto, "La Figura del Donaire," in Kanellos, ed., *Mexican American Theatre*, p. 46.

31. When her company was at the Teatro Hispano, La Chata once employed musician Desi Arnaz, paying him seventy-five dollars a week.

32. This last performance, to benefit war veterans, was held at Immaculate Heart of Mary Parish Hall in San Antonio. The event included a special mass and reception. For more on La Chata, see the "La Chata Scrapbooks," at the San Antonio Conservation Society, San Antonio, Texas.

33. For more information see Richard A. García, "The Mexican American Mind: A Product of the 1930s," pp. 67–93.

34. For example, in the novel *Mexican Village* (1945), Niggli portrays life in a Mexican rural community. The novel is structured around ten absorbing stories set in Hidalgo, one of the five villages in the Sabinas Valley of Northern México.

In 1953, Hollywood produced the film *Sombrero*, a romantic musical featuring Ricardo Montalbán, based on this novel. The movie was filmed in Mexico, in the state of Morelos, near Cuernavaca. Norman Foster, the film's top-flight director, lived in Mexico City for several years before returning to Hollywood.

35. *Soldadera* was originally produced by the Carolina Playmakers at Chapel Hill, North Carolina (February 27–29, 1936). A few years later, Josefina Niggli included it as "Soldadera: A Play of the Mexican Revolution" in her *Mexican Folk Plays* (Chapel Hill: University of North Carolina Press, 1938), pp. 53–114. *Soldadera* was also included in Margaret Mayorga's *The Best One-Act Plays of 1937* (New York: Dodd, Mead, 1938). The next year, Niggli's play *This Is Villa* was published in Mayorga's *The Best One-Act Plays of 1938* (New York: Dodd, Mead, 1939). The foreword to Niggli's collection of folk plays was written by the well-known Mexican dramatist Rodolfo Usigli. Other plays in this collection include "Tooth Shave: A Mexican Folk Comedy," "The Red Velvet Goat: A Tragedy of Laughter and A Comedy of Tears," "Azteca: A Tragedy of Pre-Conquest Mexico," and "Sunday Costs Five Pesos: A Comedy of Mexican Village Life."

36. Koch, introduction to *Mexican Folk Plays* by Josefina Niggli (Chapel Hill: University of North Carolina Press, 1938), p. vii. This edition of *Mexican Folk Plays* is the basis of my analysis and it is the source of the material I quote here (appropriate page numbers are included in parentheses following each quote).

37. Ibid., p. x.

38. Paula W. Shirley, "Josefina Niggli," in *Dictionary of Literary Biography Yearbook 1980* (Detroit: Gale Research, 1981), pp. 279–286. For more information on Niggli, see also my entry "Josefina Niggli," *The New Hand Book of Texas*, vol. 4 (Austin: Texas State Historical Association, 1996), pp. 1013–1014.

39. See "Foreword," in Niggli, *Mexican Folk Plays*, p. xix.

40. Shirley, "Josephina Niggli," p. 286.

41. Unless otherwise indicated, the verses of "La Adelita" and others that I include elsewhere in this discussion are taken from Dromundo's *Francisco Villa y La Adelita*. Later in this chapter, the discussion is based on verses of the song that are presented in Josefina Niggli's play, *Soldadera*.

42. This verse was taken from the version in Herrera-Sobek's *Mexican Corrido*, p. 107.

43. This term was used to refer to Francisco "Pancho" Villa's troops; they were also known as the Villistas.

44. Dromundo, *Francisco Villa*, p. 36.

45. Anna Macías, *Against All Odds: The Feminist Movement in Mexico to 1940* (Westport: Greenwood, 1982), p. 3.

46. Octavio Paz, *The Labyrinth of Solitude and Other Writings*, trans. Lysander Kemp, et al. (New York: Grove Weidenfeld, 1985), p. 81.

47. Ibid., p. 81.

48. Ibid. The verb *chingar* literally translates as "to fuck." As a Mexican signifier, however, chingar is used in many different contexts. Octavio Paz uses it as a cultural marker of a colonized people.

49. Emma Pérez, "Sexuality and Discourse: Notes from a Chicana Survivor," in *Chicana Lesbians: The Girls Our Mothers Warned Us About*, ed. Carla Trujillo (Berkeley: Third Woman, 1991), p. 168.

50. The year Niggli went to Chapel Hill, she became an active participant in the Carolina Playmakers, acting, directing, designing costumes, and writing.

51. This song also appeared in a southern, Zapatista version, ridiculing Carranza, his glasses, and his beard. During the Mexican Revolution, four songs—"La Adelita," "La Valentina," "La Cucaracha," and "El Pato"—gained a popularity that continues today.

52. Niggli returned to the subject of Pancho Villa in a later play, *This Is Villa*. There she depicts him as a man of many contradictions: cruel, violent, and indecent; sensitive, generous, and brilliant. While in *Soldadera* she presents the heroism of women-soldiers, in her later play, she explores various types of people involved in the Revolution: the intellectual, the killer, and the faithful soldier. When Villa kills the faithful soldier's fiancée on their wedding day, the would-be groom chooses to kill himself rather than avenge the death of his beloved.

53. Niggli includes a note after these verses to point out that the song "La Adelita" "holds the same place that Annie Laurie did to English soldiers during the World War."

54. Jane Flax, "Postmodernism and Gender Relations in Feminist Theory," in *Feminism/Postmodernism*, ed. Linda J. Nicholson (New York: Routledge, 1990), p. 45.

55. It is important to point out that the Revolution increased contacts between the indigenous population and other Mexicans, as indigenous people left their own communities to fight and *mestizos* came into their areas.

56. Carmen Salazar Parr and Genevieve M. Ramírez, "The Female Hero in Chicano Literature," in *Beyond Stereotypes: The Critical Analysis of Chicana Literature* (Binghamton: Bilingual Press/Editorial Bilingüe, 1985), p. 50.

57. Walter Spearman, *The Carolina Playmakers: The First Fifty Years* (Chapel Hill: University of North Carolina Press, 1970), p. 16.

58. Herrera-Sobek, *Mexican Corrido*, p. 108.

59. Consult Gustavo Casasola, *Biografía ilustrada del General Francisco Villa 1878–1966* (Mexico: Editorial Gustavo Casasola, 1969), p. 67. The same page also includes other pictures of women soldiers. In one, the woman is playing a cornet; in the other, a female soldier is standing next to her man. Although this is the only page in the book that portrays female soldiers, Casasola includes other pictures of female soldiers in his *Historia gráfica de la Revolución: 1900–1960*, 4 vols. (Mexico: Editorial F. Trillas, 1960).

60. See Soto, *Modern Mexican Women*, pp. 43–45. *Soldaderas* were also known as *galletas* (cookies) during the Revolution.

61. Soto has pointed out that Zapata's movement attracted women from all social classes and from all parts of Mexico. She notes, "Paulina Maraver Cortés, a professor and former Maderista, with Nachita Vázques, initiated the agrarian movement in the state of Puebla." (*Modern Mexican Women*, pp. 44, 46)

62. Macías, *Against All Odds*, p. 49. Macías' book examines the history of the feminist movement in Mexico from 1890 to 1940 and assesses the contributions of three significant women: journalist Juana Belén Gutiérrez de Mendoza (1875–1942); school teacher Dolores Jiménez y Muro (1848–1925); and the private secretary of President Carranza, Hermila Galindo de Topete (1896–1954). Macías' work is one of the best feminist contributions in Mexico.

63. A second aristocratic rebel was Elisa Acuña, who financed the publication of her work *La Guillotina* (The Guillotine) with her own money During the Revolution, she was forced to leave Mexico, but she later returned and joined the Zapatistas.

64. Clara Lomas, ed., *The Rebel: Leonor Villegas de Magnon* (Houston: Arte Público, 1994), p. xi. This book is introduced and annotated by Lomas, who discovered this work and others by the same author.

65. Ibid., p. xvii.

66. Herrera-Sobek, *Mexican Corrido*, p. 104.

67. Ibid.

68. Ibid., p. 106.

69. The Padua Hills Theatre, located three miles north of the Claremont Colleges in Claremont, California, was built in 1930, on land that once had been part of the great Rancho San José, as a community center and home of the Claremont Community Players. The Claremont Community Players made Padua Hills one of the outstanding examples of the little theater movement in the United States, but the impact of the Great Depression forced them to abandon the Padua. Ironically, the same dire economic conditions that forced this group to leave gave the Mexican Players the opportunity to become the major entertainment component of the institute. Consult Norma Blakeslee Hopland, "History of Padua Hills Theatre," *Pomona Valley Historian* 9 (Spring 1973), pp. 46–66; and my article, "Contemporizing Performance: Mexican California and the Padua Hills Theatre," *Mester* 2 (Spring 1994), pp. 5–30.

70. Padua Hills Theatre Collection at Pomona Public Library. Charles A. Dickinson was a director of the theatre for many years until his death in 1950. His association with the Padua began when he was a graduate student in Claremont. He wrote most of the plays that were performed by the Mexican Players during the 1930s.

71. This narrative is documented in one of the scrapbooks located in the Padua Hills Theatre Collection at Pomona Public Library. Most of the plays produced by the Padua Hills Theatre remain unpublished.

72. Prints of this type were created for sale on the Day of the Dead (November 2). Consult Roberto Berdecio and Stanley Appelbaum, eds., *Posada's Popular Mexican Prints: 273 Cuts by José Guadalupe Posada* (New York: Dover, 1972).

73. Other figures represented in Posada's work were Emiliano Zapata, Francisco I. Madero, and dictator Porfirio Díaz.

74. This period incorporates different cultural, social, and political trends throughout the Southwest. However, in the 1930s, Mexican American thought emerged as a symbol of the rising middle class who wanted assimilation. The League of United Latin American Citizens (LULAC), founded in Texas but with chapters throughout the Southwest, promoted this ideology. This organization emphasized the virtues of Mexican culture and advocated for constitutional rights for all Mexicans living in the U.S. The Mexican American middle class demanded equal access to education and other institutions and an end to discrimination against Mexicans. For more information about the Mexican American experience, consult Acuña, *Occupied America*, pp. 198–250, and Richard A. García, "The Mexican American Mind: A Product of the 1930s," in *History, Culture and*

Society: Chicano Studies in the 1980s (Ypsilanti: Bilingual Press/Editorial Bilingüe, 1983), pp. 67–93.

75. Teresa de Lauretis, *The Technologies of Gender: Essays on Theory, Film, and Fiction* (Bloomington: Indiana University Press, 1987), p. 26.

3. Chicana Identity and Performance Art

1. Diana Taylor, "Opening Remarks," in Taylor and Villegas, eds., *Negotiating Performance*, p. 14.

2. Gloria Anzaldúa, "Opening Remarks," in Anzaldúa, ed., *Making Face, Making Soul/haciendo caras*, p. xxii.

3. See Chapter 5 for a discussion of the technology of self-representation. That chapter expands the theoretical notion of performance presented here and, in analyzing the work of Monica Palacios and Carmelita Tropicana, raises questions about "queer theory."

4. Jeanie Forte, "Women's Performance Art: Feminism and Postmodernism," in *Performing Feminisms: Feminist Critical Theory and Theatre*, ed. Sue-Ellen Case (Baltimore: Johns Hopkins University Press, 1990), p. 251.

5. Other significant contributors to Chicana/o theater include Josefina López, Denise Chávez, and Edit Villarreal. See Chapter 4 for further discussion.

6. Cherríe Moraga, *Giving up the Ghost: Teatro in Two Acts* (Los Angeles: West End, 1986).

7. In an interview, Estela Portillo-Trambley confessed that she created the lesbian character doña Josefa for economic reasons: "The plot is about lesbians; I knew nothing about them, but I was going to sell it. Well, it got published, it appeared in four anthologies, I get invited to talk about it, it gets analyzed to death, and it's a play I wrote in a very short time and for a terrible reason. I was just being mercenary." Quoted in Juan Bruce-Novoa, *Chicano Authors: Inquiry by Interview* (Austin: University of Texas Press, 1980), p. 170.

8. Yvonne Yarbro-Bejarano, "The Female Subject in Chicano Theater: Sexuality, 'Race,' and Class," in Case, ed., *Performing Feminisms*, p. 145.

9. Sue-Ellen Case alludes directly to this transition in her piece, "Seduced and Abandoned: Chicanas and Lesbians in Representation," in Taylor and Villegas, eds., *Negotiating Performance*, pp. 88–101.

10. Yarbro-Bejarano's essay (see note 8) traces this evolution as she reviews the history of Chicano theater. She studies the early texts, noting their cultural nationalism, and then traces the shift in interests that led to the exploration of alternative spaces in the 1980s.

11. Luis Valdez, *Early Works: Actos* (Houston: Arte Público, 1990), p. 7.

12. Broyles-González, *El Teatro Campesino*, p. 163.

13. *El Grito: A Journal of Contemporary Mexican-American Thought*, founded in 1967 by Octavio Romano, a professor at the University of California at Berkeley, was a key publication during the Chicano movement. This journal included scholarly work oriented toward challenging Anglo American scholarship and criticizing its effect on Chicanos. It also included creative works, such as poetry and art.

14. For more information on the Chicano movement, consult Acuña, *Occupied America*, pp. 307–354.

15. *Raza* studies is a renowned program at San Francisco State University.

16. Juanita Domínguez, "Yo soy Chicano," in *The Chicano Manifesto*, ed. Armando Rendón (New York: Collier, 1971), p. 182. Also quoted by Angie Chabram-Dernersesian, "And Yes . . . The Earth Did Part: On the Splitting of Chicana/o Subjectivity," in *Building with Our Hands: New Directions in Chicana Studies*, ed. Adela de la Torre and Beatríz M. Pesquera (Berkeley: University of California Press, 1993), pp. 34–35.

17. Valdez went on to become an independent playwright and film director after the Chicano movement. He and El Teatro Campesino became more involved in television and movie productions, as well as in producing plays he authored himself. He produced *Zoot Suit* (1978), *Corridos* (1982), and *I Don't Have to Show You No Stinking Badges* (1986). *Zoot Suit* was a tremendous success in Los Angeles; the musical did not hold the same appeal in New York City, however. Right after its opening at the Winter Garden Theatre on Broadway (March 1979), *Zoot Suit* closed. Despite this failure, Valdez went on to success as a movie director and screenwriter with *La Bamba* (1987). In the late 1980s and early 1990s, Valdez edited his most successful plays (e.g., *Zoot Suit*, *Corridos*, and *I Don't Have to Show You No Stinking Badges*) for publication; he also included some of his older, previously published plays, such as *Bernabé* (1976) and *The Shrunken Head of Pancho Villa* (1974). For more biographical detail on Valdez, see Nicolás Kancllos, "Luis Miguel Valdez," in *Dictionary of Literary Biography: Chicano Writers*, Vol. 122 (Detroit: Bruccoli Clark Layman, 1992), pp. 281–292.

18. Chabram-Dernersesian, "And Yes . . . The Earth Did Part," p. 37.

19. Yvonne Yarbro-Bejarano, "The Female Subject in Chicano Theater: Sexuality, 'Race' and Class," in Case, ed., *Performing Feminisms*, p. 132.

20. Yarbro-Bejarano, like Broyles-González, has made excellent contributions to feminist criticism regarding the Chicana subject in representation and her role in the history of Chicano theater. While both critics are concerned with questions of subordination in gender relations, Yarbro-Bejarano's approach to Chicano culture more directly emphasizes questions of sexuality and the influence of heterosexual hierarchy in male/female relationships.

21. Case, *Performing Feminisms*, p. 11.

22. Broyles-González, *El Teatro Campesino*, p. xiii.

23. These were collective performances which enacted the sociocultural and political experience of the Chicano community.

24. Broyles-González, *El Teatro Campesino*, p. 135.

25. Catharine Mackinnon, "Feminism, Marxism, Method, and the State: An Agenda for Theory," in *Modern Feminisms: Political, Literary, Cultural*, ed. Maggie Humm (New York: Columbia University Press, 1992), p. 117.

26. Norma Alarcón, "Chicanas' Feminist Literature: A Re-vision through Malintzín, Or, Malintzín: Putting Flesh Back on the Object," in Anzaldúa and Moraga, eds., *This Bridge Called My Back*, p. 186.

27. The Aztecs' nickname for Cortés—they called him *El Malinche*—is significant because it not only makes central the power of Malinche, but also deconstructs the male-female relational patterns according to a patriarchal model. Moreover, the meaning inherent in the sign of La Malinche/El Malinche signals the development of real structural changes in pre-Hispanic and postcolonial social relationships.

28. Cherríe Moraga, *Loving in the War Years: Lo que nunca pasó por sus labios* (Boston: South End, 1983), p. 99.

29. Tey Diana Rebolledo and Eliana S. Rivero, "Myths and Archetypes," in Rebolledo and Rivero, eds., *Infinite Divisions*, p. 193.

30. Ibid.

31. Gloria Anzaldúa, *Borderlands/La Frontera: The New Mestiza* (San Francisco: Spinsters/Aunt Lute, 1987), p. 80.

32. Chabram-Dernersesian, "And, Yes. . . .The Earth Did Part," p. 39.

33. In the introduction to *Latinas on Stage: Practice and Theory*, ed. Alicia Arrizón and Lillian Manzor (Third Woman Press, forthcoming), Lillian Manzor and I enumerate some of the most frequently recurring motifs in Latina theater.

34. Anzaldúa, *Borderlands/La Frontera*, p. 79.

35. Norma Alarcón, "Cognitive Desires: An Allegory of/for Chicana Critics," in *Listening to Silence*, ed., Shelly Fisher Fishkin (New York: Oxford University Press, 1994), p. 270.

36. Ibid.

37. See Chapter 4 for an analysis of the role of borders in Latina identity.

38. This passage and others in this chapter are from a videotape Margie Waller made of "Fierce Tongues: Women of Fire," a multimedia event organized by Luis Alfaro and Monica Palacios and held at Highways Performance Space in Santa Monica, California, January 21–23, 1994. As a participant, I was able to get permission from the artists to use the film.

39. Laura Esparza, "I DisMember the Alamo: A Long Poem for Performance," in Arrizón and Manzor, eds., *Latinas on Stage*. Esparza has performed this piece since 1991, not only in the United States, but also in Mexico and Spain. Note that the pagination cited in this chapter corresponds to that of the original manuscript. The book is expected to be out soon.

40. John Wayne directed, starred in, and produced the movie *The Alamo* in 1960.

41. Acuña, *Occupied America*, pp. 10–11.

42. Peggy Phelan, *Unmarked: The Politics of Performance* (New York: Routledge, 1993), p. 2.

43. Marguerite Waller, "Pocha or Pork Chop?: An Interview with Theater Director and Performance Artist Laura Esparza," in Arrizón and Manzor, eds., *Latinas on Stage*, p. 238.

44. The performance discussed here was presented on January 23, 1994 at Highways Performance Space in Santa Monica, California.

45. Among the many artists who participated in this event at Highways were Laura Aguilar (photographer), Dyan Garza (multimedia artist), Evelina Fernández (writer, actress, and producer), Elia Arce (performance artist), and Dolores Chavez.

46. Peter Stallybrass and Allon White, *The Politics and Poetics of Transgression* (Ithaca: Cornell University Press, 1986), pp. 10–11.

47. Mary Russo, "Female Grotesques: Carnival and Theory," in *Feminist Studies: Critical Studies*, ed. Teresa de Lauretis (Bloomington: Indiana University Press, 1986), p. 219.

48. Ibid., p. 217.

49. Mikhail Bakhtin, *Rabelais and His World*, trans. Helen Iswolsky (Cambridge: MIT Press, 1968), p. 90.

50. Luis Alfaro is a performance artist. He writes poetry, plays, and short stories. Currently, he is the coordinator (with Diane Rodriguez) for the Mark Taper Forum's Latino Theatre Initiative.

51. Jill Dolan, *The Feminist Spectator as Critic* (Ann Arbor: University of Michigan Press, 1988).

52. Case, *The Domain-Matrix*, p. 29.

53. This passage was not included in the final text to be published in *Latinas on Stage*. However, Esparza performed this section many times before writing the final script of her piece. The text included here is from a videotape produced by Marguerite Waller in 1992.

54. Peggy Phelan, who teaches in the Department of Performance Studies at New York University, points out that Newt Gingrich has threatened to "zero out" NEA funding by 1997. See her "Open Letter," *Theater Topics*, 6, no. 2 (1996), p. 105. In response to such threats and newly implemented government policies on the arts, an ad hoc coalition of organizations, institutions, and individuals (including artists, activists, art administrators, students, and faculty) recently created ARTNOW. This group hopes to organize nationally to demand the strongest possible federal support for the arts. Their efforts culminated in an April 1997 demonstration on the Mall, directly opposite the Capitol building in Washington, D.C.

55. Jeanie Forte, "Women's Performance Art: Feminism and Postmodernism," in Case, ed., *Performing Feminisms*, p. 251.

56. Diamond, "Introduction," in Elin Diamond, ed., *Performance and Cultural Politics*, p. 6.

57. Ibid.

58. Michel Foucault, *The History of Sexuality: Vol. 1, An Introduction*, trans. Robert Hurley (New York: Vintage, 1990), p. 95.

59. See, for example, Foucault's account in his *Discipline and Punish* (New York: Vintage, 1979). For a critque of Foucault's theories of power relations, see Sandra Lee Bartky, *Femininity and Domination: Studies in the Phenomenology of Oppression* (New York: Routledge, 1990). She considers Foucault's power analysis, "as a whole," to be embedded in that sexism "which is endemic throughout Western political theory" (p. 65).

60. Judith Butler, "Performative Acts and Gender Constitution: An Essay in Phenomenology and Feminist Theory," *Theatre Journal*, 40, no. 4 (1988), p. 519.

61. Ibid., p. 520.

62. Ibid.

63. Diamond, "Introduction," in Elin Diamond, ed., *Performance and Cultural Politics*, pp. 4–5.

64. Waller, "Pocha or Pork Chop?: An Interview with Theater Director and Performance Artist Laura Esparza," p. 239.

4. Cross-Border Subjectivity and the Dramatic Text

1. Case, *The Domain-Matrix*, p. 25.

2. Ibid.

3. "Opening Remarks," in Taylor and Villegas, eds., *Negotiating Performance*, p. 13.

4. INTAR was founded in 1967 as ADAL (Latin American Group). Since its formation, this organization has been dedicated to producing works by Latin American authors. By 1977, under the name INTAR, the company had acquired equity status as a professional theatre on the East Coast and in the Midwest (New York and Chicago) and also in the Southwest.

5. For more information on Milcha Sánchez-Scott and her dramaturgy, consult *Necessary Theater: Six Plays about the Chicano Experience*, ed. Jorge Huerta (Houston: Arte Público, 1989), pp. 76–81; and *On New Ground: Contemporary Hispanic-American Plays*, ed. M. Elizabeth Osborn (New York: Theater Communications Group, 1987), pp. 244–247.

6. "Coyote" is a widely used term for a smuggler who makes money helping people cross illegally from Mexico into the United States. Some coyotes charge between $300 and $500 per person.

7. Milcha Sánchez-Scott, "Latina," in Huerta, ed., *Necessary Theater*, pp. 76–141.

8. On those occasions, Sánchez-Scott played this actress's part. See Osborn, ed., *On New Ground*, p. 246.

9. *Latina* was also produced at California State University, Long Beach, in 1983, directed by Elena Gutiérrez, as her master's thesis project. See Huerta, ed., *Necessary Theater*, p. 76.

10. Jeremy Blahnik seems to be a co-author of the final, published version of *Latina*. In *Necessary Theater* both names are acknowledged, with Sánchez-Scott as the first author. Sánchez-Scott has described Blahnik as her guide and mentor in writing the play.

11. See Ron Pennington, "Curtain Calls," *The Hollywood Reporter* (May 15, 1980), p. 18.

12. Ibid.

13. Ibid.

14. Ibid.

15. In an interview conducted in 1980, Milcha Sánchez-Scott is referred to as "the actress Milcha Scott." Later, she became known in the Latino community as Sánchez-Scott, the Latina dramatist. I suspect that after the success of *Latina*, Sánchez-Scott came to accept her own *Latinidad*, much as Sarita does by the end of *Latina*. See Pennington, "Curtain Calls," p. 18.

16. Those who prefer "Latin" are said to be trying to evoke an association with Italians or the French, groups that are accorded greater toleration because of their alleged sophistication and romantic nature. Moreover, as Europeans, these groups have had a different history than Mexicans and Central or South Americans.

17. Huerta, ed., *Necessary Theater*, p. 76.

18. Anzaldúa, *Borderlands/La Frontera*, p. 86.

19. In this context, metadiscourse is the system of signs that helps the audience to visualize the text in terms of its implied theatrical performance.

20. Sánchez-Scott is aware of the potential dangers of these stereotypes: "This play poses problems for me because all of the women are maids and that is what we always play on television, in the movies. I have trouble promoting my own play if it will promote stereotypes." Quoted in Huerta, ed., *Necessary Theater*, p. 77.

21. The Mexican-origin population of the United States includes Mexican Americans and Chicanos (citizens of Mexican origin), permanent residents, and undocumented immigrants. As U.S. citizens, Mexican Americans and/or Chicanos differ in their cultural, social, and political status from Mexican residents, documented and undocumented.

22. Anzaldúa, *Borderlands/La Frontera*, p. 55.

23. "Opening Remarks," in Taylor and Villegas, eds., *Negotiating Performance*, p. 7.

24. Evelyn Glenn Nakano, "From Servitude to Service Work: Historical Continuities in the Racial Division of Paid Reproductive Labor," in *Unequal Sisters*, 2nd ed., ed. Vicki L. Ruiz and Ellen Carol Dubois (New York: Routledge, 1994), p. 406.

25. Interview conducted on October 17, 1994. Ms. Ramírez has been in Los Angeles since 1987. I met with her a few times at a coffeehouse in Beverly Hills. She explained that her name was a pseudonym she used for her own protection as an undocumented worker.

26. Dolores Prida, "The Show Does Go On," in Horno Delgado, Ortega, Scott, and Sternbach, eds., *Breaking Boundaries*, p. 188.

27. "The Show Does Go On," p. 183.

28. Ibid.

29. Ibid.

30. Reprinted in Dolores Prida, *Beautiful Señoritas and Other Plays* (Houston: Arte Público Press), pp. 17–67. *Coser y cantar* was first staged at Duo Theater in New York City on June 25, 1981. This production was directed by María Norman, who also played the role of She; Elizabeth Peña played Ella. The play has had many subsequent productions throughout the U.S. and in Puerto Rico. The theater magazine *Tramoya* also published *Coser y cantar* (in 1990). Other plays included in this anthology are *Beautiful Señoritas*, *Savings*, *Pantallas*, and *Bótanica*. These plays mark Prida's creative evolution over twelve years (1978–1990), representing with humor the complexity of identity, gender relations, ethnicity, and social class.

31. Alberto Sandoval, "Dolores Prida's *Coser y cantar*: Mapping the Dialectics of Ethnic Identity and Assimilation," in Horno-Delgado, Ortega, Scott, and Sternbach, eds., *Breaking Boundaries*, p. 203.

32. This is a typical reaction among Latinos who have never associated with people from the barrios. As an instructor in Chicano Studies, I often find that at the beginning of the term, middle-class students who are taking their first Chicano Studies course express similarly negative impressions of Chicano culture.

33. Guillermo Gómez-Peña, "The Multicultural Paradigm: An Open Letter to the National Arts Community," in Taylor and Villegas, eds., *Negotiating Performance*, p. 19.

34. Stuart Silverstein, "Domestics: Hiring the Illegal Hits Home," *Los Angeles Times* (October 28, 1994), p. 1. Computer analysis of 1990 U.S. census data by *Los Angeles Times* analyst Sandra Poindexter revealed that immigrants accounted for more than 58% of the state's domestic workers, with the figure rising to 80% in Los Angeles County and nearly 69% in Orange County. According to the census data, California's immigrant domestic workers, both documented and undocumented, come from the following places: Mexico (33%), El Salvador (28.7%), Guatemala

(17.4%), Asia (5%), Honduras (3.5%), South America (3.1%), Europe (2%) and other (7.3%).

35. Ibid., p. 1.

36. Josefina López, "Simply María or the American Dream," in *Shattering the Myth: Plays by Hispanic Women*, ed. Linda Feyder (Houston: Arte Público, 1992), pp. 115–141. The play's title deliberately echoes the name of a television soap opera (telenovela), *Simplemente Maria*, that was very popular across Latin America and in the U.S. (through the Spanish International Network) in the 1980s. López's play was first produced by the California Young Playwrights Project at the Gaslamp Quarter Theater in San Diego, California, on January 13, 1988. In 1990, the play went on tour with Teatro Campesino and was adapted for television (PBS). Teatro Campesino produced the play a second time in 1992 in Los Angeles.

37. Renato Rosaldo, *Culture and Truth: The Remaking of Social Analysis* (Boston: Beacon, 1989), p. 214.

38. Ibid., p. 211.

39. Ibid., p. 214.

40. Anzaldúa, *Borderlands/La Frontera*, p. 3.

41. Gloria Anzaldúa, "Chicana Artists: Exploring *Nepantla*, el lugar de la frontera," in *NACLA: Report on the Americas* 27, no. 1 (1993), p. 39. This number was a special issue entitled *Latin American Women: The Gendering of Politics and Culture*.

42. Ibid.

43. Ibid.

44. Gloria Anzaldúa, "La Prieta," in Anzaldúa and Moraga, eds., *This Bridge Called My Back*, pp. 198–209.

45. Ibid., p. 209.

46. Ibid., p. 209.

47. Cherríe Moraga, *Heroes and Saints and Other Plays* (Albuquerque: West End, 1994). This collection includes: "Giving up the Ghost," "Shadow of a Man," and "Heroes and Saints."

5. Self-Representation

1. Case, *The Domain-Matrix*.

2. See, for example, her introduction in *Performance and Cultural Politics*, ed. Elin Diamond, pp. 1–12.

3. Judith Butler, *Bodies That Matter: On the Discursive Limits of "Sex"* (New York: Routledge, 1993), p. 195.

4. Ibid., p. 12.

5. I am aware of the current political controversy surrounding the term "queer," including the fact that some uses attempt to diminish the importance of specificity. My use of the term is associated with a cultural space which recognizes the possibility of gay, lesbian, and other forms of sexual identity intolerable to the heterocentricism of our dominant society. In this chapter, I use the term "queer" in discussing the work of Monica Palacios and Carmelita Tropicana as a way to engage the standard opposition of "queer" and "nonqueer" (or heterosexual) while emphasizing the "queerness" embedded in my own reading. Thus, within the

relevance of specificity, "queer" refers to lesbian sexuality and the way I am dealing with it.

6. Lynda Hart, "Identity and Seduction: Lesbians in the Mainstream," in *Acting Out: Feminist Performances,* ed. Lynda Hart and Peggy Phelan (Ann Arbor: University of Michigan Press, 1993), p. 124.

7. Trujillo, ed., *Chicana Lesbians,* p. ix.

8. Adela Alonso, "Contributors Page," in *The Sexuality of Latinas,* ed. Norma Alarcón, Ana Castillo, and Cherríe Moraga (Berkeley: Third Woman, 1989), p. 185.

9. Yvonne Yarbro-Bejarano, "Expanding the Categories of Race and Sexuality in Lesbian and Gay Studies," in *Professions of Desire: Lesbian and Gay Studies in Literature,* ed. George E. Haggerty and Bonnie Zimmerman (New York: Modern Language Association of America, 1995), p. 133.

10. Leigh Gilmore, *Autobiographics: A Feminist Theory of Women's Self-Representation* (Ithaca: Cornell University Press, 1994), p. 67.

11. Yarbro-Bejarano, "Expanding the Categories of Race and Sexuality in Lesbian and Gay Studies," in Haggerty and Zimmerman, eds., *Professions of Desire,* p. 130.

12. Lizbeth Goodman, *Contemporary Feminist Theatres: To Each Her Own* (New York: Routledge, 1993), p. 118.

13. Judith Butler, *Bodies That Matter: On the Discursive Limits of "Sex,"* p. 93.

14. Shane Phelan, *Getting Specific: Postmodern Lesbian Politics* (Minneapolis: University of Minnesota Press, 1994), p. 55.

15. Ibid., p. 24.

16. Chela Sandoval, "U.S. Third World Feminism: The Theory of Method and Oppositional Consciousness in the Postmodern World," *Genders* 10 (1991), pp. 1–24.

17. Adrienne Rich, "Foreword," in *The Coming Out Stories* (Watertown: Persephone, 1980), p. xiii.

18. Ibid., p. 51.

19. Consult Sigmund Freud, *Three Essays on the Theory of Sexuality,* trans. by James Strachey (New York: Basic Books, 1975).

20. Simone de Beauvoir, *The Second Sex* (New York: Alfred A. Knopf, 1989), p. 424. The emphasis is given in the original text.

21. Claudia Card, "Lesbian Attitudes and *The Second Sex,*" in *Hypatia: A Journal of Feminist Philosophy* 8: 3 (1985), 209.

22. Adrienne Rich, "Compulsory Heterosexuality and Lesbian Existence," *Signs: Journal of Women in Culture and Society* 5, no. 4 (1980), pp. 631–660. See also the new reprint with a foreword in *The Lesbian and Gay Studies Reader,* ed. Henry Abelove et al. (New York: Routledge, 1993), pp. 227–254.

23. Adrienne Rich, "Compulsory Heterosexuality and Lesbian Existence," in Abelove et al., p. 227.

24. The text of this performance is in Monica Palacios, "Latin Lezbo Comic: A Performance about Happiness, Challenges, and Tacos," in Arrizón and Manzor, eds., *Latinas on Stage.* Palacios' first performance of *Latin Lezbo* was in 1992 at Highways, Santa Monica, California. That same year, her performance was featured on the Public Broadcasting System (PBS). Palacios also performed at UC

Riverside on March 2, 1993. Her performance was a major event during the celebration of "Semana de la Mujer." Co-sponsored by MECHA and the Chicano Student Program, Palacios' performance attracted more than 150 people to the campus theater. After this performance, she was invited to return to UC Riverside (in 1994 and 1995) by the Gay, Lesbian, and Bisexual Student Program.

25. Note that the pagination here and elsewhere in this chapter refers to the original manuscript. The book is expected to be out soon.

26. Antonia Villaseñor, "Dos Lenguas Listas: An Interview with Monica Palacios," forthcoming in Arrizón and Manzor, eds., *Latinas on Stage*, p. 278.

27. Yvonne Yarbro-Bejarano, "The Lesbian Body in Latina Cultural Production," in *¿Entiendes?: Queer Readings, Hispanic Writings*, ed. Emilie L. Bergmann and Paul Julian Smith (Durham: Duke University Press, 1995), p. 192. In this essay, Yvonne Yarbro-Bejarano relates the work of Palacios to other Latina artists. She uses the work of Cherríe Moraga, Ester Hernández, and Marcia Ochoa to talk about cultural productions and the lesbianization of the heterosexual icons of popular culture.

28. Comments of Monica Palacios after she performed *Latin Lezbo Comic* at UC Riverside in 1993.

29. Yarbro-Bejarano, "The Lesbian Body in Latina Cultural Production," in Bergmann and Smith, eds., *¿Entiendes?* p. 194.

30. Sue-Ellen Case, "Performing Lesbian in the Space of Technology: Part I," *Theatre Journal* 47, no. 1 (1995), p. 3.

31. Ibid., p. 18.

32. I am referring to the production of the play directed by Anita Mattos and José Gaudalupe Saucedo, performed at San Francisco's Theatre Rhinoceros (February–March 1989). This was the second time the play had been produced. The cast consisted of Linda Huey (Corky), Anna Olivarez (Amalia), and Belinda Ramirez (Marisa). *Giving up the Ghost* was published first as an individual text (in 1986) by West End Press in Los Angeles. Later, it was included in *Heroes and Saints and Other Plays* (1994).

33. See Yvonne Yarbro-Bejarano's "The Female Subject in Chicano Theater: Sexuality, 'Race,' and Class," in Case, ed., *Performing Feminisms*, pp. 131–149.

34. Carmelita Tropicana, "Milk of Amnesia/Leche de Amnesia," *The Drama Review* 39, no. 3 (1995), p. 94.

35. Carmelita Tropicana is the staged identity of Alina Troyano. She initiated her artistic career in New York, where she currently resides. She has become well known in the East Village performance scene, mainly in queer and feminist spaces, such as the Club Chandelier and the WOW Cafe. Carmelita Tropicana, as an invention of Alina, was born by accident. Almost a decade ago, the M.C. at the WOW cafe did not show up and Alina was encouraged to go on stage as a replacement. She went on as Carmelita Tropicana, and—as she has pointed out—has never come off since. For more information, consult Alisa Solomon, "The WOW Cafe," *The Drama Review* 29, no. 1 (1985), 92–101. Also consult Lillian Manzor "Too Spik or Too Dyke: Carmelita Tropicana," *Ollantay: Theater Magazine* (Winter/Spring 1994), pp. 39–55.

36. David Román, "Carmelita Tropicana Unplugged," *The Drama Review* 39, no. 3 (1995), p. 85.

37. Peggy Phelan, *Unmarked: The Politics of Performance* (New York: Routledge, 1993), p. 5.

38. Ibid.

39. This self-description is a reminder of Betacourt's role in *Memorias de la Revolución/ Memories of the Revolution* (1987), unpublished manuscript. In this play, produced in collaboration with Uzi Parnes, Tropicana is in a boat heading toward Miami when she meets Pingalito.

40. Lillian Manzor, "From Minimalism to Performative Excess: The Two Tropicanas," in Arrizón and Manzor, eds., *Latinas on Stage*. Pérez Prado has been called the father of *mambo*. He started playing in the 1940s, but he received little attention in Cuba. In 1949, he moved to Mexico, where the *mambo* became a popular form of dance. Currently, the *mambo* is considered one of the most typical rhythms in Cuba.

41. Ibid., p. 518.

42. Román, "Carmelita Tropicana Unplugged," p. 90.

43. Ibid., p. 91.

44. José Esteban Muñoz, "'No es fácil': Notes on the Negotiation of Cubanidad and Exilic Memory in Carmelita Tropicana's *Milk of Amnesia*," *The Drama Review: The Journal of Performance Studies* 39, no. 3 (1995), p. 78.

45. Norma Alarcón, "Cognitive Desires: An Allegory of/for Chicana Critics," in Hedges and Fishkin, eds., *Listening to Silences*, p. 270.

46. Román, "Carmelita Tropicana Unplugged," p. 91.

47. Ibid.

48. Manzor, "From Minimalism to Performative Excess," in Arrizón and Manzor, eds., *Latinas on Stage*, p. 529.

49. Ibid., p. 502.

50. Sue-Ellen Case, "Tracking the Vampire," *Differences* 3, no. 2 (1991), 3.

51. Troyano had used the subtitle of this movie before, in her *Memorias de la Revolución*. There the Virgin appeared to Carmelita and made a pact with her. After telling Carmelita in German, "your art is your weapon," she made Tropicana promise that she would never touch a man. See Román, "Carmelita Tropicana Unplugged," p. 88.

52. Chavela Vargas sings traditional Mexican *rancheras* and *boleros*. Her music is more popular in intellectual circles than among the masses; she has become internationally known among feminists and lesbians. Her unique style and powerful voice reinscribe a feminist perspective in genres which have been dominated by males. Chavela's voice is deep and defiant.

53. José Esteban Muñoz, "Flaming Latinas: Ela Troyano's *Carmelita Tropicana: Your Kunst Is Your Waffen*," in *The Ethnic Eye: Latino Media Arts*, ed. Chon A. Noriega and Ana M. López (Minneapolis: University of Minnesota Press, 1996), pp. 129–142.

54. Ibid., p. 139.

55. Tomás Ybarra-Frausto, "Rascuachismo: A Chicano Sensibility," in *CARA: Chicano Art, Resistance and Affirmation*, ed. Richard Griswold del Castillo, Teresa Mckenna, and Yvonne Yarbro-Bejarano (Los Angeles: Wight Art Gallery, 1990), p. 155.

56. Ibid., p. 156.

57. Case, "Tracking the Vampire," p. 3.

58. Ibid.

59. In addition to using tacos as an "ingredient" in the title of her performance piece, Palacios also throws a dozen tortillas to her audience at one point in her show.

60. Case, "Tracking the Vampire," p. 2.

Bibliography

Books and Anthologies

Abel, Elizabeth. "Race, Class, and Psychoanalysis? Opening Questions." In *Conflicts in Feminism*, ed. Marianne Hirsch and Evelyn Fox Keller. New York: Routledge, 1990.

Abel, Elizabeth, ed. *Writing and Sexual Difference*. Chicago: University of Chicago Press, 1982.

Acuña, Rodolfo, *Occupied America. A History of Chicanos*. 3rd ed. New York: Harper Collins, 1988.

Agosín, Marjorie. "Literature." In *Latinas of the Americas*, ed. K. Lynn Stoner. Westport: Greenwood, 1990.

Alarcón, Norma. "Chicana's Feminist Literature: A Re-vision through Malintzín, Or, Malintzín: Putting Flesh Back on the Object." In *This Bridge Called My Back: Writing by Radical Women of Color*, ed. Gloria Anzaldúa and Cherríe Moraga. New York: Kitchen Table, 1981.

———. "Cognitive Desires: An Allegory of/for Chicana Critics." In *Listening to Silences*, ed. Shelly Fisher Fishkin. New York: Oxford University Press, 1994.

———. "Latina Writers in the United States." In *Spanish American Women Writers: A Bio-Bibliographical Source Book*, ed. Diane E. Marting. Westport: Greenwood, 1990.

———. "The Theoretical Subject(s) of *This Bridge Called My Back* and Anglo-American Feminism: Creative and Critical Perspectives by Women of Color." In *Making Face, Making Soul/haciendo caras: Creative and Critical Perspectives by Women of Color*, ed. Gloria Anzaldúa. San Francisco: Aunt Lute, 1990.

———. "Traddutora, Traditora: A Paradigmatic Figure of Chicana Feminism." In *Changing Our Power: An Introduction to Women's Studies*, ed. Jo Whitehorse Cochran, Donna Langston, Carolyn Woodward. Dubuque: Kendal/Hunt, 1988.

———. "What Kind of Lover Have You Made Me Mother?" In *Women of Color: Perspectives on Feminism and Identity*, ed. Audrey T. McCluskey. Occasional Papers Series, Vol. 1, No. 1. Bloomington: Women's Studies Program, Indiana University, 1985.

Alarcón, Norma, Ana Castillo, and Cherríe Moraga, eds. *The Sexuality of Latinas.* Berkeley: Third Woman, 1989.

Alarcón, Norma, and Sylvia Kossnar. *Bibliography of Hispanic Women Writers*, Chicano-Riqueño Studies Bibliography Series, No. 1. Bloomington: Chicano-Riqueño Studies, 1980.

Alcoff, Linda, and Elizabeth Potter. *Feminist Epistemologies.* New York: Routledge, 1993.

Anaya, Rodolfo A., and Francisco Lomelí, eds. *Aztlán: Essays on the Chicano Homeland.* Albuquerque: Academia/El Norte, 1989.

Anderson, Benedict. *Imagined Communities: Reflections on the Origin and Spread of Nationalism.* London: Verso, 1983.

Andrade, Elba, and Hilde F. Cramsie, eds. *Dramaturgas latinoamericanas contemporáneas.* Madrid: Editorial Verbum, 1991.

Anzaldúa, Gloria. *Borderlands/La Frontera: The New Mestiza.* San Francisco: Spinsters/Aunt Lute, 1987.

Anzaldúa, Gloria, ed. *Making Face, Making Soul/haciendo caras: Creative and Critical Perspectives by Women of Color.* San Francisco: Aunt Lute, 1990.

Anzaldúa, Gloria and Cherríe Moraga, eds. *This Bridge Called My Back: Writings by Radical Women of Color.* New York: Kitchen Table, 1981.

Aparicio, Frances R., and Susana Chávez-Silverman. *Tropicalizations: Transcultural Representations of Latinidad.* Hanover: University Press of New England, 1997.

Arrizón, Alicia, and Lillian Manzor, eds. *Latinas on Stage: Practice and Theory.* Berkeley: Third Woman, forthcoming.

Auslander, Philip. *Presence and Resistance: Postmodernism and Cultural Politics in Contemporary American Performance.* Ann Arbor: University of Michigan Press, 1993.

Austin, Gayle. *Feminist Theories: For Dramatic Criticism.* Ann Arbor: University of Michigan Press, 1990.

Bakhtin, Mikhail, *The Dialogic Imagination.* Austin: University of Texas Press, 1981.

———. *Rabelais and His World.* Trans. Hélène Iswosky. Bloomington: Indiana University Press, 1984.

Barthes, Roland. *Camera Lucida.* Trans. Richard Howard. New York: Hill & Wang, 1981.

Bartky, Sandra Lee. *Femininity and Domination: Studies in the Phenomenology of Oppression.* New York: Routledge, 1990.

Beauvoir, Simone de. *The Second Sex.* Trans. and ed. H. M. Parshley. New York: Alfred A. Knopf, 1989.

Behar, Ruth, ed. *Bridges to Cuba/Puentes a Cuba.* Ann Arbor: University of Michigan Press, 1996.

Bennett, Susan. *Performing Nostalgia: Shifting Shakespeare and the Contemporary Past.* New York: Routledge, 1996.

Berdecio, Roberto, and Stanley Appelbaum, eds. *Posada's Popular Mexican Prints: 237 Cuts by José Guadalupe Posada*. New York: Dover, 1972.

Bergmann, Emilie, et al. *Women, Culture, and Politics in Latin America*. Berkeley: University of California Press, 1990.

Bharucha, Rustom. *Theatre and the World: Performance and the Politics of Culture*. New York: Routledge, 1990.

Boal, Augusto. *Teatro del oprimido*. Mexico City: Editorial Nueva Imagen, 1980.

Bonilla Martínez, Natasha, ed. *La Frontera/The Border: Art about the Mexico/United States Border Experience*. Trans. Gwendolyn Gómez. San Diego: Centro Cultural de la Raza and Museum of Contemporary Art, 1993.

Brecht, Bertolt. *Brecht on Theatre: The Development of an Aesthetic*. Ed. John Willet. New York: Hill and Wang, 1964.

Brennan, Teresa. *History after Lacan*. New York: Routledge, 1993.

——. *The Interpretation of the Flesh: Freud and Femininity*. New York: Routledge, 1992.

Brodribb, Somer. *Nothing Mat(t)ers: A Feminist Critique of Postmodernism*. North Melbourne: Spinifex, 1992.

Brody, Janet Esser, ed. *Behind the Mask in Mexico*. Santa Fe: Museum of New Mexico, 1988.

Broyles-González, Yolanda. *El Teatro Campesino: Theater in the Chicano Movement*. Austin: University of Texas Press, 1994.

Bruce-Novoa, Juan. *Chicano Authors: Inquiry by Interview*. Austin: University of Texas Press, 1980.

Butler, Judith. *Bodies That Matter: On the Discursive Limits of Sex*. New York: Routledge, 1993.

——. *Excitable Speech: A Politics of the Performative*. New York: Routledge, 1997.

——. *Gender Trouble: Feminism and the Subversion of Identity*. New York: Routledge, Chapman & Hall, 1990.

Canning, Charlotte. *Feminist Theaters in the U.S.A.* New York: Routledge, 1996.

Cárdenas de Dwyer, Carlota. "The Development of Chicano Drama and Luis Valdez." In *Modern Chicano Writers*, ed. Joseph Sommers and Tomás Ybarra-Frausto. Englewood Cliffs: Prentice-Hall, 1979.

Casasola, Gustavo. *Biografía Ilustrada del General Francisco Villa 1878–1966*. Mexico City: Editorial Gustavo Casasola, 1969.

——. *Historia Gráfica de la Revolución: 1900–1960*. 4 vols. Mexico City: Editorial F. Trillas, 1960.

Case, Sue-Ellen. *The Domain-Matrix: Performing Lesbian at the End of Print Culture*. Bloomington: Indiana University Press, 1996.

——. *Feminism and Theatre*. New York: Methuen, 1988.

——. "Toward a Butch-Femme Aesthetic." In *Making a Spectacle: Feminist Essays on Contemporary Women's Theatre*, ed. Lynda Hart. Ann Arbor: University of Michigan Press, 1989.

Case, Sue-Ellen, ed. *Performing Feminisms: Feminist Critical Theory and Theatre*. Baltimore: John Hopkins University Press, 1990.

Case, Sue-Ellen, and Janelle Reinelt, eds. *The Performance of Power: Theatrical Discourse and Politics*. Iowa City: University of Iowa Press, 1991.

Castillo, Debra A. "Rosario Castellanos: 'Ashes without a Face.'" In *De/Colonizing the Subject: The Politics of Gender in Women's Autobiography*, ed. Sidonie Smith and Julia Watson. Minneapolis: University of Minnesota Press, 1992.

Castro-Klarén, Sara, "La crítica literaria feminista y la escritora en Latina América." In *La sartén por el mango*, ed. Patricia E. González and Eliana Ortega. Rio Piedras, Puerto Rico: Edición Huracán, 1985.

Castro-Klarén, Sara, Sylvia Molloy, and Beatriz Sarlo, eds. *Women Writing in Latin America*. Boulder: Westview, 1991.

Cevallos-Candau, Francisco Javier, Jeffrey A. Cole, et al. *Coded Encounters: Writing, Gender, and Ethnicity in Colonial Latin America*. Amherst: University of Massachusetts Press, 1994.

Chabram-Dernersesian, Angie. "And, Yes . . . the Earth Did Part: On the Splitting of Chicana/o Subjectivity." In *Building with Our Hands: New Directions in Chicana Studies*, ed. Adela de la Torre and Beatríz M. Pesquera. Berkeley: University of California Press, 1993.

Chinoy, Helen Krich, and Linda Walsh Jenkins, eds. *Women in American Theatre*. New York: Theatre Communication Group, 1987.

Cixous, Hélène, and Catherine Clément. *The Newly Born Woman*. Trans. Betsy Wing. Minneapolis: University of Minnesota Press, 1991.

Colombres, Adolfo. *Sobre la cultura y el arte popular*. Buenos Aires: Ediciones del Sol, 1987.

Conley, Verena Andermatt. *Cixous, Hélène: Writing the Feminine*. Lincoln: University of Nebraska Press, 1991.

Cotera, Marta P. *The Chicana Feminist*. Austin: Information Systems Development, 1977.

———. *Diosa y Hembra: The History and Heritage of Chicanas in the U.S.* Austin: Information Systems Development, 1976.

Crimp, Douglas, ed. *AIDS: Cultural Analysis/Cultural Activism*. Cambridge: MIT Press, 1988.

Cypess, Sandra M. *La Malinche in Mexican Literature: From History to Myth*. Austin: University of Texas Press, 1991.

———. "Tradition and Innovation in the Writing of Puerto Rican Women." In *Out of the Kumbla: Caribbean Women and Literature*, ed. Carole Boyce Davies and Elaine S. Fido. Trenton, N.J.: Africa World Press, 1990.

Dauster, Frank. *The Double Strand: Five Contemporary Mexican Poets*. Lexington: University Press of Kentucky, 1987.

Davis, Angela. *Women, Race and Class*. London: Women's Press, 1982.

Davis, Tracy. *Actresses as Working Women: Their Social Identity in Victorian Culture*. New York: Routledge, 1991.

———. "Shotgun Wedlock: Annie Oakley's Power Politics in the Wild West." In *Gender in Performance: The Representation of Difference in the Performing Arts*, ed. Laurence Senelick. Hanover: University Press of New England, 1992.

de la Cruz, Sor Juana Inés. *Obras completas*. 3 vols. Ed. Alfonso Méndez Plancarte and Alberto G. Salceda. México City: Fondo de Cultura Económica, 1951–1957.

de la Roche, Elisa. *¡Teatro Hispano!: Three Major New York Companies*. New York: Garland, 1995.

de la Torre, Adela, and Beatríz M. Pesquera, eds. *Building with Our Hands: New Directions in Chicana Studies.* Berkeley: University of California Press, 1993.

de Lauretis, Teresa. *The Practice of Love: Lesbian Sexuality and Perverse Desire.* Bloomington: Indiana University Press, 1994.

———. *Sexual Difference: A Theory of Social-Symbolic Practice.* Bloomington: Indiana University Press, 1987.

———. *Technologies of Gender: Essays on Theory, Film, and Culture.* Bloomington: Indiana University Press, 1987.

Diamond, Elin, ed. *Performance and Cultural Politics.* New York: Routledge, 1996.

Dolan, Jill. *The Feminist Spectator as Critic.* Ann Arbor: University of Michigan Press, 1988.

———. *Presence and Desire: Essays on Gender, Sexuality, Performance.* Ann Arbor: University of Michigan Press, 1993.

Donaldson, Laura E. *Decolonizing Feminisms: Race, Gender, and Empire-Building.* Chapel Hill: University of North Carolina Press, 1992.

Doty, Alexander. *Making Things Perfectly Queer: Interpreting Mass Culture.* Minneapolis: University of Minnesota Press, 1993.

Douglas, Carol Anne. *Love and Politics: Radical Feminist and Lesbian Theories.* San Francisco: Ism, 1990.

Dromundo, Baltasar. *Francisco Villa y La Adelita.* Durango: Victoria de Durango, 1936.

DuBois, Ellen Carol, and Vicki L. Ruiz, eds. *Unequal Sisters: A Multicultural Reader in U.S. Women's History.* New York: Routledge, 1990.

Echols, Alice. "The New Feminism of Yin and Yang." In *Powers of Desire: The Politics of Sexuality,* ed. Ann Snitow, Christine Stansell, and Sharon Thomson. New York: Monthly Review, 1983.

Ecker, Gisela, ed. *Feminist Aesthetics.* Trans. Harriet Anderson. Boston: Beacon, 1985.

Fanon, Frantz. *Black Skin, White Masks.* Trans. Charles Markmann. New York: Grove, 1967.

Finney, Gail. *Women in Modern Drama: Freud, Feminism, and European Theater at the Turn of the Century.* Ithaca: Cornell University Press, 1989.

Flores, Arturo. *El Teatro Campesino de Luis Valdez (1965–1980).* Madrid: Editorial Pliegos, 1990.

Flores, Juan. *Divided Borders: Essays on Puerto Rican Identity.* Houston: Arte Público, 1993.

Foucault, Michel. *The History of Sexuality: Vol. 1, An Introduction.* Trans. Robert Hurley. New York: Vintage, 1990.

———. *The History of Sexuality: Vol. 2, The Use of the Pleasure.* Trans. Robert Hurley. New York: Vintage, 1990.

———. *The History of Sexuality: Vol. 3, The Care of the Self.* Trans. Robert Hurley. New York: Vintage, 1988.

———. *Power/Knowledge: Selected Interviews and Other Writings 1972–1977.* Trans. Colin Gordon, et al. Brighton: Harvester, 1980.

Franco, Jean. "Beyond Ethnocentrism: Gender, Power, and the Third-World Intelligentsia." In *Marxism and the Interpretation of Culture,* ed. Cary Nelson and Laurence Grossberg. Chicago: University of Illinois Press, 1988.

———. "Killing Priests, Nuns, Women, Children." In *On Signs*, ed. Marshall Blonsky. Baltimore: Johns Hopkins University Press, 1985.

———. *Plotting Women: Gender and Representation in Mexico*. New York: Columbia University Press, 1989.

Fregoso, Rosa Linda. *The Bronze Screen: Chicana and Chicano Film*. Minneapolis: University of Minnesota Press, 1993.

Freud, Sigmund. *Three Essays on the Theory of Sexuality*. Trans. James Strachey. New York: Basic Books, 1975.

———. "The Uncanny." In *Collected Papers*, ed. Ernest Jones, vol. 4. New York: Basic Books, 1959.

Frye, Marilyn. *The Politics of Reality: Essays in Feminist Theory*. Freedom, Calif.: Crossing, 1983.

Fusco, Coco. *English Is Broken Here: Notes on Cultural Fusion in the Americas*. New York: New Press, 1995.

Fuss, Diana, ed. *Essentially Speaking: Feminism, Nature and Difference*. New York: Routledge, 1989.

———. *Inside/Out: Lesbian Theories, Gay Theories*. New York: Routledge, 1991.

Gallop, Jane. *The Daughter's Seduction: Feminism and Psychoanalysis*. Ithaca: Cornell University Press, 1982.

García, Canclini, Néstor. *Las culturas híbridas: Estrategias para entrar y salir de la modernidad*. México D.F.: Editorial Grijalbo, 1990.

———. *Las culturas populares en el capitalismo*. México D.F.: Editorial Nueva Imagen, 1982.

García, Richard A. "The Mexican American Mind: A Product of the 1930s." In *History, Culture and Society: Chicano Studies in the 1980s*. Ypsilanti: Bilingual Press/Editorial Bilingüe, 1983.

Garfield, Evelyn Picon, ed. *Women's Voices from Latin America*. Detroit: Wayne State University Press, 1987.

Garner, Stanton B. *Bodied Spaces: Phenomenology and Performance in Contemporary Drama*. Ithaca: Cornell University Press, 1994.

Gilmore, Leigh. *Autobiographics: A Feminist Theory of Women's Self-Representation*. Ithaca: Cornell University Press, 1994.

Goodman, Lizbeth. *Contemporary Feminist Theatres: To Each Her Own*. New York: Routledge, 1993.

Grahn, Judy. *Another Mother Tongue: Gay Words, Gay Worlds*. Boston: Beacon, 1985.

Gray, John, ed. *Black Theatre and Performance: A Pan-African Bibliography*. New York: Greenwood, 1990.

Gross, Elizabeth. *Space, Time and Perversion*. New York: Routledge, 1995.

Gutiérrez-Jones, Carl. *Rethinking the Borderlands: Between Chicano Culture and Legal Discourse*. Berkeley: University of California Press, 1995.

Hadley-García, George. *Hispanic Hollywood: The Latins in Motion Picture*. New York: Citadel, 1990.

Haraway, Donna J. *Simians, Cyborgs, and Women: The Reinvention of Nature*. New York: Routledge, Chapman, and Hall, 1991.

Harding, Sandra. *The Science Question in Feminism*. Ithaca: Cornell University Press, 1986.

Hart, Lynda. *Fatal Women: Lesbian Sexuality and the Mark of Aggression*. Princeton: Princeton University Press, 1994.

Hart, Lynda, and Peggy Phelan, eds. *Acting Out: Feminist Performances*. Ann Arbor: University of Michigan Press, 1993.

Hernandez, Mike, and Sky Renfro, "Packing, Pissing and Passing." In *Dragger: On Butch Women*, ed. Lily Burana, Roxie, and Linnea Due. Pittsburgh: Cleis, 1994.

Herrera-Sobek, María. *The Mexican Corrido: A Feminist Analysis*. Bloomington: Indiana University Press, 1990.

Herrera-Sobek, María, ed. *Beyond Stereotypes: The Critical Analysis of Chicana Literature*. Binghamton: Bilingual Press/Editorial Bilingüe, 1985.

Herrera-Sobek, María, and Helena María Viramontes. *Chicana Creativity and Criticism: Charting New Frontiers in American Literature*. Houston: Arte Público, 1988.

Herrera-Sobek, María. *Chicana (W)rites: On Word and Film*. Berkeley: Third Woman, 1995.

Hicks, D. Emily. *Border Writing: The Multidimensional Text*. Minneapolis: University of Minnesota Press, 1991.

hooks, bell. *Feminist Theory: From Margin to Center*. Boston: South End, 1984.

———. *Yearning: Race, Gender, and Cultural Politics*. Boston: South End, 1990.

Horno-Delgado, Asunción, et al., eds. *Breaking Boundaries: Latina Writing and Critical Readings*. Amherst: University of Massachusetts Press, 1989.

Huerta, Jorge. *Chicano Theater: Themes and Forms*. Ypsilanti: Bilingual Review, 1982.

Irigaray, Luce. *This Sex Which Is Not One*. Trans. Catherine Porter. Ithaca: Cornell University Press, 1985.

Issak, Jo Anna. *Feminism and Contemporary Art: The Revolutionary Power of Women's Laughter*. New York: Routledge, 1996.

Jaggar, Alison M. *Feminist Politics and Human Nature*. New Jersey: Rowman & Allanheld, 1983.

Jagose, Annamarie. *Lesbian Utopics*. New York: Routledge, 1994.

Jameson, Fredric. "Americans Abroad: Exogamy and Letters in Late Capitalism." In *Critical Theory, Cultural Politics, and Latin American Narrative*, ed. Steven M. Bell, Albert H. LeMay, and Leonard Orr. Notre Dame: University of Notre Dame Press, 1993.

Jenkins, Ron. *Subversive Laughter: The Liberating Power of Comedy*. New York: Free Press, 1994.

Kaminsky, Amy K. *Reading the Body Politic: Feminist Criticism and Latin American Women Writers*. Minneapolis: University of Minnesota Press, 1993.

Kanellos, Nicolás. *A History of Hispanic Theatre in the United States: Origins to 1940*. Austin: University of Texas Press, 1990.

Kershaw, Baz. *The Politics of Performance: Radical Theatre as Cultural Intervention*. New York: Routledge, 1992.

Keyssar, Helene. *Feminist Theatre: An Introduction to Plays of Contemporary British and American Women*. New York: Grove, 1985.

Kintz, Linda. *The Subject's Tragedy: Political Poetics, Feminist Theory and Drama*. Ann Arbor: University of Michigan Press, 1992.

Lacan, Jacques. *Écrits: A Selection*. Trans. Alan Sheridan. New York: W. W. Norton, 1977.

———. *Feminine Sexuality*, ed. Juliet Mitchell and Jacqueline Rose, trans. Jacqueline Rose. New York: W. W. Norton, 1982.

Lapovsky, Elizabeth, and Madeline D. Davis. *Boots of Leather, Slippers of Gold: The History of a Lesbian Community*. New York: Penguin Books, 1994.

Lomas, Clara, ed. *The Rebel: Leonor Villegas de Magnon*. Houston: Arte Público, 1994.

López, Tiffany Ana, ed. *Growing Up Chicana/o*. New York: William Morrow, 1993.

Macías, Anna. *Against All Odds: The Feminist Movement in Mexico to 1940*. Westport: Greenwood, 1982.

Mackinnon, Catharine. "Feminism, Marxism, Method, and the State: An Agenda for Theory." In *Modern Feminisms: Political, Literary, Cultural*, ed. Maggie Humn. New York: Columbia University Press, 1992.

Malpede, Karen, ed. *Women in Theatre: Compassion and Hope*. New York: Drama Book Publishers, 1983.

Marting, Diane E., ed. *Spanish American Women Writers: A Bio-Bibliographical Source Book*. Westport: Greenwood, 1990.

Matovina, Timothy M. *The Alamo Remembered: Tejano Accounts and Perspectives*. Austin: University of Texas Press, 1995.

McCullough, Rita I. *Sources: An Annotated Bibliography of Women's Issues*. Manchester: Knowledge, Ideas and Trends, 1991.

McRobbie, Angela. *Postmodernism and Popular Culture*. New York: Routledge, 1994.

Merrim, Stephanie, ed. *Feminist Perspectives on Sor Juana Inés de la Cruz*. Detroit: Wayne State University Press, 1991.

Miller, Beth, ed. *Women in Hispanic Literature: Icons and Fallen Idols*. Berkeley: University of California Press, 1983.

Miller, Francesca. *Latin American Women and the Search for Social Justice*. Hanover: University Press of New England, 1991.

Minh-ha, Trinh T. *Woman Native Other*. Bloomington: Indiana University Press, 1989.

Mirandé, Alfredo, and Evangelina Enríquez. *La Chicana: The Mexican-American Woman*. Chicago: University of Chicago Press, 1979.

Mohanty, Chandra Talpade, Ann Russo, and Lourdes Torres, eds. *Third World Women and the Politics of Feminism*. Bloomington: Indiana University Press, 1991.

Monsiváis, Carlos. *Escenas de pudor y livianidad*. Mexico City: Editorial Grijalbo, 1988.

Moraga, Cherríe. *The Last Generation: Prose and Poetry*. Boston: South End, 1993.

———. *Loving in the War Years: Lo que nunca pasó por sus labios*. Boston: South End, 1983.

Muñoz, José Esteban, "Flaming Latinas: Ela Troyano's *Carmelita Tropicana: Your Kunst Is Your Waffen*." In *The Ethnic Eye: Latino Media Arts*, ed. Chon A. Noriega and Ana M. López. Minneapolis: University of Minnesota Press, 1996.

Nakano, Evelyn Glenn. "From Servitude to Service Work: Historical Continuities in the Racial Division of Paid Reproductive Labor." In *Unequal Sisters*, 2nd ed., ed. Vicki L. Ruiz and Ellen Carol Dubois. New York: Routledge, 1994.

Napier, David. *Foreign Bodies: Performance, Art, and Symbolic Anthropology.* Berkeley: University of California Press, 1992.

Nathan, Debbie. *Women and Other Aliens: Essays from the U.S.-Mexico Border.* El Paso: Cinco Puntos, 1991.

Nestle, Joan. *The Persistent Desire: A Femme-Butch Reader.* Boston: Alyson, 1992.

Nicholson, Linda J., ed. *Feminism/Postmodernism.* New York: Routledge, 1990.

Olmos, Margarita Fernández, and Lizabeth Paravisini-Gebert, eds. *Pleasure in the World: Erotic Writing by Latin American Women.* New York: White Pine, 1993.

Paredes, Américo. *With His Pistol in His Hand: A Border Ballad and Its Hero.* Austin: University of Texas Press, 1958.

Paredes, Raymund. "The Origins of Anti-Mexican Sentiment in the United States." In *New Directions in Chicano Scholarship.* Santa Barbara: Center for Chicano Studies, 1984.

Parker, Andrew, et al. *Nationalisms and Sexualities.* New York: Routledge, 1992.

Pavis, Patrice. *Theatre at the Crossroads of Culture.* New York: Routledge, 1992.

Paz, Octavio. *The Labyrinth of Solitude and Other Writings.* Trans. Lysander Kemp, et al. New York: Grove Weidenfeld, 1985.

Peden, Margaret Sayers, trans. *A Woman of Genius: The Intellectual Autobiography of Sor Juana Inés de la Cruz.* Salisbury: Lime Rock, 1982.

Peña, Manuel. *The Texas-Mexican Conjunto: History of Working Class Music.* Austin: University of Texas Press, 1985.

Pharr, Suzanne. *Homophobia: A Weapon of Sexism.* Little Rock: Women's Project, 1988.

Phelan, Peggy. *Unmarked: The Politics of Performance.* New York: Routledge, 1993.

Phelan, Shane. *Getting Specific: Postmodern Lesbian Politics.* Minneapolis: University of Minnesota Press, 1994.

Ramírez, Elizabeth Cantú. *Footlights Across the Border: A History of Spanish-Language Professional Theater in Texas.* New York: Peter Lang, 1990.

Rebolledo, Tey Diana, and Eliana S. Rivero. *Infinite Divisions: An Anthology of Chicana Literature.* Tucson: University of Arizona Press, 1993.

Reinelt, Janelle G., and Joseph R. Roach, eds. *Critical Theory and Performance.* Ann Arbor: University of Michigan Press, 1992.

Rich, Adrienne. "Compulsory Heterosexuality and Lesbian Existence." In *Lesbian and Gay Studies Reader*, ed. Henry Abelove, Michèle Aina Barale, and David M. Halperin. New York: Routledge, 1993.

———. "Foreword." In *The Coming out Stories*, ed. Susan J. Wolfe, et al. Watertown: Persephone, 1980.

Ríos-Bustamante, Antonio. "Latino Participation in the Hollywood Film Industry, 1911–1945." In *Chicanos and Film: Representation and Resistance*, ed. Chon Noriega. Minneapolis: University of Minnesota Press, 1992.

Román, David. *Acts of Intervention: Performance, Gay Culture and AIDS.* Bloomington: Indiana University Press, 1998.

Rosaldo, Renato. *Culture and Truth: The Remaking of Social Analysis.* Boston: Beacon, 1989.

Russo, Mary. "Female Grotesques: Carnival and Theory." In *Feminist Studies: Critical Studies*, ed. Teresa de Lauretis. Bloomington: Indiana University Press, 1986.

Rutherford, Jonathan, ed. *Identity, Community, Culture, Difference.* London: Lawrence & Wishart, 1990.

Saldívar, José David. *The Dialectics of Our America: Genealogy, Cultural Critique, and Literary History.* Durham: Duke University Press, 1991.

Sánchez, Rosaura, and Rosa Martínez Cruz. *Essays on la Mujer.* Los Angeles: Chicano Studies Research Center, 1977.

Sánchez, Rosaura, and Beatrice Pita, eds. *Who Would Have Thought It? María Amparo Ruiz de Burton.* Houston: Arte Público, 1995.

Sedgwick, Eve Kosofsky. *Epistemology of the Closet.* Berkeley: University of California Press, 1990.

Seibel, Beatriz. *Historia del Circo.* Buenos Aires: Ediciones del Sol, 1993.

Showalter, Elaine, ed. *The New Feminist Criticism: Essays on Women, Literature and Theory.* New York: Pantheon, 1985.

Smyth, Cherry. *Lesbian Talk: Queer Notions.* London: Scarlet, 1992.

Sommer, Doris. *Foundational Fictions: The National Romances of Latin America.* Berkeley: University of California Press, 1991.

Soto, Shirlene. *The Emergence of the Modern Mexican Woman: Her Participation in Revolution and Struggle for Equality 1910–1940.* Denver: Arden, 1990.

Souhami, Diana. *Gertrude and Alice.* San Francisco: Harper Collins, 1991.

Spearman, Walter. *The Carolina Playmakers: The First Fifty Years.* Chapel Hill: University of North Carolina Press, 1970.

Spelman, Elizabeth V. *Inessential Woman: Problems of Exclusion in Feminist Thought.* Boston: Beacon, 1988.

Spivak, Gayatri Chakravorty. *In Other Worlds: Essays in Cultural Politics.* New York: Routledge, 1988.

———. *Outside in the Teaching Machine.* New York: Routledge, 1993.

———. *The Postcolonial Critic: Interviews, Strategies, Dialogues.* New York: Routledge, 1990.

Stallybrass, Peter, and Allon White. *The Politics and Poetics of Transgression.* Ithaca: Cornell University Press, 1986.

Stam, Robert. *Subversive Pleasures: Bakhtin, Cultural Criticism, and Film.* Baltimore: Johns Hopkins University Press, 1989.

Stanton, Domna C., ed. *Discourses of Sexuality: From Aristotle to AIDS.* Ann Arbor: University of Michigan Press, 1992.

Stein, Edward. *Forms of Desire: Sexual Orientation and the Social Constructionist Controversy.* New York: Routledge, 1990.

Sten, María. *Vida y muerte del teatro náhuatl.* Xalapa: Universidad Veracruzana, 1982.

Stevens, Evelyn P. "Marianismo: The Other Face of Machismo." In *Male and Female in Latin America*, ed. Ann Pescatello. Pittsburgh: University of Pittsburgh Press, 1973.

Taylor, Diana. *Disappearing Acts: Spectacles of Gender and Nationalism in Argentina's "Dirty War."* Durham: Duke University Press, 1996.

———. *Theatre of Crisis: Drama and Politics in Latin America*. Lexington: University Press of Kentucky, 1991.

———. "Transculturating Transculturation." In *Interculturalism and Performance*, ed. Bonnie Marranca and Gautam Dasgupta. New York: PAJ, 1991.

Taylor, Diana, and Juan Villegas, eds. *Negotiating Performance: Gender, Sexuality, and Theatricality in Latin/o America*. Durham: Duke University Press, 1994.

Trujillo, Carla, ed. *Chicana Lesbians: The Girls Our Mothers Warned Us About*. Berkeley: Third Woman, 1991.

Valdez, Luis, and S. Steiner, eds. *Aztlán: An Anthology of Mexican American Literature*. New York: Random House, 1972.

Versényi, Adam. "The Mexican Revolution: Religion, Politics, and Theater." In *Crucibles of Crisis: Performing Social Change*, ed. Janelle Reinelt. Ann Arbor: University of Michigan Press, 1996.

———. *Theatre in Latin America: Religion, Politics and Culture from Cortés to the 1980s*. Cambridge: Cambridge University Press, 1993.

Vidal, Hernán, ed. *Cultural and Historical Grounding of Hispanic and Luso-Brazilian Feminist Literary Criticism*. Minneapolis: Institute for the Study of Literature and Ideology, 1989.

Warner, Michael, ed. *Fear of Queer Planet: Queer Politics and Social Theory*. Minneapolis: University of Minnesota Press, 1993.

Weed, Elizabeth, and Naomi Schor, eds. *Feminism Meets Queer Theory*. Bloomington: Indiana University Press, 1997.

Weiss, Judith, Leslie Damasceno, et al. *Latin American Popular Theatre*. Albuquerque: University of New Mexico Press, 1993.

West, Cornel. "The New Cultural Politics of Difference." In *Out There: Marginalization and Contemporary Cultures*, ed. Russell Ferguson, et al. New York: New Museum of Contemporary Art, 1990.

Winsbro, Bonnie. *Supernatural Forces: Belief, Difference and Power in Contemporary Works by Women*. Amherst: University of Massachusetts Press, 1993.

Yarbro-Bejarano, Yvonne. "Expanding the Categories of Race and Sexuality in Lesbian and Gay Studies." In *Professions of Desire: Lesbian and Gay Studies in Literature*, ed. George E. Haggerty and Bonnie Zimmerman. New York: Modern Language Association of America, 1995.

———. "The Lesbian Body in Latina Cultural Production." In *¿Entiendes?: Queer Readings, Hispanic Writings*, ed. Emilie L. Bergmann and Paul Julian Smith. Durham: Duke University Press, 1995.

Ybarra-Frausto, Tomás, "La Figura del Donaire." In *Mexican American Theatre: Then and Now*, ed. Nicolás Kanellos. Houston: Arte Público, 1983.

———. "I Can Still Hear the Applause. La Farándula Chicana: Carpas y Tandas de Variedad." In *Hispanic Theatre in the United States*, ed. Nicolás Kanellos. Houston: Arte Público, 1984.

———. "Rascuachismo: A Chicano Sensibility." In *CARA: Chicano Art, Resistance and Affirmation*, ed. Richard Griswold del Castillo, Teresa Mckenna, and Yvonne Yarbro-Bejarano. Los Angeles: Wight Art Gallery, 1990.

Young, Ann Venture, ed. *The Image of Black Women in Twentieth Century South American Poetry: A Bilingual Anthology*. Washington: Three Continents, 1987.

Articles, Interviews, and Other Writings

Alcoff, Linda. "Cultural Feminism versus Post-Structuralism: The Identity Crisis in Feminist Theory." *Signs: A Journal of Women in Culture and Society* 13, no. 3 (spring 1988).

Anzaldúa, Gloria. "Chicana Artists: Exploring *Nepantla,* el lugar de la frontera." *NACLA: Report on the Americas* 27, no. 1 (1993).

Aparicio, Frances R. "On Multiculturalism and Privilege: A Latina Perspective." *American Quarterly* 46, no. 4 (1994).

Arismendi, Yareli. "Whatever Happened to the Sleepy Mexican? One Way to Be a Contemporary Mexican in a Changing World Order." *The Drama Review: The Journal of Performance Studies* 38, no. 1 (1994).

Arrizón, Alicia. "Contemporizing Performance: Mexican California and the Padua Hills Theatre." *Mester* 2 (1994).

———. "Josefina Niggli." *The New Hand Book of Texas.* Vol. 4. Austin: Texas State Historical Association, 1996.

———. "Soldaderas and the Staging of the Mexican Revolution." *The Drama Review: The Journal of Performance Studies* 42, no. 1 (1998).

Blakeslee, Norma Hopland. "History of Padua Hills Theatre." *Pomona Valley Historian* 9 (1973).

Boorman, Joan. "Contemporary Latin American Dramatists." *Rice University Studies* 64, no. 1 (1978).

Bouknight, Jon. "Language as Cure: An Interview with Milcha Sánchez-Scott." *Latin American Theatre Review* 23, no. 2 (1990).

Burns, Judy, and Jerri Hurlbutt. "A Conversation with Lisa Mayo of Spiderwoman Theater." *Women and Performance: A Journal of Feminist Theory* 5, no. 2 (1992).

Butler, Judith. "Performative Acts and Gender Constitution: An Essay in Phenomenology and Feminist Theory." *Theatre Journal,* 40, no. 4 (1988).

Card, Claudia. "Lesbian Attitudes and *The Second Sex.*" *Hypatia: A Journal of Feminist Philosophy* 8, no. 3 (1985).

Case, Sue-Ellen. "Classic Drag: The Greek Creation of Female Parts." *Theatre Journal,* 37 (1985).

———. "Performing Lesbian in the Space of Technology: Part I." *Theatre Journal* 47, no. 1 (1995).

———. "Performing Lesbian in the Space of Technology: Part II." *Theatre Journal* 47, no. 3 (1995).

———. "Tracking the Vampire." *Differences: A Journal of Feminist Studies* 3, no. 2 (1991).

Castedo-Ellerman, Elena. "Feminism or Femininity? Six Women Writers Answer." *Americas* 30, no. 10 (1978).

Christian, Barbara. "The Race for Theory." *Feminist Studies* 14, no. 1 (spring 1988).

Cixous, Hélène. "Castration or Decapitation." Trans. Annette Kuhn. *Signs: A Journal of Women in Culture and Society* 7 (1981).

Cockcroft, Eva. "Women in the Community Mural Movement." *Heresies* 1 (1977).

Cypess, Sandra Messinger. "From Colonial Constructs to Feminist Figures: Re/Visions by Mexican Women Dramatists." *Theatre Journal* 42, no. 4 (1989).

———. "Women Dramatists of Puerto Rico." *Revista/Review Interamericana* 9, no. 1 (1979).

Davy, Kate. "Constructing the Spectator: Reception, Context and Address in Lesbian Performance." *Performing Arts Journal* 2, no. 1 (1984).

———. "Outing Whiteness: A Feminist/Lesbian Project." *Theatre Journal* 47, no. 2 (1995).

———. "Visibility Troubles and Literate Perverts." *Women and Performance: A Journal of Feminist Theory* 7, no. 1 (1994).

de Lauretis, Teresa. "Eccentric Subjects: Feminist Theory and Historical Consciousness." *Feminist Studies* 16 (1990).

———. "Sexual Indifference and Lesbian Representation." *Theatre Journal* 40 (1988).

Desmond, Jane. "Mapping Identity onto the Body." *Women and Performance: A Journal of Feminist Theory* 6, no. 2 (1993).

Diamond, Elin. "Mimesis, Mimicry, and the 'True-Real,'" *Modern Drama* 32 (March 1988).

Dolan, Jill. "Breaking the Code: Musings on Lesbian Sexuality and the Performer." *Modern Drama* 32 (March 1989).

———. "Desire Cloaked in a Trenchcoat." *The Drama Review: The Journal of Performance Studies* 33 (1989).

———. "The Dynamics of Desire: Sexuality and Gender in Pornography and Performance." *Theatre Journal* 40 (1988).

———. "Gender Impersonation Onstage: Destroying or Maintaining the Mirror of Gender Roles." *Women and Performance: A Journal of Feminist Theory* 2, no. 2 (1985).

Duggan, Lisa. "Making It Perfectly Queer." *Socialist Review* 22, no. 1 (January–March 1992).

Feliciano, Wilma. "'I Am a Hyphenated American': Interview with Dolores Prida." *Latin American Theatre Review* 29, no. 1 (1995).

———. "Language and Identity in Three Plays by Dolores Prida." *Latin American Theatre Review* 28, no. 1 (1994).

Flores, Juan, and George Yúdice. "Living Borders/Buscando América: Languages of Latino Self-Formation." *Social Text* 24 (1990).

Fornes, María Irene. "I Write These Messages That Come." *The Drama Review: The Journal of Performance Studies* 21, no. 4 (1977).

Forte, Jeanie. "Realism, Narrative, and the Feminist Players—A Problem of Reception." *Modern Drama* 32, no. 1 (1989).

———. "Women's Performance Art: Feminism and Postmodernism." In Sue-Ellen Case, *Performing Feminisms: Feminist Critical Theory and Theatre*. Baltimore: John Hopkins University Press, 1990.

Franco, Jean. "Self-Destructing Heroines." *Minnesota Review* 22 (1984).

Fusco, Coco. "The Other History of Intercultural Performance." *The Drama Review: The Journal of Performance Studies* 38, no. 1 (1994).

Gallop, Jane. "The Problem of Definition." *Genre* 20 (1987).

García-Vásquez, Guadalupe. "¡Hasta no Verte, Aztlán!" *Women and Performance: A Journal of Feminist Theory* 7, no. 2; 8, no. 1 (1995).

Gimenez, Martha E. "Latinos/Hispanics. . . .What Next!: Some Reflections on the Politics of Identity in the U.S." *Heresies* 27 (1993).

Goldberg, Marianne. "The Body, Discourse, and the Man Who Envied Women." *Women and Performance: A Journal of Feminist Theory* 3, no. 2 (1987–1988).

Goldman, Shifra. "The Iconography of Chicano Self-Determination: Race, Ethnicity, and Class." *Art Journal* 49, no. 2 (1990).

Gómez-Peña, Guillermo. "A Binational Performance Pilgrimage." *The Drama Review: The Journal of Performance Studies* 35, no. 3 (1991).

———. "Death on the Border: A Eulogy to Border Art." *High Performance: A Quarterly Magazine for the New Arts* 12 (1991).

———. "The New World Border: Prophecies for the End of the Century." *The Drama Review: The Journal of Performance Studies* 38, no. 1 (1994).

Hart, Lynda, and Peggy Phelan. "Queerer Than Thou: Being and Deb Margolin." *Theatre Journal* 47, no. 2 (1995).

Huerta, Jorge. "Algunos pensamientos sobre el teatro hispánico en los Estados Unidos." *Gestos: Teoría y Práctica del Teatro Hispánico* 2, no. 4 (1987).

Jiménez, Reynaldo L. "Cuban Women Writers and the Revolution: Toward an Assessment of Their Literary Contributions." *Folio* 11 (1978).

Jiménez-Muñoz, Gladys M. "The Elusive Signs of African-ness: Race and Representation among Latinas in the United States. *Border/Lines* 29, no. 30 (1993).

Kanellos, Nicolás. "Hispanic Theatre in the United States: Post-War to the Present." *Latin American Theatre Review* 25, no. 2 (1992).

Kaplan, E. Ann. "Feminism(s)/Postmodernism(s): MTV and Alternate Women's Videos and Performance Art." *Women and Performance: A Journal of Feminist Theory* 6, no. 1 (1993).

Koppen, Randi S. "'The Furtive Event': Theorizing Feminist Spectatorship." *Modern Drama* 35, no. 3 (1992).

Lee, Muna. "Puerto Rican Women Writers: The Record of One Hundred Years." *Books Abroad* 8, no. 1 (1934).

Lindstrom, Naomi. "Feminist Criticism of Latin American Literature: Bibliographic Notes." *Latin American Research Review* 15, no. 1 (1980).

Lobo, Luiza. "Women Writers in Brazil Today." *World Literature Today* 61, no. 1 (1987).

Manzor, Lillian. "From Minimalism to Performative Excess: The Two Tropicanas." In *Latinas on Stage: Practice and Theory*, ed. Alicia Arrizón and Lillian Manzor. Berkeley: Third Woman, forthcoming.

———. "Too Spik or Too Dyke: Carmelita Tropicana." *Ollantay: Theater Magazine* 2, no. 1 (1994).

———. "Who Are You Anyways? Gender, Racial and Linguistic Politics in U.S. Cuban Theater." *Gestos: Teoría y Práctica del Teatro Hispánico* 6, no. 11 (1991).

Manzor, Lillian, and Inés María Martiatu Terry. "VI Festival Internacional de Teatro de La Habana: A Festival against All Odds." *The Drama Review: The Journal of Performance Studies* 39, no. 2 (1995).

Marrero, María Teresa. "Chicano-Latino Self-representation in Theater and Performance Art." *Gestos: Teoría y Práctica del Teatro Hispánico* 6, no. 11 (1991).

———. "In the Limelight: The Insertion of Latina Theater Entrepreneurs, Playwrights and Directors into the Historical Record." *Ollantay: Theater Magazine* 4, no. 1 (1996).

Pennington, Ron. "Curtain Calls." *The Hollywood Reporter*, May 15, 1980.

Perricone, Catherine. "A Bibliographic Approach to the Study of Latin American Women Poets." *Hispania* 71, no. 2 (1988).

Phelan, Peggy. "Feminist Theory, Poststructuralism, and Performance." *The Drama Review: The Journal of Performance Studies* 32, no. 1 (1988).

———. "Open Letter." *Theater Topics* 6, no. 2 (1996).

Reinelt, Janelle. "Beyond Brecht: Britain's New Feminist Drama." *Theatre Journal* 38 (1986).

———. "Feminist Theory and the Problem of Performance." *Modern Drama* 32 (March 1989).

Resnick, Susan. "Presencias: Latin American Filmmakers in the Feminine Plural." *Women and Performance: A Journal of Feminist Theory* 2, no. 1 (1984).

Román, David. "Carmelita Tropicana Unplugged." *The Drama Review: The Journal of Performance Studies* 39, no. 3 (1995).

Román, David, and Alberto Sandoval. "Caught in the Web: Latinidad, AIDS, and Allegory in *Kiss of the Spider Woman, the Musical*." *American Literature* 67, no. 3 (September 1995), pp. 553–585.

Sánchez, Rosaura. "Corridos: A New Folk Musical." *Crítica* 1, no. 2 (1985).

Sandoval, Alberto, and Nancy Saporta Sternbach. "Rehearsing in Front of the Mirror: Marga Gomez's Lesbian Subjectivity as a Work-in-Progress." *Women and Performance: A Journal of Feminist Theory* 8, no. 2 (1996).

Seibel, Beatriz. "La mujer en el teatro argentino." *Gestos: Teoría y Práctica del Teatro Hispánico* 4, no. 8 (1989).

Shea, Maureen. "A Growing Awareness of Sexual Oppression among Contemporary Latin American Women Writers." *Confluencia: Revista Hispánica de Cultura y Literatura* 4, no. 1 (1988).

Shirley, Paula W. "Josefina Niggli." In *Dictionary of Literary Biography Yearbook 1980*, Detroit: Gale Research, 1981.

Silverstein, Stuart. "Domestics: Hiring the Illegal Hits Home." *Los Angeles Times*, October 28, 1994.

Solomon, Alisa. "The WOW Cafe." *The Drama Review: The Journal of Performance Studies* 29, no. 1 (1985).

Steele, Cynthia. "Toward a Socialist Feminist Criticism of Latin American Literature." *Ideologies and Literature* 4, no. 16 (1983).

Sullivan, Constance. "Re-Reading the Hispanic Literary Canon: The Question of Gender." *Ideologies and Literature* 4, no. 2 (1983).

Taylor, Diana. "'High Aztec': or Performing Anthro Pop: Jesusa Rodríguez and Liliana Felipe in *Cielo de abajo*." *The Drama Review: The Journal of Performance Studies* 37, no. 3 (1993).

———. "Negotiating Performance." *Latin American Theatre Review* 26, no. 2 (1993).

Trujillo, Marcela. "The Dilemma of the Modern Chicana Artist and Critic." *Heresies* 2, no. 4 (1979).

Ugalde, Sharon Keefe. "Process, Identity, and Learning to Read: Female Writing and Feminist Criticism in Latin America Today." *Latin American Research Review* 24, no. 1 (1989).

Venegas, Sybil. "Conditions for Producing Chicana Art." *Chismearte* 1, no. 4 (1977–1978).

Waller, Margie. "Pocha or Pork Chop?: An Interview with Theater Director and Performance Artist Laura Esparza." In *Latinas on Stage: Practice and Theory*, ed. Alicia Arrizón and Lillian Manzor. Berkeley: Third Woman, forthcoming.

Yarbro-Bejarano, Yvonne. "Chicanas' Experience in Collective Theatre: Ideology and Form." *Women and Performance: A Journal of Feminist Theory* 2, no. 2 (1985).

———. *"Teatropoesia* by Chicanas in the Bay Area: Tongues of Fire." *Revista Chicano-Riqueña* 11, no. 1 (1983).

Yarbro-Bejarano, Yvonne, and Tomás Ybarra-Frausto. "Zoot Suit y el movimiento chicano." *Plural* 9, no. 7 (1980).

Zimmerman, Marc. "Latin American Literary Criticism and Immigration." *Ideologies and Literature*, 4, no. 16 (1983).

Performance, Dramatic Texts, and Works on Other Cultural Practices

Antush, John V., ed. *Nuestro New York: An Anthology of Puerto Rican Plays*. New York: Penguin, 1994.

Assunção, Leilah. *Boca Molhada de Paixão Calada/Moist Lips, Quiet Passion*. In *Three Contemporary Brazilian Plays*, ed. Joe Bratcher and Elzbieta Szoka. Austin: Host, 1988.

Bustamante, Nao. *Indigurrito*. Performed at Highways Performance Space, Santa Monica, Calif., January 23, 1994.

Case, Sue-Ellen, ed. *Lesbian Practice/Feminist Performance*. New York: Routledge, 1996.

Cassady, Marsh, ed. *Great Scenes from Women Playwrights: Classic and Contemporary Selections for One to Six Actors*. Colorado Springs: Mariwether, 1995.

Castellanos, Rosario. "The Eternal Feminine." In *Rosario Castellanos Reader*, ed. Maureen Ahern. Austin: University of Texas Press, 1988.

Cruz, Migdalia. "Telling Tales." In *Telling Tales and Other One Act Plays*, ed. Eric Lane. New York: Penguin, 1993.

Cuello, José. "Latinos and Hispanics: A Primer on Terminology." Nov. 19, 1996, *Midwest Consortium for Latino Research* ("MCLR-L@msu.edu").

Davis, Jill, ed. *Lesbian Plays*. Vol. 1. London: Methuen, 1987.

Diosdado, Ana. *Yours for the Asking*. Trans. Patricia W. O'Connor. University Park: Pennsylvania State University Press, 1994.

Esparza, Laura. "I DisMember the Alamo: A Long Poem for Performance." In *Latinas on Stage: Practice and Theory*, ed. Alicia Arrizón and Lillian Manzor. Berkeley: Third Woman, forthcoming.

Esteves, Sandra María. *Bluestown Mockingbird Mambo*. Houston: Arte Público, 1990.

———. *Tropical Rain: A Bilingual Downpour*. New York: African Caribbean Poetry Theater, 1984.

———. *Yerba Buena*. New York: Greenfield Review, 1980.

Farhoud, Abla. "When I Was Grown Up." *Women and Performance: A Journal of Feminist Theory* 5, no. 1 (1990).

Feitlowitz, Marguerite, ed. and trans. *Information for Foreigners: Three Plays by Griselda Gambaro*. Evanston: Northwestern University Press, 1992.

Feyder, Linda, ed. *Shattering the Myth: Plays by Hispanic Women.* Houston: Arte Público, 1992.

Fornes, María Irene. *María Irene Fornes Plays.* New York: PAJ, 1986.

Fusco, Coco, and Nao Bustamante. "Stuff." *The Drama Review: The Journal of Performance Studies* 41, no. 4 (1997), pp. 63–82.

Gambaro, Griselda. "Antígona furiosa." *Gestos: Teoría y Práctica del Teatro Hispánico* 3, no. 5 (1988).

———. "El Despojamiento." *Tramoya* 21 (1981).

———. "Sólo un aspecto." *La Palabra y el Hombre* 8, 1973.

———. *Teatro: las paredes, el desatino, los siameses.* Buenos Aires: Editorial Argonauta, 1979.

———. *Teatro 1: Real envido, la malasangre, del sol naciente.* Buenos Aires: Ediciones de la Flor, 1984.

———. *Teatro 2: Dar la vuelta, información para extranjeros, puesta en claro, suceda lo que pasa.* Buenos Aires: Ediciones de la Flor, 1987.

Garza, Roberto I., ed. *Contemporary Chicano Theatre.* Notre Dame: University of Notre Dame Press, 1976.

Gómez-Peña, Guillermo. "Border Brujo: A Performance Poem." *The Drama Review: The Journal of Performance Studies* 35, no. 3 (1991).

Hernández, Josefina. "The Mulattos' Orgy." In *Voices of Change in Spanish American One-Act Plays,* ed. William I. Oliver. Austin: University of Texas Press, 1971.

Huerta, Jorge, ed. *Six Plays about the Chicano Experience.* Houston: Arte Público, 1989.

Leguizamo, John. *Spic-O-Rama: A Dysfunctional Comedy.* New York: Bantam, 1994.

López, Josefina. *Real Women Have Curves.* Seattle: Rain City Projects, 1988.

Mayo, Lisa, Gloria Miguel, and Muriel Miguel. "Reverb-ber-ber-rations." *Women and Performance: A Journal of Feminist Theory* 5, no. 2, (1992).

Moraga, Cherríe. *Giving Up the Ghost.* Los Angeles: West End, 1986.

———. *Heroes and Saints and Other Plays.* Albuquerque: West End, 1994.

Niggli, Josefina, *Mexican Folk Plays.* Chapel Hill: University of North Carolina Press, 1938.

Osborn, Elizabeth M., ed. *On New Ground: Contemporary Hispanic-American Plays.* New York: Theatre Communications Group, 1987.

Palacios, Monica. "Latin Lezbo Comic: A Performance about Happiness, Challenges, and Tacos." In *Latinas on Stage: Practice and Theory,* ed. Alicia Arrizón and Lillian Manzor. Berkeley: Third Woman, forthcoming.

Perkins, Kathy S., and Roberta Uno, eds. *Contemporary Plays by Women of Color.* New York: Routledge, 1996.

Portillo-Trambley, Estela. *Sor Juana and Other Plays.* Ypsilanti: Bilingual Press/ Editorial Bilingüe, 1986.

Prida, Dolores. *Beautiful Señoritas and Other Plays.* Houston: Arte Público, 1991.

———. "Screens." In *Cuban Theatre in the United States: A Critical Anthology,* ed. Luis González Cruz and Francesca M. Colecchia. Tempe: Bilingual Press Review, 1992.

Rainer, Yvonne. "The Man Who Envied Women." *Women and Performance: A Journal of Feminist Theory* 3, no. 2, (1987/1988).

Rosenberg, Joe, ed. *¡Aplauso!: Hispanic Children's Theater.* Houston: Arte Público, 1995.

Tropicana, Carmelita. "Milk of Amnesia/Leche de Amnesia." *The Drama Review: The Journal of Performance Studies* 39, no. 3 (1995).

Uno, Roberta, ed. *Unbroken Threads: An Anthology of Plays by Asian American Women.* Amherst: University of Massachusetts Press, 1993.

Valdez, Luis. *Early Works: Actos.* Houston: Arte Público, 1990.

———. *Zoot Suit and Other Plays.* Introduction by Jorge Huerta. Houston: Arte Público, 1992.

Index

Page numbers in italics refer to illustrations.

ALICIA ARRIZÓN, Associate Professor of Ethnic Studies at the University of California at Riverside, teaches courses in U.S. Latina/o literature and theater as well as Chicano cultural studies and critical theory. Her writings on theater and performance have been published in *The Drama Review: The Journal of Performance Studies, Ollantay: Theater Magazine*, and *Mester: Literary Journal*.